Land of the Cosmic Race

Land of the Cosmic Race

RACE MIXTURE, RACISM, AND
BLACKNESS IN MEXICO

CHRISTINA A. SUE

OXFORD
UNIVERSITY PRESS

OXFORD

UNIVERSITY PRESS

Oxford University Press is a department of the University of Oxford.
It furthers the University's objective of excellence in research, scholarship,
and education by publishing worldwide.

Oxford   New York
Auckland   Cape Town   Dar es Salaam   Hong Kong   Karachi
Kuala Lumpur   Madrid   Melbourne   Mexico City   Nairobi
New Delhi   Shanghai   Taipei   Toronto

With offices in
Argentina   Austria   Brazil   Chile   Czech Republic   France   Greece
Guatemala   Hungary   Italy   Japan   Poland   Portugal   Singapore
South Korea   Switzerland   Thailand   Turkey   Ukraine   Vietnam

Oxford is a registered trademark of Oxford University Press
in the UK and certain other countries.

Published in the United States of America by
Oxford University Press
198 Madison Avenue, New York, NY 10016

© Oxford University Press 2013

Library of Congress Cataloging-in-Publication Data

Sue, Christina A.
Land of the cosmic race : race mixture, racism, and blackness in
Mexico / Christina A. Sue.
p. cm.
Includes bibliographical references and index.
ISBN 978–0–19–992548–3 (hardcover: alk. paper) — ISBN 978–0–19–992550–6
(pbk.: alk. paper)
1. Ethnicity—Mexico. 2. Mestizaje—Mexico. 3. Miscegenation—Mexico.
4. Mestizos—Race identity—Mexico. 5. Blacks—Race identity—Mexico.
6. National characteristics, Mexican. 7. Race awareness—Mexico. 8. Racism—Mexico.
9. Mexico—Race relations. I. Title.
F1392.A1S84 2013
305.800972—dc23
2012022986

ISBN 978–0–19–992548–3
ISBN 978–0–19–992550–6

To my mom, Diane Muriel Sue, for everything

CONTENTS

ACKNOWLEDGMENTS

The intellectual inspiration for this book grew out of conversations with many. However, my relationships with Jonathan Warren and Eddie Telles deserve special mention.

Jonathan introduced me to the enigma of race in Latin America and (perhaps unintentionally) converted me to sociology. I have learned a great deal from him. One of the best writers I know, he provided a model for clever and stimulating academic writing. Jonathan has also been a great mentor; his self-deprecating style and calm demeanor have consistently helped keep me grounded.

Eddie has enormously impacted my intellectual development. His unabated belief in me as a scholar and the importance of this book provided a constant source of fuel throughout this particular academic marathon. I feel fortunate to have benefited from his mentorship, generosity, and intellectual insight.

Although barely recognizable as the dissertation it once was, this book was largely conceived during my graduate career at the University of California–Los Angeles (UCLA). There, I had an incredible team of colleagues and friends including Rubén Hernández-León, David Lopez, Mark Sawyer, Nancy Yuen, Noriko Milman, Christina Chin, Faustina DuCros, Leisy Ábrego, Chinyere Osuji, Meera Deo, David Fitzgerald, David Cook-Martín, Angie Jamison, and Rob Jansen, who all left their mark on me or this book in their own way. Others, such as Ángel Yepez, Rubén Yepez, Josephine Lam, Carlos Godoy, and Andrea Weiss, provided friendship, guidance, and support during my time in Los Angeles.

As any ethnographer knows, we are nothing without the help and goodwill of those whose worlds we seek to understand. I am forever indebted to the subjects of this book, whose names I cannot reveal here. Not only did they tolerate my consistent and invasive presence in their lives, but they also somehow made me feel welcome in the process. Many of them assisted me in countless ways, donating copious amounts of time and patience without expecting anything in return. In particular, I owe my gratitude to my main informants who deserve special recognition for the immense role they played in making this research possible. I extend an anonymous, yet heartfelt, "gracias" for their guidance, assistance, and friendship. Also in the broader "field" of Mexico, I thank Concepción Meléndez Hernández, Leopoldo Hernández Díaz, Patricia Navarro Gutiérrez, and Alberto Miranda Meléndez for their friendship and for accompanying me during my multiple treks across Mexico in search of potential field sites. I thank José Luis Ramírez Coronel for his support and personal sacrifice during the initial years of this project.

I am also grateful for the support of a number of scholars who have facilitated this research over the years, including Stan Bailey, Tanya Golash-Boza, Sagrario Cruz-Carretero, Bobby Vaughn, Patricia Ponce, Kali Argyriadis, Odile Hoffman, Christian Rinaudo, Marco Polo Hernández Cuevas, Tianna Paschel, Wendy Roth, and Regina Martínez Casas. I thank the anonymous reviewers at Oxford University Press for their thoughtful comments. Finally, without the generous financial support from the Andrew W. Mellon Foundation, the University of California Institute for Mexico and the United States (UC MEXUS), UCLA, and the University of Colorado (CU), this research would not have been possible.

My colleagues at CU have been an invaluable source of support and encouragement during the writing process. Jason Boardman, Liam Downey, Leslie Irvine, and Janet Jacobs have graciously taken on a mentoring role for me in the department. Joanne Belknap, Patti Adler, Sara Steen, Mike Radelet, Joyce Nielson, and Rick Rogers have also supported me in various capacities. I am especially grateful for my network of wonderful junior faculty colleagues including Stef Mollborn, Isaac Reed, Hillary Potter, and Jenn Bair. It has been an honor to begin my career as an assistant professor alongside Sanyu Mojola, whose perspective on my work, and sociology more broadly, always leaves me thinking. Amy Wilkins has also been a rich source of scholarly exchange and a close friend. Amy was one of the few individuals who read the manuscript in its entirely. Her comments were invaluable, as is her unrelenting enthusiasm for my work. I have also benefited from a strong network of Latin Americanists at CU. I am particularly thankful for the on-campus presence of Rob Buffington, an excellent resource on Mexican history. I also thank the members of the Latin American Studies Center working group for providing a space for intellectual dialogue on the topic of race and gender in Latin America.

Fernando Riosmena has been a key source of intellectual exchange and emotional support. The mixture of his philosophies of cautious optimism and *patientia vincit omnia* proved the perfect recipe for maintaining my sanity during the process of finalizing the book manuscript, submitting it for review, and waiting. His spontaneous humor and well-timed comic relief kept me afloat during the most trying times. For this, among many other things, I am deeply grateful. Reaching deeper into history, my friends from childhood, Talia Kaye and Erika Isaacs, have always been there for me, offering good cheer, shoulders to lean on, and a healthy escape from the world of academia.

Over the course of this book project and beyond, my family has provided unwavering love and support. My sister, Jennifer Sue, even across the distance, has always cheered me on and made sure we kept in contact even when life constraints would have it otherwise. My brother and sister-in-law, Joe and Heather Foster, have given steady encouragement and a place to crash, when needed. The main source of my family support has come from my parents, Diane and David Sue. They demonstrate, over and over again, the true meaning of "unconditional" love. I was able to count on them during the many unexpected twists and turns that my life took over the course of writing this book. My mom, in particular, has made my academic career possible and my emotional health sustainable. In big and small ways, she has sacrificed much of her own life to make mine easier. This book would not exist without her support.

Life happened (literally) during the course of writing this book. The birth of my twin sons, Adrián and Joaquín, brought the biggest curveball life had yet to offer me. Parenting twins, starting a career as an assistant professor, becoming a single mother, and writing a book presented a tricky combination. Despite all imaginable challenges, Adrián and Joaquín have remained my loyal and loving companions. They provided me with perspective, energy, and constant entertainment during the book-writing process. But most importantly, every morning, they let me know that the sun is up.

1 | Introduction

L EADERS OF A NATION STRIVE to maximize their power and influence. To this end, they often create a belief system to justify, legitimize, and support their rule. They then disseminate these beliefs or ideologies to their target audience—national constituents. In early twentieth-century Mexico, in the wake of the Mexican Revolution, government officials and intellectuals promulgated a national ideology geared toward fostering nationalist sentiment, obliterating internal perceptions of racial inequality, and situating Mexico among the league of modern nations. They exalted Mexico's mestizo (mixed-race) population, declared Mexico free from racism, and erased blackness from the image of the Mexican nation. One century later, these aspects of Mexican racial ideology endure.

In 2005, the Mexican government issued a commemorative postage stamp featuring a popular black comic book character, a boy named Memín Penguín (see Figure 1.1).[1] United States government officials and African American leaders vehemently criticized Mexican officials' endorsement of what they considered to be a racist image.[2] Former U.S. presidential press secretary Scott McClellan stated: "Racial stereotypes are offensive, regardless of their origin...Images such as those of Memín do not have a place in the modern world."[3] The charges of racism were fiercely denied by Mexican government leaders. For example, former Mexican presidential spokesperson Rubén Aguilar declared that, far from being racist, Memín promotes "family values and plurality."[4] This modern-day controversy not only highlights cross-national differences in understandings of race but also illustrates the persistence of Mexico's official stance that the country is free of racism.

Mexican national ideology serves as a powerful conceptual backdrop for non-elite[5] Mexicans as they think through and manage "race"[6] in their every-day lives. However, in the process of constructing their identities and creating

FIGURE 1.1 The comic book character, Memín Penguín, was included as part of a postage stamp series issued by the Mexican government to commemorate Mexican comics.

discourses about race, non-elite Mexicans often end up socially reproducing the national belief system. Thus, the relationship between national ideology and popular thought is mutually reinforcing. In this book, I focus on the non-elite side of this ideological equation. I show how urban Mexican mestizos of mixed European, indigenous, and sometimes African heritage[7] understand and negotiate race and how these dynamics relate to Mexico's official ideology. In doing so, I engage the broader themes of racial identity, racial group-boundary construction, racial attitudes, interracial marriage and multiracial family dynamics, racial discrimination, and racial inequality.

Silvia's Story

Silvia is fifty-four-years old.[8] Her dark-brown skin and tightly curled hair suggest some African heritage. A widow, Silvia lives alone in a small house on the outskirts of a working-class neighborhood in the Port of Veracruz, a city located on the Gulf Coast of Mexico. She spends her days working at a local day care center and her free time enjoying the city. On occasion, Silvia visits the city's most prominent attraction, the beach, but avoids it when the sun is out. After several informal interactions, Silva agreed to be interviewed and graciously invited me into her home for our conversation. We were joined by her older sister, Angelica, who shares Silvia's phenotype.

Silvia articulated an unstable and intermittent black identity. When I asked directly about her racial identification, she struggled to find a term. When Angelica came to her aid, offering "mestiza"[9] as a response, Silvia accepted the suggestion with a nod and then launched into a detailed description of her maternal grandmother who was an "authentic Spaniard." Only later did she drop a quick reference to her black maternal grandfather. The tardiness of this admission was significant. In this conversation and others, Silvia vacillated between describing herself as black (*negra*) and *morena*,[10] a term that literally translates to brown but that can function as a euphemism for the term black. When I asked Silvia directly about her color, she described herself as "*morena*, but almost, almost black." Then she laughed uneasily. When characterizing the local population, she said, "The majority of *us* are *moreno*." However, when recounting a story of her love affair with an American, she informed me that his family was opposed to their relationship because she is black. She described black people in Veracruz as being upbeat and liking to dance, commenting that she is always compelled to dance when hearing music. However, Silvia discussed Mexico's history of African slavery entirely in the abstract. She did not claim this history as her own, nor did she link it to her personal identity. In fact, Silvia mentioned that I would not find many black people in the Port of Veracruz because "*they* are in Jalapa," the state's capital.

Silvia's connection to blackness strengthened during discussions of racism. She commented on her childhood growing up in a mixed-color family, a common experience in Mexico. According to both Silvia and Angelica, one of their white sisters used to call them a host of racial epithets such as "ugly, big-mouthed blacks." They described how this sister treated Angelica as her "black slave." Even worse, their own father engaged in differential treatment, providing their lighter-skinned sisters with extra attention, resources for furthering their education, and coveted luxury items. At this point in the conversation, Silvia's usual light-hearted demeanor had dissipated and was replaced with a somber and depressed tone.

Silvia's relationship to her blackness is complex and her racial identity fluid and situational. For example, while the term *negra* evoked strong negative emotions when discussing the treatment from her white sister, it flooded Silvia with positive memories of her deceased husband, who called her *negrita*[11] as a term of endearment. Fondly resurrecting her husband's memory, Silvia shared that he was "not too light or too dark" and that he was lighter than she, a point she continually emphasized. Soon after describing him, Silvia led me to a wall decorated with a few small, framed photographs of her husband. While I was looking at the images, Angelica, seated on the couch, loudly stated: "He wasn't *moreno*." As if to decode her sister's message, Silvia clarified: "He wasn't black like me." I leaned in to more closely inspect the photographs. I could feel both Silvia and Angelica's eyes upon me, awaiting my assessment of his color. I turned my head toward Silvia and nodded, confirming, "He was lighter than you." As if to signal an accomplished mission, Silvia returned to her seat.

Later, I asked Silvia about her preferences for romantic partners. The ensuing exchange was punctuated with giggles and jokes as the sisters playfully entertained ideas about potential partners for Silvia. After the joking subsided, Silvia offered a more serious response, saying she would like to marry a Veracruzano, but not someone who is "very, very black." She explained: "I am not racist, but what happens is that the people who are very, very, very black, very *moreno*, do not share…my chemistry." Silvia was also unenthusiastic about the idea of an indigenous partner, saying that she would rather remain single. In this instance, her concern revolved around cultural, as opposed to "chemistry"-based incompatibilities. According to Silvia, indigenous men do not allow women to work and have freedom.

Partner choice involves implications for potential offspring, a point of which Silvia was well aware. Solidifying her position regarding the undesirability of a black partner, she explained: "If I had a child, and he [the father] is black and with me being black, how is the baby going to come out? I thought about that….The poor babies will later be called *negros*." Referencing the child-care center where she works, Silvia added: "It happens with everyone in the daycare. One little one tells another, 'Get away *negra*'—'You are very black, get away from here.'" Silvia continued to provide examples of how color matters in Mexico, intent on demonstrating that her concerns are not a figment of her imagination. According to Silvia, not only do lighter-skinned children think they are better than those with brown skin, but some of Silvia's coworkers also reinforce this perspective, favoring children with light skin and blue or green eyes and withholding affection from darker-skinned children.

Despite her lived experiences with discrimination, Silvia assured me that she does not feel inferior because of her color. To the contrary, she is proud. She asserted: "Well, I didn't do what Memín Pinguín did, cover my face with powder—or put power on myself like the black girl in the movie.[12] What for? The blackness isn't going to come off of a person.... I have always felt content with my color...." But as our conversation wound down and I prepared to leave, I asked Silvia if I could take her picture. She consented but then quickly excused herself, disappearing into her bedroom. When she emerged ready for the photograph, her face was covered with a foundation makeup so light it gave the appearance of a white mask.

Silvia's life story represents the main substantive themes of this book—*mestizaje* (race mixture),[13] racism,[14] and blackness—in microcosmic form. It demonstrates how individuals negotiate these issues in Mexico, a society that privileges whiteness and is stratified by race and color. At a deeper level, Silvia's narrative exposes the entanglement of interconnected dynamics that surround race and color in Mexico. It touches upon the broader issues of racial identity construction, racial attitudes,[15] interracial marriage[16] and family dynamics, and racial discrimination.[17] Moreover, it shows the dilemmas individuals face when negotiating race and racism in a particular ideological context. As seen with Silvia, Mexicans' lived experiences are replete with attitudes and events that contradict Mexico's national ideology, which asserts that race mixture is positive and that racism is nonexistent and positions blackness outside the borders of the imagined Mexican community. Individuals like Silvia are thus faced with the task of crafting a racial identity and making sense of their everyday experiences within a complex web of ideological contradictions. This book is largely concerned with the process through which individuals respond to, manage, and resolve the dilemmas posed by these contradictions.

The context for the questions driving this book can be described as follows. A powerful national ideology pervades Mexican society. This ideology not only communicates messages about race but also conveys ideas about what it means to be Mexican. Within this context, Mexicans are constantly negotiating race in their everyday lives, forming thoughts and discourses about race, and constructing their racial as well as their national identities. Therefore, one wonders: How do individuals manage their identities, attitudes, and lived experiences in the context of the national system of beliefs? Furthermore, how do they respond when their identities, attitudes, and experiences contradict the national ideology? In answering these questions, I paint a detailed picture of the process by which non-elite Mexicans develop and articulate a racial common sense—a popular understanding of race and color—within Mexico's racialized ideological context. I show how Mexicans navigate the sea of contradictions that arise when their lived experiences conflict with the national stance and how their navigation strategies largely uphold, protect, and reproduce the national ideology. Thus, I illustrate the mechanisms through which ideology and the social hierarchy are reproduced.[18]

This book centralizes the racial common sense of Mexican mestizos. In Mexico, not only are mestizos the numerically dominant group, but they also symbolize quintessential Mexicanness. As such, mestizos are the primary targets and intended consumers of Mexican national ideology. Despite this, their role in the Mexican story of race remains largely untold. Instead, studies have focused on the indigenous population[19] and the indigenous–mestizo boundary.[20] This traditional emphasis has multiple consequences: (1) It neglects the mestizo experience, which is representative of the vast majority of the Mexican population;[21] (2) it treats mestizo as a monolithic category, overlooking the role of color within this group; and (3) it neglects the issue of blackness, both as a separate racial category and as an element of the mestizo population (traditionally defined as a Spanish–indigenous mixture). This book expands our knowledge of the Mexican racial terrain by addressing color dynamics within the mestizo population and the question of blackness in Mexico.

Race, Ethnicity, and Color

To understand Mexican racial dynamics and related inequality, it is essential to address color (a term I use to refer to various phenotypic markers including skin tone, hair texture, eye color, and facial features). Despite this, scholars have virtually ignored the role of color in Mexican society. Instead, racial inequality is typically analyzed through the lens of mestizos versus the indigenous.[22] This approach neglects the significant color-based stratification within the mestizo category. A remnant from Mexico's colonial past, Mexico is a pigmentocracy in which light-skinned individuals with European features dominate the top positions of society and dark-skinned individuals of indigenous or African descent are overrepresented at the bottom rungs of society.[23] In many regions of Mexico, light-skinned mestizos are much more likely to own large companies, live in mansions, and possess the finest luxury goods, while dark-skinned mestizos disproportionately experience life in *casas de cartón* (shanty housing) and struggle to put food on the table. This pigmentocratic arrangement is reproduced through contemporary practices of discrimination.[24]

Despite these color-based realities, there has been little research on the topic. This book addresses this shortcoming by illustrating how color matters in mestizo Mexico.

My emphasis on color dynamics among mestizos (i.e., dynamics within a racial-group boundary) has important implications for how scholars think about race and ethnicity. In his seminal work, Fredrik Barth (1969) challenged conventional scholarly wisdom, which viewed ethnic groups as culture-bearing units. He proposed that, to better understand ethnicity, we should look at how ethnic-group boundaries are formed and maintained. In other words, he encouraged an emphasis on "the ethnic *boundary* that defines the group, not the cultural stuff that it encloses."[25] Scholars have subsequently turned their attention to racial- and ethnic-group boundary dynamics.[26] In Latin America, however, these boundaries are often fluid and ambiguous, making an exclusive focus on boundaries more difficult. Moreover, within-boundary and weak-boundary dynamics play a major role in the creation and reproduction of inequality. In this book, I focus not on the "cultural stuff" but on the color dynamics that exist within the boundaries of the mestizo category.[27]

Scholars contentiously debate the analytic distinction between race and ethnicity[28] and, more recently, between race and color.[29] In Latin America, the black experience is generally analyzed within the framework of race, while indigenous populations are viewed from the perspective of ethnicity. However, there are a number of problems with this division, including the fact that the category indian was intricately tied to the emergence of the race concept.[30] Therefore, I use race as an umbrella term to reference dynamics related to both blackness and indigeneity. Furthermore, I treat color as an analytic subset of race.

The color hierarchy that exists in Mexico, a country in which the vast majority of the population is of mixed heritage, was developed based on an orientation to the *racialized* categories of white, indigenous, and, to some degree, black. Color has become salient precisely because racial ancestry is assumed to be relatively constant. In other words, a perceived similarity in *racial* makeup has heightened the importance of color as a distinction-making marker; color, therefore, has become a proxy for the degree to which an individual represents particular *racial* poles. For this reason, I treat color as one manifestation of race.

In the text I typically use color when emphasizing dynamics related to phenotype and race when speaking at a broader and more abstract, analytic level. Following scholars who use terms such as ethno-racial to describe overlapping concepts,[31] I frequently employ the single encompassing term race-color to simultaneously reference racial and color dynamics. Due to the complex and slippery nature of the race versus color distinction, there are instances in which I deviate from the aforementioned practices, but, in these cases, I justify my reasoning through in-text or endnote references. When drawing from specific conversations with individuals or referring to the literature, I employ the terminology used in those contexts.

Ideology, Common Sense, and the Reproduction of Inequality

The stories and everyday discourses presented in this book illustrate how ideology functions in society and how "racial formation" occurs at the microsocial level (Omi and Winant 1994). Understanding national ideology and its inner workings is important due to its role in maintaining state hegemony and societal power structures.[32] Most groups in power do not rule through threat of force but instead encourage subordinates to embrace a worldview or ideology that justifies the current social order.[33] They use "symbolic violence" (Bourdieu 2001) to create a system in which the dominated adopt the dominant point of view. Therefore, at its core, the study of ideology is the study of power and inequality.

Scholars have theorized extensively about ideology, emphasizing how *elites* develop and maintain dominant ideologies.[34] However, ideology cannot survive without popular support; non-elites need to adopt and continually reproduce ideology to ensure its success.[35] In other words, although ideologies often represent the social, economic, and cultural goals of a dominant group, the social force behind ideology lies in the popular realm.[36] Thus, popular-level conceptions of ideologies, often referred to as "common sense" (Gramsci 1971), are central components of the process of ideological reproduction. Analysis of common sense, as expressed through everyday discourse, illuminates how systems of domination are reproduced.[37] By focusing on common sense, this book exposes the popular-level mechanisms involved in the process of ideological reproduction.

Ideology and common sense are complex social forces, steeped in contradiction. Not only are contradictions present within national ideology itself,[38] but also individuals' lived experiences are oftentimes inconsistent with elite ideology. Additional contradictions arise during the process through which elite ideology is disseminated, received, and interpreted by the populace—or otherwise transformed into common sense.[39] Thus, common sense ends up representing an amalgam of ideas derived from elite ideology and those borne out of lived experience, producing a system wrought with disorganization and contradiction.[40] Non-elites are thus tasked with making sense of their identities, attitudes, and lived experiences amid this chaos. In this book, I map out the internal life of the ideological realm, demonstrating how individuals engage in "ideological work" (Berger 1981) through the deployment of a racial common sense that strategically manages contradictions that arise between their lived experiences and their nation's racial ideology.[41]

The ways that non-elites manage ideological contradictions have important implications for systems of inequality. Their strategies of ideological management can fuel the reproduction of an inequitable social order, a process I highlight in this book. Under these conditions, social dominance becomes a cooperative game.[42] That being said, despite my emphasis on how non-elite Mexicans continuously create and deploy a common sense that validates and legitimizes official ideology, this book is *not* a story about how citizens are duped by their leaders into passively accepting elite ideology. Instead, it is a story about how Mexicans actively reproduce the national ideology, even when bombarded with social realities that contradict it. We see how Mexicans carefully balance the symbolic importance of ideology with their lived realities and cultivate a common sense that simultaneously protects the national ideology while avoiding a complete invalidation of their identities and experiences. They creatively draw on particular aspects of national ideology to construct their identities, understand the world around them, and make sense of their lives.[43]

Nevertheless, the question provoked by my findings remains: *Why would non-elites facilitate their own subordination?* The traditional explanation, most closely associated with Karl Marx, is that of false consciousness. This theory contends that the consciousness of the subordinate class obscures and misrepresents the realities associated with its exploitation, thus preventing massive mobilization to challenge systems of inequality. However, although the collective strategies and processes I outline often end up buttressing elite ideology and perpetuating racial inequality, I argue that the situation cannot be explained with a false consciousness framework. In concluding the book, I propose an alternate explanation, emphasizing the link between the reproduction of Mexico's race-based national ideology and the fortification of individuals' identities as Mexican. This connection is far from insignificant, given the tentacular and powerful reach of Mexican nationalism.

Race and National Ideology in Latin America

National narratives strongly influence how race operates at the popular level.[44] In spite of this, the study of state-sponsored racial ideology in Mexico has been largely neglected both in the sociological literature on race and in the literature on race in Latin America. Regarding the former, the United States has represented the paradigmatic case for sociological theorizing on race.[45] Until recently, much less was known about how race and racial ideology operate in Latin America. Within the Latin American context, race scholars have concentrated on Afro-Latin America—countries such as Brazil and the Spanish-speaking Caribbean, which are characterized by a black–white racial continuum. Mestizo America, which includes Mexico, Guatemala, Peru, and other countries where racial dynamics primarily revolve around the indigenous–mestizo distinction, has received less attention. We know little about race and related ideology in Mexico, despite the fact that Mexico's ideology of *mestizaje* has served as a model for similar ideologies throughout Latin America.[46]

Scholars such as van den Berghe (1967) view the relative neglect of the study of race in Mexico as justified. In his classic theorization of comparative race relations, van den Berghe claims that Mexico represents an exceptional "nonracial" system, where race has ceased to be meaningful. Furthermore, he writes: "...The dual process of miscegenation and hispanization have so homogenized the Mexican population that race and ethnic relations in the country have received scant attention from social scientists" (p. 42). Van den Berghe's stance helps explain the longstanding academic neglect on the topic.[47] In this book, I work to fill this void by presenting a comprehensive ethnographic account of how race-color and related discrimination function in contemporary mixed-race Mexico. Before expounding on the details of my research, I present a discussion of the origins and development of contemporary Mexican national ideology.

Antecedents of Contemporary Mexican Racial Ideology: The Colonial Period to the Revolution

Mexico's experience with race dates back to the colonial period (1519–1821). Upon arrival to the Americas, Spanish colonizers quickly erected socio-political institutions to facilitate the expansion, colonization, and control of the territory. As part of their colonization efforts, they created two republics—one for Spaniards and one for the various indigenous groups that they encountered—to ensure their separation. Although indians initially provided an important source of labor for the colonizers, their numbers soon declined significantly due to war and disease. This loss of labor spurred the importation of Africans to Mexico; slaves arrived throughout the sixteenth, seventeenth, and eighteenth centuries, with the majority of imports occurring during the seventeenth century. Approximately 200,000 African slaves are estimated to have reached Mexico's shore, although this is likely an undercount because many slaves were imported illegally.[48] Slaves mainly entered Mexico through the port of Veracruz, although they later migrated throughout the country.[49] They primarily worked in mines, on sugar haciendas, as ranchers, and as domestic servants.[50] For much of colonial history, blacks outnumbered whites in Mexico.[51]

Early in the colonial period, social contact between Europeans, indians, and Africans was regulated through segregationist ideologies and practices, though segregation was difficult to enforce.[52] The blurring of boundaries that resulted from increasing race mixture concerned colonial authorities.[53] As Katzew (2004) notes: "The stability of the Spanish social order rested on the difference between Spaniards and indians, the maintenance of internal stability within each republic, and the effective restriction of rights and obligations of the Africans and the racially mixed. Policing ethnic boundaries was paramount for the preservation of the Spanish body politic" (p. 40). In an attempt to maintain social order amid various degrees of mixture, colonial authorities developed an elaborate caste system based on race, culture, and socioeconomic status. In this system, Spaniards were positioned on top, followed by mixed-race individuals, and then indians and Africans. Color played an important role in how individuals were treated within this classification scheme.[54]

During the eighteenth century, *casta* paintings (visual representations of race mixture between indians, Spaniards, and Africans) were commissioned by Spanish functionaries and exported to Europe.[55] In addition to illustrating taxonomy and exotic portrayals of the New World, these images categorizing individuals based on their racial background, powerfully displayed the role of phenotype in socio-racial classification. Unlike the caste system in India, however, the Spanish system did not rigidly structure social relations nor was it strictly applied in the legal realm.[56] The system survived until Mexico's War of Independence (1810–1821), at which time legal distinctions pertaining to race were abolished,[57] along with slavery. Although the caste system was abandoned, the value placed on whiteness remained.[58]

In the years following Mexico's independence from Spain, leaders of the newly independent nation faced the challenge of creating a unified citizenry in the wake of a highly segregated and hierarchical colonial system. They were also tasked with delineating the characteristics of the new nation and defining its citizenry.[59] Elites were particularly concerned with how to integrate the marginalized and impoverished indigenous populations into this vision. Prominent liberal thinkers such as José Maria Luis Mora attributed indigenous poverty to the paternalistic system and communal land orientation that existed during colonial times. They believed that the nation could prosper only if indigenous communities lost their corporate status and assimilated into the broader nation. Under this philosophy, leaders of a fledgling Mexico disbanded organizations aimed at protecting indigenous communities and revoked indigenous collective land rights.[60]

Mexican elites were also preoccupied with how to transform their country, which was bankrupt and had a divided multiracial citizenry, into a prosperous, unified nation.[61] The nation's leaders, however, lacked a clear vision regarding Mexico's future, as seen in the ongoing struggle between liberals and conservatives. This antagonism reached a zenith in the mid-nineteenth century. As liberals gained power, they implemented a series of laws and developed a constitution aimed at creating a federalist government, secularizing the country, privatizing property, and establishing equality under the law. Internal strife intensified as conservatives and those negatively affected by these changes railed against them. From 1858 to 1861, under the contested presidency of Benito Juárez, a liberal and an indian, the country engaged in civil war. In 1861, when the war ended, Juaréz was officially declared president. However, the country was in financial ruin, and Juárez was forced to suspend payment on Mexico's foreign debt, which resulted in a French invasion and the establishment of a French monarchy in Mexico between 1864 and 1867. When the French withdrew from the country and Juárez fully regained the presidency, his party was splintered and his administration under fire. The national treasury was debilitated and local strife plagued the country.[62] Concerns that had haunted national leaders earlier that century—how to create a modern, developed, and unified nation—remained.

These concerns came to a head in 1876 when Porfirio Díaz ascended to the presidency. Many believed Díaz's rule would mark a turning point in Mexico's long (yet unsuccessful) pursuit of modernity.[63] Indeed, Díaz's reign (1876–1911) was characterized by an agenda of economic development and modernization, under the banner of "order and progress." Although the goals of modernization and national unification remained unchanged from previous years, the circumstances confronting Díaz were somewhat new. For example, European scientific racist thought, which equated whiteness with progress and indigeneity, blackness, and racial hybridity with backwardness, was gaining international momentum. European theorists viewed a country's racial composition as a major predictor of its capacity for growth and civilization.[64] Although Porfirian intellectuals varied in their interpretations of scientific racism, many espoused ideas of white superiority.[65] In their eyes, Mexico's mixed and predominately nonwhite population was blocking the country's progress.[66]

In response, Porfírio Díaz and his technocrats implemented oppressive practices targeting the indigenous population, including forceful assimilation, land privatization, and the dispossession of indigenous communities.[67] Furthermore, they actively recruited European immigrants in hopes of whitening (and thus modernizing) the country.[68] However, Díaz's efforts fell short. His socioeconomic policies generated increasing social unrest and his attempts to attract European immigrants largely failed.[69] New solutions were in order. Shortly after the turn of the twentieth century, intellectuals such as Justo Sierra, Andrés Molina Enríquez, and Manuel Gamio had already begun challenging Eurocentric racist views by extolling the virtues of the mestizo.[70] This trend foreshadowed a significant shift in the official stance on race—a change originating during the tumultuous period of the Mexican Revolution (1910–1920).

The Mexican Revolution and Post-revolutionary Racial Ideology

Porfirio Díaz's relentless and uncompromising quest for modernization exacerbated social inequality; wealth, power, and land were concentrated in the hands of foreigners and a few Mexican metropolitan elites.[71] Toward the end of Díaz's reign, real wages declined; mining, timber, and textile industries experienced a significant downturn, leaving many workers unemployed; and agriculture suffered, leading to widespread famine and food riots.[72] Díaz, abiding by his belief in the free market, provided little relief for the Mexican people. Conditions were ripe for a massive uprising. In 1910, the country erupted in civil warfare.

Revolutionaries came from all walks of life and levels of society, united by anti-Díaz sentiment and a social justice agenda. In 1911, Díaz stepped down and Francisco I. Madero assumed the presidency. However, social turmoil increased as Madero continued to privatize landholdings and marginalized his most powerful supporters, including Pancho Villa and Emiliano Zapata, by not affording them a prominent role in the new political scene.[73] Law and order broke down as popular protests swept across the country. Much of the revolutionary activity took place in the rural and the indigenous areas that were hardest hit by land privatization policies. During the course of the Revolution, Mexico also endured two U.S. military invasions of its territory.

After ten years of political chaos and much bloodshed, the Mexican Revolution came to a close. Post-revolutionary leaders faced the difficult task of repairing the damage done by the war and rebuilding the country. They needed to tackle the issue of indigenous marginalization, which had come to the fore during the Revolution.[74] Further complicating matters, post-revolutionary elites were forced to contend with the still prominent theories of scientific racism, which deemed Mexico's largely nonwhite, racially mixed population as a barrier to modernization. Additionally, they faced the challenge of uniting a once-again divided citizenry and fostering national pride in the war's aftermath. The task of creating a coherent nation had never been more daunting.[75]

The nation's problems, brought to the fore by the Revolution and the dilemmas posed in its aftermath, spawned new thinking on race and a new national ideology. The guiding principles of post-revolutionary leaders included integrating all Mexicans into the nation and rejecting foreign influence over Mexico. Mexican leaders were determined to cultivate their source of strength from within.[76] In contrast to the forced assimilation of the indigenous population imposed during Díaz's reign, post-revolutionary elites pursued non-coercive policies aimed at respecting indigenous culture and integrating indians into the national community.[77] The indigenous population, long considered an obstacle to the country's progress, was valorized for its historical contribution to Mexican society and as an ancestral root of the mestizo population; indigenous heritage became a mark of national distinction.[78]

Three Pillars of Post-revolutionary Ideology

These changes in elite thought on race served as a basis for the development of Mexico's post-revolutionary national ideology, which included the following ideological pillars: (1) *mestizaje,* the embracement of race mixture and lauding of the mestizo;[79] (2) nonracism, the contention that racism does not exist in the country;[80] and (3) nonblackness, the marginalization, neglect, or negation of Mexico's African heritage.[81] Not only did these pillars emerge in response to changing perspectives on race, but they were also instrumental in solving the dilemmas posed by scientific racism and national disunity.

Pillar 1: Mestizaje

Post-revolutionary elites challenged traditional views of scientific racism, which equated racial hybridity with racial inferiority, by reframing race mixture as something positive and arguing that the mestizo represented a culturally and biologically superior race.[82] Furthermore, they touted hybridity as a national asset, a shared characteristic that should engender pride among all Mexicans.[83] The *mestizaje* ideology provided the basis for a much needed sense of national unity and became a rallying point for nationalist sentiment.[84] Through this process, racial ideology became fused with understandings of national identity; the mestizo was lauded as the quintessential Mexican.[85]

José Vasconcelos, Mexican writer, philosopher, and politician, popularized the ideology of *mestizaje*. In his classic text *The Cosmic Race* ([1925]1997), Vasconcelos predicted the global dominance of the mestizo race. Rather than simply espousing *mestizaje*-centered rhetoric in intellectual circles, his appointment as Minister of Education (1921–1924) provided him the opportunity to institutionalize and widely disseminate his vision. During his tenure, Vasconcelos built schools, created institutes, and sent cultural missionaries to remote parts of the country to provide schooling for rural, indigenous populations.[86] The nationalized Mexican education system became a central vehicle for the transmission of state ideology to the populace;[87] teachers became the soldiers of the Revolution. The explicit purpose of the national curriculum was to create a new Mexican identity, foster a love of country, and inculcate an official historical narrative.[88] Vasconcelos also supported a national mural movement that glorified the revolutionary ideals.[89] The *mestizaje* ideology, which continues to exist, was intricately linked to the development of another pillar of Mexican national ideology—the belief that the country is free of racism.

Pillar 2: Nonracism

As in other parts of Latin America, Mexico's *mestizaje* ideology provided the basis for an ideology of nonracism. Government officials and intellectuals argued that racism cannot exist in a racially mixed society.[90] Driven by this belief, elites concluded that there was no need to document race and thus removed the race question after Mexico's 1921 census.[91] Like the *mestizaje* ideology, the nonracism pillar was instrumental in cultivating nationalist sentiment. Drawing on a tried and true nation-building strategy, Mexican leaders deployed symbolic boundaries[92] in relation to an external "other" against which all Mexicans could assert their opposition.[93] The United States represented a convenient "other," especially given the outcome of the Mexican–American War (1846–1848) in which the United States acquired substantial Mexican territory.[94] The flames of anti-American sentiment were further fanned by Díaz's pro-foreign stance and the U.S. military interventions that took place during the Revolution.

Post-revolutionary elites capitalized on the contentious nature of U.S.–Mexico relations, positioning Mexico as the symbolic nemesis to the United States in the realm of race relations. Designating the United States as the epitome of racism was an easy task given the segregationist racial practices in existence in the U.S. South during that time. Mexican elites argued that the mixed-race nation of Mexico, unlike the United States, was free from the racist virus.[95] As with the *mestizaje* ideology, the nonracism pillar was tied to understandings of nation—being Mexican signified not engaging in racism and living in a country where racism did not exist. More importantly, Mexican elites worked to foster a strong sense of national pride surrounding the characterization of Mexico as a nonracist nation. Over the course of the twenty and twenty-first centuries, Mexican intellectuals such as Luis Cabrera (1977), Alfonso Caso (1971), and Enrique Krauze (2009, 2011), have continued to contend that Mexico is free of racism.

Pillar 3: Nonblackness

The final pillar, nonblackness, represents the minimization or erasure of blackness from the Mexican national image, both as a separate racial category and as a component of the mestizo population. Mexican leaders reclaimed the country's indigenous past as part of nation-building efforts but largely ignored blacks in these new narratives, a pattern seen in other countries within mestizo America.[96] Mexico's nonblackness ideology was strongly tied to the *mestizaje* pillar, as blacks were perceived as having been absorbed into the population through the process of race mixing.[97] The post-revolutionary ideology of *mestizaje* clinched the belief that the black population had disappeared through biological and cultural integration;[98] not only did the *mestizaje* ideology bolster the notion that extensive race mixture had taken place, but it also constructed the mestizo as the by-product of a Spanish–indigenous mixture.

Thus, the nonblackness pillar signals both a marginalization of the historic role of blacks in Mexico and a negation of the African heritage of Mexico's mixed-race population. At best, blackness has been treated as an element of Mexico's population on a trajectory toward disappearance (Vasconcelos [1925]1997) or as a regional issue (i.e., affecting states such as Veracruz) but not constituting a "national problem" (Cabrera 1977: 281). The fact that there has been no official measurement of the black population in Mexico since Independence reinforces these assumptions. As with the other two pillars, because the nonblackness ideology was consolidated in the context of nation-building efforts, it has implications for understandings of nation—being Mexican means not being black.

The erasure of the African element in Mexican national consciousness continued throughout the "cultural phase" of the Mexican Revolution (1920–1986).[99] Even in current Mexican society, blackness does not exist in the collective imaginings of the nation.[100] It should be noted, however, that the nonblackness pillar is less central to Mexican national ideology compared with the *mestizaje* and nonracism pillars. It is more of a latent ideology, which surfaces from time to time, without figuring as prominently on the national ideological landscape.

The ideological pillars of *mestizaje*, nonracism, and nonblackness remained prominent throughout the twentieth century and are still alive today.[101] To provide just one example, during the 1990s, in reports submitted to the United Nations (UN) International Convention on the Elimination of All Forms of Racial Discrimination, a global organization dedicated to combating racism, the Mexican government cited the absence of racism in Mexico as a justification for not implementing antiracist legislation. The report referenced Mexico's mixed-race population as evidence that racism does not exist. This same report reproduced the nonblackness pillar by defining Mexico's mestizo population as a Spanish–indigenous mixture.[102]

The Whitening Undercurrent and Embedded Contradictions

The valorization of whiteness seen during colonial times and throughout the nineteenth century, persist in post-revolutionary Mexico, despite the symbolic centering of mixed-race individuals. Similar to other regions of Latin America,[103] the ideology of *mestizaje* and the privileging of whiteness comfortably coexist. This compatibility can be seen in the original conceptualization of *mestizaje* ideologies. Early twentieth-century Latin American leaders not only treated *mestizaje* as beneficial in terms of producing a superior mestizo race but also viewed it as an avenue for whitening through the eventual elimination of blacks and indians.[104] Thus, post-revolutionary ideology possessed a strong undercurrent valorizing whiteness, a dynamic that is still prevalent in contemporary Mexico.

The coexistence of whitening and *mestizaje* philosophies illustrates how ideologies themselves house internal contradictions. On the surface, the *mestizaje* discourse appears to challenge notions of white superiority; in fact, it was touted as a great homogenizing and equalizing force. However, one of the primary motivations behind the ideology was to whiten the population-at-large and "bleach out" Mexico's nonwhite populations. Also contradictory is the fact that, while the mixed-race, brown-skinned individual became the esteemed national representative, the white phenotype was (and still is) very much prized. Further contradiction surrounds the nonracism and *mestizaje* pillars. Although the nonracism ideology presumes an explicit rejection of race-driven thought, mestizophiles employed scientifically racist notions to justify mestizo superiority. In other words, rather than challenging biological understandings of race, they simply rearranged the racial hierarchy, placing mestizos on top. Given these internal inconsistencies, not only do non-elites need to manage contradictions that arise between their lives and the national ideology, but they also need to deal with the contradictions present in the ideologies themselves.

This book speaks to such complexities by identifying the processes through which Mexicans negotiate race-color in their everyday lives and how they do so within an ideological terrain littered with contradiction. It addresses questions such as: How do individuals construct their identities in an ideological context that privileges whiteness while simultaneously touting brown-skinned mestizos as the Mexican prototype? How do individuals interpret the widespread societal preference for light-skinned partners within the context of a pro-mixture national ideology? How do individuals in intercolor relationships and members of mixed-color families negotiate color?[105] How do Mexicans reconcile the existence of Mexicans of African descent in a nation where the term "black Mexican" is an oxymoron and where mestizo is defined as a Spanish–indigenous mixture? Moreover, how do Mexicans of African descent construct their identities in this context? Finally, how do Mexicans make sense of their experiences with racism in a country where these experiences are not supposed to exist? In addressing these questions, I demonstrate how Mexicans use complex strategies to manage contradictions in a way that leaves the national ideology intact and simultaneously reinforces their Mexican identity.

Research Site and Methodology

I collected ethnographic data between 2003 and 2005 in the cities of the Port of Veracruz and Boca del Río, both located in the metropolitan area of Veracruz. Each region in Mexico has a unique history and racial make-up. The Veracruz population is descended from Europeans, indians, and Africans. The vast majority of the population is mestizo, although there is a very small indigenous population (which is fairly comparable to similarly sized metropolitan areas).[106] The most unique element of the Veracruz racial landscape is its African root. The Port of Veracruz was the major gateway for the African slaves brought to Mexico,[107] and the more recent arrival of Cuban immigrants, many of African descent.[108] Because of this regional history, a higher proportion of the Veracruz population is of African descent compared with most other regions of Mexico.[109] Furthermore because of the regional connection between Veracruz and the Caribbean (Cuba in particular),[110] Veracruz is associated with blackness in the national consciousness,[111] a dynamic I discuss further in chapter 6.

The Veracruz metropolitan area is an interesting site to study race and color for a variety of reasons. First, the population's mixed European, indigenous, and African heritage results in the manifestation of a wide range of racial dynamics. Furthermore, there is much phenotypic variation within the mixed-race population, lending itself to the study of color. Consistent with many other regions in Mexico, the phenotype of Veracruz mestizos ranges from individuals with very light skin and European features to those with very dark skin and clearly defined indigenous or African-origin features. Like in Mexico more broadly, these color distinctions correlate with different positions in the socioeconomic hierarchy. Although some mixed-race Veracruzanos have features suggesting African ancestry, most fall within the general range of phenotypes common to mestizos in other regions of Mexico. Finally, the urban, cosmopolitan nature of Veracruz facilitates the transmission of national ideology to the populace and studying a setting such as Veracruz can help us understand how race and color operate in urban Mexico. Much of our knowledge on race is derived from studies of rural areas despite the fact that over three-fourths of Mexicans live in urban areas.[112]

My findings are primarily based on thirteen months of participant observation and 112 semi-structured interviews conducted in Veracruz. While living in the area, I interacted with, observed, and participated in the daily lives and activities of Veracruzanos both in public and private settings. Participant observation allowed me to explore the everyday importance of race and color as it arose naturally in the field, while interviews allowed me to understand how Veracruzanos discursively deal with these issues. My interview sample was generated using the snowball technique, a form of convenience sampling.[113] I purposely selected respondents who vary in terms of color, age, class, education, gender, and neighborhood to tap into various kinds of experiences.[114] Each interview lasted between one and three hours; the broad goal was to understand how Veracruzanos experience, perceive, and frame issues related to race and color. Interview questions covered the topics of racial and color identity construction and classification, racial stereotypes, attitudes on race mixture, understandings of blackness, and experiences with and perceptions of racism and color discrimination, among other things.

I supplemented interview data with that gathered in five focus groups (involving four to seven participants) where I screened the 1948 Mexican film classic *Angelitos Negros* (Little Black Angels), a mainstream Mexican cultural icon.[115] In this film, a famous singer courts and marries a blond woman whose African heritage has been hidden from her. When their first child is born black, she is rejected by her white mother. This film provides an excellent research tool in that it confronts the frequently silenced issues of racism and blackness in Mexico. After screening the film, I allowed for open discussion among the group members and then posed a few general questions such as:

- Which character do you empathize with and why?
- Did what happened in the movie resonate with any of your personal experiences or the experiences of someone you know?
- Do you think this movie addresses issues that exist today in Mexico?

Finally, I administered 105 student surveys about race and color to students at a low-income, public high school where two of my main informants worked. The survey included questions such as:

- What race do you consider yourself?
- What color do you consider yourself?
- For you, what is racism?
- Have you or someone you know had problems with racism?
- Have you witnessed another person being discriminated against because of his or her color?
- Do you think color discrimination exists in Mexico?
- Do you think racism exists in Mexico?

The vast majority of my respondents asserted a mixed-race heritage and would therefore be officially classified as mestizo. However, they often did not use the term mestizo to describe themselves, a finding I discuss in chapter 3. None of the people I interviewed (with possibly one exception) met the official criteria for being a member of the indigenous population (e.g., speaking an indigenous language, living in an indigenous community, or practicing indigenous traditions). Approximately one-fifth of my respondents were considered to be part black or black by other Veracruzanos, although self-identification within this group varied, a topic I cover in chapter 6.

I primarily refer to respondents using color descriptors, except when I am explicitly examining processes of identity construction or when other classification markers are directly relevant to the discussion. Although it is customary to gauge race based on self-identification, I use color descriptors because they more directly reflect individuals' positions in the race-color hierarchy and how they are treated in society,[116] dynamics of central concern to my research. I classified each respondent using the following color categories: light, light-brown, medium-brown, and dark-brown.[117] These descriptions are not meant to be definitive but instead are used to give readers a general idea of where individuals fall on the Veracruz race-color continuum. When making group-level distinctions, I sometimes refer to *brown-skinned* mestizos or *brown-skinned* individuals, a reference encompassing those with a light-brown to dark-brown hue, and *light-skinned* mestizos or *light-skinned* individuals, referring to those whom I classified as light. When possible, I translate race-color terminology into English for ease of reading, although I retain the Spanish term in cases where an English translation does not adequately capture the appropriate meaning (e.g., when race-color terms are used in the form of a noun). Rough translations of local race-color terms are *güero/a, blanco/a* (white); *claro/a* (light); *moreno claro/a, apiñonado/a* (light brown); *moreno/a* (brown); *moreno oscuro/a* (dark brown); *negro/a* (black); mestizo/a (mixed race); and *indígena/indio* (indigenous or indian).[118] When Veracruzanos reference an individual or group in a particular way, I use their terminological classifications. I discuss terminology in more depth in chapter 2.

Fieldwork Issues

Gaining access in Veracruz was relatively easy. In my initial trip, I was accompanied by a family from the state of Jalisco who had local contacts in the area. Through these contacts I was able to locate a room for rent in a house owned by Sandra and Pepe, two high school teachers. Over the course of three weeks, I spent time getting acquainted with Veracruz, establishing a social network, and collecting preliminary data. I then exited the field and returned within a year for a twelve-month period. On this trip I was accompanied by my partner. We initially stayed with Sandra and Pepe and later found an apartment. Despite my exit from their home, Sandra and Pepe served as main informants throughout my time in the field. They facilitated my entrée into various communities and invited me into their social circles. They were particularly helpful in introducing me to members of the education community and various school settings.

Early in my fieldwork I made concerted attempts to integrate myself into a variety of social networks. These efforts culminated in the development of three additional "sets" of main informants. Each set of informants led very different lives; they were located in different parts of the city and were positioned differently in terms of occupation, educational background, family structure, and color composition. Jorge and Mía, a dentist and a nurse, respectively, and their two daughters lead a typical middle-class lifestyle. This family was instrumental in orienting me to Veracruz and helping me establish local contacts during my initial months in the field. Also helpful was Laura, a working-class single mother of two, who mans a newspaper stand owned by her mother. I spent many hours with Laura, becoming well acquainted with her family as well as her broad customer base. Finally, I met Anahí and Martín at a party organized by Laura's sister. Martín is a navy captain, and Anahí is a stay-at-home mother of two. Martín was resourceful in helping me gain access to his closed occupational circle while Anahí integrated me into her family's daily activities and included me in her many social gatherings. Out of these networks, my own social network emerged. Although this network introduced me to the lives of many working-, middle-, and upper-middle class folks, it did not extend into the top social strata of Veracruz.

Wealthy Veracruzanos proved more difficult to access. I found members of the upper class to be initially guarded and suspicious toward me and my research. My access was also constrained by structural barriers. For example, upper-class men are often involved in the management of companies or businesses and work long hours. Therefore, most of my contact was with upper-class women. Furthermore, the socially exclusive and insular nature of wealthy neighborhoods and social clubs was not conducive to informal observation. Despite these barriers, I eventually gained access to members of the Veracruz upper class and was able to interview approximately twenty individuals of this social stratum. Much of my success was due to the persistence of two "advocates," themselves members of the upper class: Carolina, a homemaker and member of Veracruz high-society; and Lili, a homemaker residing in the wealthiest neighborhood in Veracruz. I met Carolina one day when she drove up to Laura's newspaper stand to buy a magazine. She later introduced me to Lili. These women went to great lengths to introduce me to their friends and family. During the process, they encountered many barriers and expressed much frustration over the inaccessibility of their social networks.

My relationships with respondents varied immensely. In some cases, we interacted on a daily basis and developed strong bonds of friendship; with others, my main contact was in the interview setting. Typically, I conducted interviews after intermittent to sustained informal interaction with individuals. The variation in the kinds and intensity of relationships reflects the large urban setting of my field site and my attempt to learn from people located in different neighborhoods, institutional settings, and socioeconomic positions. In other words, as opposed to the traditional anthropological model of studying a small community, where it is feasible to have sustained contact with most informants, the urban setting of Veracruz produced a variety of researcher-informant relationship models.

Positioning Myself

One's position vis-à-vis his or her respondents always plays a role in the research process and the kind of data gathered. I am a U.S. citizen who self-identifies as biracial (Chinese–white). My racial identity was ambiguous to Veracruzanos, although they did not typically identify me as part Chinese. Many respondents assumed I am Mexican American because of my Spanish fluency and Mexican partner. Regardless of the ambiguity surrounding my racial status, Veracruzanos clearly viewed me as a light-skinned "American." They placed me in the ranks of the middle- or upper-middle class (an accurate assessment) and recognized my status as well educated because of my role in the field.

All positionalities have benefits and drawbacks. The methods literature has traditionally focused on the benefits of racial "insider" status,[119] although newer scholarship explicates racial "insider" limitations[120] and the benefits of "outsider" status.[121] In my experience, my outsider status created some initial barriers in terms of access and the development of rapport. However, my nationality and skin color also granted me certain unanticipated field-work privileges. Having light skin and holding U.S. citizenship are markers of status in Mexico. In Veracruz, a highly status-conscious society, individuals are eager to associate, and be associated with, individuals of high status. This dynamic worked to my advantage, allowing me to access and participate in a wide variety of social networks and settings. Furthermore, I discovered (rather late in my fieldwork) that upper-class respondents felt an affinity with me based on our mutual engagement in activities that marks one as "cultured," such as traveling to particular places or visiting specific cultural sites. I was able to use my cultural capital to open doors and establish rapport in that community. My status as a national outsider brought other advantages. I was able to ask the "stupid" questions or those in which the answers would be presumed obvious to any Mexican. For example, I had the freedom to ask "Who is Benito Juárez?" and "What does *moreno* mean?" without expectations that I should already know the answer. I was also permitted to engage in detailed inquiry about Veracruz society, in a way that an insider would not. Furthermore, my performed role as an ignorant outsider solicited highly detailed, in-depth responses and explanations to my questions.

Finally, my position as a young, married, female student also enhanced my access. Many Veracruzanos feel a moral obligation to assist others in the pursuit of education. Older individuals took it upon themselves to watch over me, in a protective role that is oftentimes reserved for daughters. Because of the intersection of my age and gender, I often found myself in situations in which men were explaining or enlightening me about particular subjects. These power-laden conversations, although not always pleasant, elicited a wealth of information. On the flip side, Veracruzanas would frequently invite me into their private, all-female social circles, providing yet another window into Veracruz life. The fact that I was married to a working-class Mexican man with brown skin also influenced how I was viewed and treated in the field. His presence broke down a number of barriers, facilitating my entrée and development of rapport in various communities. However, because I was married to a Mexican, I was also often expected to understand and conform to Mexican gender roles. That being said, my "American" status shielded me from full expectations of gender norm conformity and provided some protection in cases when I breached the norms. Still, I was careful to not stray too far beyond the boundaries of social expectations.

Plan of the Book

In chapter 2, I map out Veracruz's complex race-color terminological terrain, providing a broad overview of the usages and connotations of common race-color terms. I also address methodological issues surrounding the use of race and color when conducting research in Latin America, demonstrating how, by employing both terms in the field, I was able to capture conceptual folk distinctions and the implications of such distinctions. For example, I show how Veracruzanos define racial classification as racist and assert color as opposed to racial identities. I also detail how race-color terms function on a continuum and how related labels convey broader meanings related to class and attractiveness. This chapter lays the conceptual and practical groundwork for understanding the terminology used throughout the book.

Chapter 3 highlights the process of mixed-race identity construction, honing in on the *mestizaje* ideological pillar. I describe how individuals manage their race-color and national identities amid the *mestizaje* pillar, the high value placed on whiteness, and the image of the prototypical Mexican as having brown skin and being of mixed European–indigenous heritage. I show how these management strategies differ by color. Light-skinned mestizos wed themselves to the nation by claiming a mixed-race status at little to no social cost, whereas brown-skinned mestizos frequently highlight their European origins to position themselves closer to whiteness. Albeit in different ways, both groups draw upon national ideology to construct their identities as mixed-race.

Also engaging the *mestizaje* pillar, chapter 4 addresses mestizos' attitudes toward interracial relationships. Here I examine the degree to which individuals conform to the pro-mixture ideological stance and how they manage attitudes that conflict with this perspective. I, once again, show how individuals' perspectives diverge by color. Brown-skinned mestizos view race mixture as advantageous when used as a vehicle to achieve whiteness, whereas light-skinned mestizos generally reject interracial relationships as a strategy to preserve their whiteness. Therefore, Veracruzanos embrace race mixture under specific circumstances but do not embrace it whole heartedly. However, individuals of all colors justify and frame objections to particular interracial pairings in a way that protects the national ideological pillars of *mestizaje* and nonracism.

Chapter 5 is the behavioral counterpart to chapter 4. In this chapter I present the perspectives and experiences of individuals engaged in intercolor relationships or who are members of mixed-color families. I diverge somewhat from the format of other chapters that emphasize the relationship between popular common sense and elite ideology. Instead, I interrogate the governmental, scholarly, and popular belief that racism is incompatible with race mixture (i.e., the conceptual interconnection of the *mestizaje* and nonracism pillars) by carefully examining dynamics within intercolor couples and mixed-color families, the symbolic vanguards of antiracism. In exposing the extremely pernicious and intimate forms of race-color prejudice and discrimination housed in these intimate interracial social units, I challenge Mexican national ideology, academic thought, and popular belief that conceptually equates race mixture with a lack of racism.

Chapter 6 focuses on the ideological pillar of nonblackness that minimizes and excludes blackness from the image of the Mexican nation. My discussion elucidates the myriad contradictions that Veracruzanos of visible African descent and the Veracruz region (given its association with blackness) present to this ideology. I illustrate how people of African descent manage their identities in an ideological context of nonblackness by evading a stable black identity. Furthermore, I show how all Veracruzanos collectively participate in distancing both their state and the nation from blackness, thereby reproducing the national ideology. They accomplish this by defining racialized blackness as foreign and by positioning Afro-Cubans and African Americans as representatives of authentic blackness. Finally, the chapter demonstrates how local attempts to reinvent blackness have failed, signaling the power that national ideology has to squelch emergent counter-discourses.

Chapter 7 examines the relationship between Veracruzanos' racial common sense and the nonracism ideological pillar. I show how people manage contradictions between their experiences with racial discrimination and a race-color hierarchy and the ideology of nonracism by silencing critical race talk, erecting symbolic boundaries vis-à-vis the United States, and deploying nonracism discursive frames. I demonstrate that individuals of all hues engage in strategies that protect the national ideology, even if it is seemingly not in their best interest to do so. I end the chapter by discussing the implications of these somewhat counterintuitive findings for theories on racial attitudes.

I conclude the book by proposing an answer to a major question provoked by many of my findings: Why do individuals expend such effort to defend and protect a government-sponsored ideology that conflicts with their own lived experiences, particularly when it appears contrary to their best interest? I explicitly reject a false-consciousness interpretation of this conundrum, arguing that it is essential to recognize the deeply intertwined relationship between Mexican racial ideology and nation-building efforts—a relationship that has spawned a deep-seated conceptual and emotional interconnection between understandings of race and nation. Put simply, by reproducing Mexican racial ideology, Mexicans reassert their Mexicanness. Understanding this piece of the puzzle is crucial to grasping the meaning and motivation behind Veracruz racial common sense. In the epilogue, I provide a brief discussion of Mexican national ideology as it stands at the beginning of the twenty-first century.

2 | Mapping the Veracruz Race-Color Terminological Terrain

URING A FOCUS GROUP CONVERSATION, six women of varying phenotypes discussed the racial insults they have overheard school-age children launch at one another. Bella, a forty-eight-year-old light-skinned high school teacher, evoked the case of her dark-brown-skinned son whose nickname is *negro*.[1]

BELLA: ...Imagine my poor *negro*...

SANDRA: No, but he is not *negro*... he is...

BELLA: ...That expression [*negro*] is for people who are my son's color because here there are not *negros-negros* [real blacks]. We call the *moreno, negro*... but I have not seen any *negros* here except for Mike (an African American).

SANDRA: But there are *negros*.

ROSALÍA: Yes.

SANDRA: Yes. You... perhaps you are meaning that—because you are looking at the *moreno* as *negro* but, he [Bella's son] is *moreno*, he is *moreno*.

ROSALÍA: There are *negro-negros*.

SANDRA: I mean *negros* (emphasis on *negros*)—

ROSALÍA: They are *morenisimos* [extremely *moreno*]...

SANDRA: ...I have seen *negros*...for example...the fishermen—

ALISA: But they are toasted.

BELLA: They are toasted. They are not *negros*... I mean, I am talking about *negritos*, not pure *negros*...

This animated and lengthy exchange (only partially quoted here) illustrates the complexities and inconsistencies surrounding Veracruz race-color terminology. Even within this small group there is disagreement over the meaning of *moreno* and *negro*. As is true in many parts of Latin America, the meaning and use of race-color terms in Veracruz are ambiguous, fluid, and situation specific.

In this chapter I unpack Veracruz's complex system of race-color terminology. I provide a broad overview of the usage of and connotations associated with various terms while trying not to sacrifice too much nuance for the sake of generalization. I begin by discussing the methodological issues surrounding the use of the terms race and color when in the field, arguing that by employing both terms scholars are better equipped to understand how they function at the popular level. I also discuss the implications of folk understandings surrounding race versus color. For example, I show how Veracruzanos' use of color talk (as opposed to race talk) avoids a conflict with the national ideology of nonracism. In the chapter I also demonstrate how race-color talk manifests within a "discourse of relativity," a finding that contributes to scholarly discussions of race-color discursive schema in Latin America. Finally, I describe how race-color terms are either employed in a racial sense or a color sense or have multiple functions and how race-color terminology is encrypted with meanings related to class and beauty.

Methodological Issues

Scholars disagree as to whether the term race or color should be used in the Latin American context. Some strongly object to the use of race, viewing it as a U.S.-based imposition, exogenous to local understandings.[2] Scholars such as Burdick (1998) and Sheriff (2001) prefer the term color, perceiving it as an *emic* (locally derived) concept. Others avoid both terms while conducting fieldwork, instead allowing local systems of classification to surface.[3] In my research, rather than assuming the foreign or local nature of these terms or avoiding them completely, I used both terms when in the field, turning the race versus color distinction into an empirical question. In other words, I did not dismiss race terminology based on its assumed foreignness, nor did I rely solely on the concept of color based on its assumed *emicness*. Instead, I sought to uncover local meanings and understandings of race and color by integrating both terms into formal and informal conversation and actively listening for the use of these terms in day-to-day conversation. With this approach, I was able to gauge Veracruzanos' reactions to both terms, to document what they consider to be race terms versus color terms, and to disentangle their thoughts on racism versus color-based discrimination. A systematic comparison of these issues allowed me to capture the distinct folk usages, connotations, and norms associated with these terms.

In Veracruz, social norms regulating race talk are distinct from those that govern color discourse. Any mention of race oftentimes connotes discrimination and hierarchical relationships.[4] Consequently, there is a social taboo against race discourse; talking about race or classifying someone racially is perceived as racist. Color, on the other hand, is seen as an individual physical descriptor, devoid of explicit social connotations of inequality. Therefore, Veracruzanos generally treat color talk as unproblematic, with the exception of *critical* discussions of color (i.e., those that reference hierarchy or discrimination). The distinct connotations and norms surrounding race and color discourse have several implications. First, while quite adept at color talk and making color distinctions, Veracruzanos are less confident or comfortable engaging in race talk. They employ descriptive color talk on an everyday basis but infrequently engage in critical race talk. Because color talk is viewed as benign, Veracruzanos can freely employ color discourse without exposing themselves to charges of racism. In other words, they can engage in color talk without threatening the nonracism pillar of national ideology.

When I asked Veracruzanos to self-identify by color, they generally responded without pause or hesitation. Their responses flowed naturally, especially compared with discussions about their racial identification. When asked about race, they exhibited reservation, uncertainty, confusion, or became noticeably uncomfortable. In some instances, they refused to provide a response, asserting that to do so would mean participating in racism. Adriana, a fifty-two-year-old light-skinned upper-class homemaker, became uncomfortable when I asked how she identifies racially. She stumbled through her response: "What? What?—Well, normal [laughs]. I don't, don't know. What?" Her repeated questioning, nervous laughter, and expressions of doubt suggest a lack of orientation towards the race concept. Giovanni, a twenty-eight-year-old light-skinned fisherman, reacted similarly. When I asked him what race he considers himself, he paused, laughed uncomfortably, and then asked me what race *I* considered him to be. Instead of responding to his question, I posed a new one, asking Giovanni about his color self-identification. Without missing a beat, he responded "white." When juxtaposing his distinct reactions to the race and color questions, it is clear that Giovanni, like others, was much more comfortable with and better oriented toward discussions of color.

My conversation with Aracely, a forty-eight-year-old working-class homemaker with light-brown skin, provided another example of how individuals' responses to race and color diverge.

CS: What race do you consider yourself?
ARACELY: Well, I don't even know.
CS: You don't identify with any race?
ARACELY: Well speaking of race, now that you mention it…Well I don't know, because my daughter in [her school textbook]…yes, yes I saw…yes I saw something about that but I don't remember right now. I saw all of the races of the towns here in Veracruz. Yes, something like race but I don't remember the name…
CS: And what color do you consider yourself?
ARACELY: I consider myself *morena*.

Aracely struggled to identify herself racially, locating her knowledge of race in institutional discourse (something being taught in school). In contrast, she readily oriented to color and easily identified herself in color terms.

Veracruzanos' discomfort with race discourse is linked with its conceptual association with racism. Exemplifying the equation of race talk with racism is Javier, a twenty-eight-year-old army employee with light-brown skin. When I asked Javier about his racial identification, he replied: "Mmmm. Well, I am not racist. I don't like to be racist. I see the whole world the same, everyone, *morenos*, blacks, whites, I see them all the same." In refusing to engage in the racial classification exercise, Javier stakes out his position as a nonracist. Beatriz, a fifty-three-year-old working-class homemaker with dark-brown skin, responded similarly to the same question: "Well, what can I tell you? I am…I am a person who does not feel superior or inferior to anyone." Beatriz implies that, to identify racially is to participate in a system of inequality. As we can see, for Veracruzanos the very mention of race or racial classification evokes the idea of racism.

Carmen, a nineteen-year-old shoe store employee with light-brown skin, became disoriented and struggled when contemplating the racial identity question: "Well…what racial category? Well, no…[short pause] Well, I am probably…in the category, or well, right now I am—I am [short pause], how can I tell you?…Well, the truth is I don't, I don't consider myself to be racist or anything like that…" Unlike some others, Carmen did not immediately reject the racial identification question based on its putatively racist nature. Instead, she made a concerted effort to produce an answer, but, being unable to respond, she proceeded to reject the question on moral grounds. In contrast, when I asked Carmen about her color, she identified as light brown, without hesitation or reservation. In a final example, observe how Jennifer, a forty-two-year-old working-class homemaker, talks about her color very differently than her race. Regarding the former, Jennifer stated: "I consider myself to be *apiñonada* [pine-colored]. I am not white, nor am I *morena*." But when I asked, "What racial category do you consider yourself to be in?" she responded: "I don't consider myself to be racist." Although Jennifer identifies her color without hesitation, she balks at identifying racially. Engagement with color discourse largely escapes charges of racism and thus does not challenge the national ideology in the same way that racial discourse does. Taken as a whole, Veracruzanos' reactions to race versus color illustrate that these concepts have distinct folk connotations; they are received, interpreted, and used very differently. These differences were unearthed based on my methodological decision to incorporate both terms in my research.

The Race-Color Continuum and the Discourse of Relativity

In colonial times, the Indians were at the lowest end of the social scale of New Spain; how brown one was signified how much indigenous blood one had in his or her veins. [The more indigenous blood], the lower the category. And the reverse—the whiter you were meant that you had more European blood, and for that you could receive better jobs and salaries. That trauma we conserve in Mexico.

—CÉSAR FERNANDO ZAPATA, *a Mexican journalist, 2004*

This quotation comes from an email exchange I had with Zapata, a Mexican journalist. As Zapata points out, like in colonial times, race-color in contemporary Mexico continues to be correlated with socioeconomic status and functions on a continuum. Unlike the United States, which is characterized by relatively discrete racial categories and hard racial-group boundaries, the Mexican system emphasizes gradations in phenotype and has soft race-color boundaries. This system is not unique to Mexico; it has been identified in other Latin American contexts.[5] Given the fluidity that accompanies Latin American racial systems, scholars have sought to identify how race and related discourse function in the region.[6] Sheriff (2001) provides an extensive analysis, outlining three major race-color discourses used in Brazil: (1) *discourses on race,* which articulate a bipolar black–white vision of race; (2) *descriptive discourse*, where color terms are used to describe appearance; and (3) *pragmatic discourse*, an etiquette-driven use of color terms that reflects a way of treating someone as opposed to describing one's color in an "objective" sense. In Veracruz, individuals employed descriptive discourse as well as another, which I refer to as the *discourse of relativity*.

Classifications associated with the discourse of relativity operate similarly to those arising from Sheriff's pragmatic discourse in the sense that they do not represent objective references to individuals' physical appearance. Speaking to this point, Sheriff (2001) describes pragmatic discourse as a "euphemistic, etiquette-driven manner of speaking" (p. 31) and further explains: "When distinctions were made between what people said [in the pragmatic discourse] and some notion of real color, the real color was always, by the standards of the discourse of color description, darker" (p. 51). Whereas Sheriff discusses the pragmatic discourse in relation to a euphemistic-driven *lightening* of individuals, the Veracruz discourse of relativity is not always etiquette-driven and can result in both lightening and darkening effects. In this section, I describe the inner workings of this discourse, building on previously identified classification systems in Latin America.

In the discourse of relativity, race-color continuums are not always constructed based on large societal populations (e.g., the Port of Veracruz) but instead on smaller, more intimate social units (e.g., family, friend, or co-worker networks). Veracruzanos deploy classifications based on the discourse of relativity in a relational sense, implicitly comparing an individual's race-color with other members in a particular social group. Because of their context-specificity, these classifications are more fluid than classifications surfacing from objective descriptive discourses. For example, under the discourse of relativity, one might be considered *negro/a* within the family but *moreno/a* in the work setting. A consequence of this relational dynamic is that, as either individual- or group-reference points change, so do color classifications.

I first became aware of the discourse of relativity while interacting with a group of men employed at a local car wash. Abram, a forty-year-old employee with medium-brown skin, hazel-colored eyes, and brown hair, confidently asserted a white identity throughout our conversation, referencing his carwash nickname of *güero*.[7] Abram's white identity and nickname were noticeably inconsistent with broader constructions of race in Veracruz; he is phenotypically darker than those typically assigned the white label. Given Abram's meager income, this inconsistency cannot be explained by a "money whitens" dynamic—the idea that higher class status lightens individuals' race-color classification. After repeatedly observing similar inconsistencies across a variety of contexts, I came to understand the logic behind Abram's claim to whiteness. The carwash setting, not Veracruz society at large, determined the boundaries of the race-color continuum. In other words, the phenotypes of the car wash employees provided the basis for comparison, determining race-color classifications in this context. As Abram represents the lighter end of the continuum at his work site (both in terms of skin color and his hazel-colored eyes), he is labeled white within this group. Although he has medium-brown skin, he is *relationally* white in this context.

This relational dynamic works not only to lighten individuals vis-à-vis more objective classifications, but also to darken them. This was true in the case of Roberto, a recent college graduate and member of the upper class. Roberto's medium-brown skin tone is comparable to that of Abram's. However, unlike Abram, Roberto self-identifies as *moreno* and has the nickname *negro*. This nickname was bestowed upon Roberto in his youth by classmates at a private school. Under the descriptive discourse, Roberto would not be considered black in Veracruz given his phenotype. Furthermore, if it was in effect, the money whitens dynamic should lighten, not darken, Roberto. However, at the private school where the vast majority of Roberto's classmates were light-skinned, he was among the darkest. Therefore, in Roberto's school context, he was *relationally* black. These contextual characterizations, products of the discourse of relativity, exist independent of how individuals are viewed (and treated) in broader society. Roberto was aware of this and shared with me that, when walking down the streets of downtown Veracruz, he does not feel particularly dark. When employing the discourse of relativity, Veracruzanos are not treating race-color classifications in an objective sense but instead are engaging in a kind of linguistic play. They exaggerate classifications, employing labels that reference the race-color continuum's poles. Veracruzanos acknowledged this exaggeration, pointing out, for example, that even though an individual is referred to as black in a particular context, she or he is not really black.

Labels arising from the discourse of relativity often manifest as nicknames or terms of endearment or are used for joking or insult purposes. Although these labels are drawn from both ends of the race-color spectrum, when expressing or deploying labels referencing the darker end of the continuum Veracruzanos typically use these labels in a pejorative sense. Alejandra, a light-skinned nineteen-year-old law student from an upper-middle class family, addresses this point. In her private university, she has observed: "The one who is *morenito* is referred to as 'the *negro*' ... They always refer to the *negro*. It is never like, 'you ugly *blanca*...' It is always like—how ugly is the *negro*? Even though the person doesn't even have to be *negro*, but just the fact of being *moreno*, they are 'the *negro*.'" Alejandra references the stigma surrounding dark labels. Furthermore, her observations illustrate how an individual classified as *moreno/a* in an objective sense can be given the pejorative label of *negro/a* simply by being the darkest in surrounding company, thus drawing a distinction between classifications surfacing from descriptive discourse and those associated with the discourse of relatively.

In addition to educational settings, the family is another common social unit within which the discourse of relativity frequently operates. It is not unusual for the lightest member of a family to be nicknamed *güero/a* and the darkest, *negro/a*. This dynamic was described by Carolina, a fifty-year-old light-skinned, upper-class homemaker. Within the family, Carolina's husband is called *negro*. However, Carolina made a point of telling me, "He is not an African black, he is dark brown," implying that her family's label should not be taken literally. Judy, a thirty-five-year-old light-skinned university professor, also referenced the relativity dynamic when discussing her family. Juxtaposing descriptive classifications with relative ones, Judy referred to her aunt as "actually *morena*" but explained how she is considered "the *negra*" of the family. According to Judy, in her light-skinned family, simply not being white warrants a *negro/a* label.

Adriana, the light-skinned, upper-middle class homemaker, provides another illustration of how the discourse of relativity functions within the family sphere. She explained how her sister, whom Adriana described as light brown, is called *negra* by family members. Justifying these differing characterizations (i.e., what her sister "is" versus what she is "called" in the family), Adriana articulated, "It is not because she is very dark...I am the oldest and am white and she was born *morenita*. So they call her the *negra*." As with others, the classification of Adriana's sister is based on comparison—in this case, comparison with her lighter-skinned sister. Given the gravitation to the extremes that accompanies the discourse of relativity, alongside Adriana's lightness, her light-brown-skinned sister becomes the black member of the family. However, labels spawned from the discourse of relativity do not have permanent sticking power. They do not carry societal implications outside of the specific social-group context. Therefore, classifications arising from the discourse of relativity are not good indicators of how individuals are viewed and treated in society at large. Just as Abram, the car washer, cannot reap the privileges associated with whiteness, Adriana's sister does not suffer the societal stigma associated with blackness.

Race versus Color Terms: Popular Uses and Understandings

Another component of Veracruz race-color terminology involves variations and overlaps in individuals' usage and understanding of particular
terms; individuals employ some terms in a racial sense, some in a color
sense, and others in both a racial and a color sense. For Veracruzanos,
race terms are linked to understandings of ancestry and imply a sense of
groupness. Color terms, on the other hand, are viewed as individual-level
physical descriptors. An example of a color term is *güero*. *Güero* generally
refers to someone with fair skin, blond hair, blue or green eyes, or some
combination of these features. The term is commonly heard in Veracruz
and is generally devoid of a sense of groupness.

An example of a racial term is mestizo, which typically refers to individuals who are non-indigenous and of mixed heritage. I refer to mestizo
as a racial term because it is constructed in relation to understandings of
ancestry and is oftentimes understood as a group-based term. In addition,
Veracruzanos almost exclusively evoked the term mestizo in reference to
my questions about race as opposed to those about color. The term mestizo
is typically seen in educational curricula, government reports, and academic
texts, but it is not part of everyday discourse. When Veracruzanos did reference the term, they often relied on information from their school lessons,
recalling that mestizo is the proper term for the offspring of a Spaniard
and an indian. Pepe, the high school teacher who is forty-seven-years old
and has light-brown skin, spoke about the foreignness of the term mestizo
in popular contexts when I asked him to explain the difference between
the terms *moreno* and mestizo. He told me: "The term *mestizaje* or mestizo is about the mixing of the two races. But we never talk about whether
or not one is mestizo...we identify people as *moreno* or white...That is
how we characterize people." Despite the fact that Pepe understands the
meaning of mestizo, he attests that it does not enter into popular forms of
classification.

Whereas *güero* and mestizo are exclusively color and racial terms, respectively, other terms such as *blanco*, *moreno*, and *negro* function as both racial
and color terms. For example, *moreno* is frequently used as a color descriptor. However, it is also employed as a euphemism for blackness; when used
in this way, it carries a racial connotation. In Table 2.1, I categorize common
Veracruz race-color terms into three groups: those that are exclusively racial;
those that are used as both racial and color terms (racial/color); and those
that are exclusively color terms.

TABLE 2.1 Usage of Common Veracruz Race-Color Terms

TERM	RACIAL	RACIAL/COLOR	COLOR
Güero			X
Blanco		X	
Apiñonado			X
Moreno claro			X
Moreno		X	
Moreno oscuro			X
Negro		X	
Mestizo	X		
Indígena/Indio	X		

I classify the terms *güero, apiñonado, moreno claro*, and *moreno oscuro* as color terms because they describe people physically and do not carry a connotation of groupness. For example, Veracruzanos do not make references such as *los morenos claros* (the light-brown-skinned people) in a group sense, nor do they use *apiñonado* to imply a particular kind of heritage. In contrast, racial terms such as mestizo and *indígena* commonly connote some level of groupness and a particular ancestral background.

Racial/color terms are more complex because of their multiple functions and meanings. With respect to the term *blanco*, Veracruzanos sometimes deploy this term in a group sense and use it to reference European heritage, markers of a racial term. Martín, the navy captain who is sixty-years-old and has dark-brown skin, provides an example. He informed me: "The big businesses and everything are owned by *gente blanca* [white people], like Spaniards..." Martín references whites as a group and his mention of Spaniards implies a reference to ancestry or national origin. These details suggest that Martín is using *blanco* in a racial sense.

Carolina, the light-skinned upper-class homemaker, also used *blanco* in a racial sense when responding to my question about what it means to be *blanco* in Veracruz:

Look. Here there are many Spanish people—the Spanish community...These Spaniards grew up and have children who married, perhaps Veracruzanos, but also children of Spaniards—maybe not Spaniards but people with *piel blanca* [white skin]. They had children and well, those are *blanco* children, you understand?...The richest, to say it like that—almost all of them are children of Spaniards.

Carolina uses *blanco* in a racial sense, demonstrated by her discussion of Spaniards, a term infused with racial, national, and ancestral connotations.

However, she also refers to people with "white skin," momentarily employing the term *blanco* in a phenotypically descriptive form, characteristic of a color usage. Also using *blanco* in a color sense is Mónica, a thirty-two-year-old working-class homemaker with medium-brown skin. As we were chatting in a public venue, Mónica referred to some passersby as *blancos*, explaining, "They are not as exposed to the sun." Her individualized description signals a color connotation.

Moreno can also be employed in both a racial and color sense. As a color term, it is ambiguous and inclusive, describing individuals of nearly all shades of brown. It is the most commonly used color term in Veracruz. Marco, a fifty-one-year-old painter with dark-brown skin, self-identifies as *moreno* in a color sense, explaining, "I am sunburned but one could say I am coffee colored." In similar form, Natalia, a twenty-three-year-old restaurant worker with light-brown skin, defined *morenos* as people who are "cinnamon colored." Both Marco and Natalia employ *moreno* as an individual, physical descriptor, devoid of specific ancestral connotations.

However, *moreno* transforms into a racial term when it is used euphemistically to refer to blackness. In this capacity, it replaces the racialized form of *negro,* a term that can sound harsh or offensive.[8] Lupe, a thirty-five-year-old middle-class beauty school student with medium-brown skin, spoke bluntly of this etiquette-driven dynamic: "Here many of us don't call them *negros*; we call them *morenos* because if you are called *negro* it will be offensive, right?" Like Lupe, Adán, a thirty-five-year-old painter with medium-brown skin, articulated the reasoning behind the *moreno-negro* substitution. This point surfaced when I asked Adán about *negros* in Veracruz. He immediately began to talk about *morenos* but then paused, recognizing the linguistic mismatch between my question and his response. At this point, he explained, "I call them *morenos* because *negros* sounds really bad." He then continued the conversation using the term *moreno,* but only after it was mutually understood that he meant *negros.* Others navigated this discursive swap in a subtler fashion, first employing the term *negro* to clarify meaning and then switching (oftentimes without any explicit explanation) to the more socially appropriate *moreno.*

Another way Veracruzanos avoid using the term *negro* is by substituting it with "Cuban." Although Cuban officially references nationality, the term is highly racialized in Veracruz and frequently carries an association with blackness in a racial sense. I elaborate on the Cuban–black relationship in chapter 6. Exemplifying this form of usage is Jennifer, the working-class homemaker with light-brown skin. She characterized an acquaintance of hers as *moreno-moreno* and then added: "His features are like a Cuban's."

Jennifer's remarks also illustrate how *moreno* (like other terms) can manifest in the form of an epizeuxis—the repetition of a word in immediate succession. In describing someone as *moreno-moreno* or *moreno-moreno-moreno*, Veracruzanos are signaling either that the person is darker than the typical *moreno* (i.e., very, very brown) or that the person is *negro*. Therefore, the epizeuxis strategy can be used in a color or racial sense, either emphasizing the degree of an individual's darkness or to confer a racialized black label.

The term *negro* also holds multiple meanings. Used racially, it refers to individuals having African ancestry or who exhibit physical markers that are equated with racialized constructions of blackness (e.g., curly hair). A racialized version of *negro* surfaced in a remark made to me by Gloria, a forty-eight-year-old middle-class retired health-care worker with light-brown skin, as she spoke of Yanga, Veracruz, a community origi-nally settled by runaway slaves. She explained that it is "a town where the first *negros* who arrived as Mexican slaves resided...they were African *negros*." Gloria's reference to *negros'* group status as slaves and their asso-ciation with Africa, signals a racialization of the term.

Negro, used in a color sense, refers to individuals who fall on the darker end of the color spectrum, regardless of ancestry; dark-brown-skinned individuals with either indigenous- or African-origin features can be labeled *negro*. Illustrating this is Miguel, a twenty-five-year-old university student with medium-brown skin. He explained: "For some-one who is *moreno*—meaning that he or she is a dark coffee tone but has indigenous features and straight hair—many people are going to call him or her *negro/a*." Miguel highlights how *negro*, used in a color sense, extends to dark-brown-skinned individuals without African ancestry. Another illustration of how *negro* operates as a color term is seen in what I refer to as the *sun discourse*, something I further dis-cuss in chapter 6. Veracruzanos often make comments about individuals "turning *negro*" or "becoming *negro*" due to high levels of sun expo-sure. Martín, the navy captain with dark-brown skin, adopted this dis-course during one of our many chats. As we sat at his kitchen table, he summoned his adolescent daughter. When she approached, he narrated her periodic transitions from *morena* to *negra*: "She always went swim-ming in Salina Cruz and was getting to be very *morena* because she was so burned...she arrived *negra–negrita* from the sunburn." Martín's description of his daughter's transition to *negra* references skin tone and is detached from notions of ancestry or groupness, which accom-pany racialized notions of blackness.

Deciphering the Code: Additional Meanings Embedded in Race-Color Terminology

Providing yet another layer of nuance to race-color terminological usage is the fact that race-color terms hold meanings that extend beyond race and color, encompassing concepts such as class and physical attractiveness. The degree to which understandings of race-color, class, and beauty overlap in the cognitive realm is revealed through two dynamics—*conceptual association* and *discursive slippage*. Regarding the former, in the Veracruz popular mind, there is a strong conceptual association between race-color, socioeconomic status, and attractiveness—lightness and European features signify wealth and beauty, whereas darkness and indigenous or African heritage are markers of poverty and unattractiveness.[9] As such, the concepts of rich, beautiful, and light/white become interchangeable, as do the concepts of poor, ugly, and dark/brown/black.[10]

Speaking about the association between race-color and class, Esteban, a twenty-nine-year-old light-skinned computer technician, explained: "I think that we Mexicans have an image that, if you are white with green eyes, you have money...you do what you want—play golf, have breakfast in luxurious places...." Along similar lines, Mateo, a fisherman with light-brown skin, stated, "Here, in general, the people with money are...pale faces...they are white." The conceptual association between wealth and whiteness is well entrenched in Veracruz society.

The equation of darkness with poverty is equally strong, as demonstrated by Julieta, a light-skinned university student in her twenties. Julieta characterizes the "lower class" as being comprised of "all *morenos*." Contemplating the historical basis of this association between race-color and class, Cristina, a twenty-year-old light-skinned law student, reflected, "Because of our past we have the idea that the blacks were slaves...and there still are people that think that the blacks are inferior...." Speaking from a different race-color and class position, yet asserting the same association, is Belinda, a forty-six-year-old working-class homemaker with dark-brown skin. Belinda explained that "*morenos* are poor...the majority are of little means...." These examples illustrate individuals' conscious articulation of a perceived connection between class and race-color in Veracruz.

Veracruzanos also draw associations between race-color and beauty. Highlighting this in the context of her own experience, Alejandra, the light-skinned upper-class law student, shared that she feels that people view her as beautiful because of her color. She referenced compliments she has received such as, "You are white...what a beautiful color" or "You are white, how nice.'" These recurring comments have led Alejandra to conclude that beauty is defined in terms of whiteness.

On the flip side, Veracruzanos oftentimes equate darkness with unattractiveness. On one occasion I watched Esperanza, a school teacher in her forties with medium-brown skin, attempt to take a picture of her adolescent son with three females. Esperanza described two of them as white and the other *morenita*. As Esperanza prepared to take the picture, the two light-skinned women struck photogenic poses. However, the dark-brown-skinned woman hesitated and then retreated out of shot range. After Esperanza took the picture and the group disbanded, Esperanza explained, in a matter-of-fact tone, that since *negros* (abandoning her previous use of *moreno*) do not have pretty faces the woman probably assumed that she should not be in the picture. In a subtler fashion, Lili, a forty-seven-year-old light-skinned upper-class homemaker, equated brownness and blackness with lower levels of attractiveness when talking about Miss Universe candidates. She opined, "The majority, well, are attractive....even if they are *morenita–morenita* or black...They are pretty within their race." Lili described one candidate from Africa as a "good-looking woman *despite* her dark skin." In our conversation, Lili positioned beautiful dark-skinned women as exceptions, exemplifying how Veracruzanos' constructions of beauty favor lightness.

An additional conversational dynamic illustrating the conceptual overlap between race-color, class, and aesthetics is that of discursive slippage. The existence of this slippage exposes the deep-seated nature of the aforementioned conceptual associations. Veracruzanos commit discursive slips frequently and do so in a seemingly unintentional manner. For example, when engaging in conversations about whites, they often supplant the term white with a class term (e.g., "people with money") or an aesthetic referent (e.g. "beautiful people") without explanation. I refer to this dynamic as a *slip* because individuals do not appear to be making a conscious effort to introduce a new term or change the conceptual basis of the conversation when they engage in this practice. Instead, they simply exchange terms without shifting meaning. This slippage does not impede everyday communication because, in the Veracruz mind, a conversation about whites is also a conversation about the rich, the powerful, and the beautiful.

Notice the fluidity surrounding the discursive swap that occurred in my conversation with Sofía, a medium-brown-skinned University of Veracruz employee in her twenties. When I asked Sofía about how black–white couples are received in Veracruz, she replied: "Mmmm...it doesn't look bad, it just looks strange because, well, here in the Port, the *people with money* almost always end up marrying *someone else with money* or someone from a *wealthy family*."[11] Here, Sofía exposes her strong cognitive association between race-color and class; my question regarding black–white couples conjured up an image of individuals from different socioeconomic backgrounds. A similar dynamic surfaced in my conversation with Julieta, a light-skinned university student, also on the topic of interracial partnerships.

> JULIETA: If you are part of the *upper class*, you are going to marry someone of the *upper class*. If you are part of the *lower class*, you are going to marry someone of the *lower class*.
> CS: There is not a lot of crossing?
> JULIETA: No.
> CS: Would you cross?
> JULIETA: Me, yes. But here the people are very, very elitist, to say it like that. If you have *white skin,* you have to be with someone with *white skin.*

Julieta flawlessly moves between using class and race-color terms, absent of explanation. Taken in isolation, we could imagine that Julieta is merely referencing two different types of intimate boundary crossings. However, many other Veracruzanos engaged in the same practice, suggesting that Julieta's discursive slip was just one manifestation of a broader, collective and deep-seated cognitive association between whiteness and economic privilege.

Although Veracruzanos typically seem unaware of their discursive slips, Silvia, the day care worker with dark-brown skin, was an exception. Silvia caught herself mid-swap while describing a hypothetical job situation: "Two people are going to look for a secretary position. Two young ladies, let's say. One goes all fixed up in a suit and the other one, even though she has the same level of skills, has a humble appearance and is not well-groomed like the other one. Even though *the ind—the most humble one* will be accepted, the one that goes nicely dressed will be accepted first." Silvia initially constructs the two hypothetical candidates based on appearance and class status. She then introduces a partially formed race-color term (*indígena/indio*) but catches herself, replacing it with her original class descriptor (humble).

Veracruzanos also commit discursive slips around descriptors of race-color and beauty. Omar, a forty-four-year-old journalist with medium-brown skin, engaged in this dynamic. In our conversation about "white people," he flawlessly (and seemingly unintentionally) replaced this phrase with "pretty people." Similar linguistic exchanges occurred when Veracruzanos discussed blacks, *morenos,* and indians. Martín, the navy captain with dark-brown skin, illustrates this phenomenon. One afternoon, Martín and I were seated at a table in his neighbor's backyard, enjoying a meal alongside his family, friends, and neighbors. Martín, being his typical loquacious self, had launched into an elaborate discussion of his experience when stationed on a military base in California. At one point, he characterized African Americans as "aggressive" and contrasted the U.S. racial situation to that of Mexico where "whites and *morenos* get along." Over the course of his reflections, he periodically replaced the terms *moreno* and white with "ugly" and "pretty," respectively. At one point he, like Silvia, caught himself, correcting his in-progress discursive slip, saying: "When a *more...feito* [ugly person] is in charge here in Mexico he becomes aggressive." At another moment he let the discursive swap stand, arguing, "It is because the *feitos...morenitos* are treated poorly in school." As Martín engaged in these discursive interchanges, the unchanged facial expressions of his listeners suggested that these swaps were neither objectionable nor out of the ordinary. Like many other Veracruzanos, Martín reproduced the association between brownness and ugliness, despite the implications of what it meant for himself, a dark brown-skinned individual.

Being "Presentable"

There are also meanings encoded in popular colloquialisms such as "being presentable" and having "good presentation/appearance." As seen in other parts of Latin America,[12] Veracruz notions of "presentation" and "appearance" are infused with meanings related to race-color, class, and beauty. These phrases can be found in newspaper job postings and on storefront signs soliciting new hires; "good presentation" is oftentimes listed as a requisite for positions involving direct interaction with customers (e.g., hotel receptionists, waiters, and waitresses). Veracruzanos also use these terms in everyday conversation. Across these contexts, presentation and appearance convey a particular meaning about race-color, class, and attractiveness—to have good presentation and appearance is to have light skin, not look impoverished, and be attractive.

Deciphering the meaning behind good presentation and appearance is much more than an intellectual exercise; a shared societal understanding of these phrases is important to the smooth functioning of the labor market. Employers need to convey their ideas of an ideal employee while discouraging applications from undesirable candidates. They need to do this without violating ideological, social, and legal norms that discourage discrimination based on race. On the other side of the equation, job seekers need to be able to determine whether they are acceptable candidates for an advertised position. If good presentation is listed as a desired or required characteristic, potential employees need to be able to decipher what the employer means by this seemingly vague term. In these situations, job seekers draw upon their racial common sense to decode such phrases.

Quite consistently, Veracruzanos informed me that, on the surface, the notion of good presentation or appearance refers to a person who is well groomed and nicely dressed. These interpretations represent the socially acceptable face of the term. However, they also spoke of a deeper meaning embedded in the ideas of presentation and appearance, one referencing the concepts of race-color, class, and beauty. The most prominent interpretation involved race-color; according to many Veracruzanos, being presentable means having light skin or being white. Bernardo, a forty-three-year-old university professor with dark-brown skin, did not hesitate to point this out, telling me: "Underlying good presentation is to have white skin." A sixteen-year-old high school student expressed a similar sentiment on a survey: "In some companies you need a good image [appearance] and if you aren't white they reject you." Additionally, Franco, a sixty-four-year-old fisherman with dark-brown skin, matter-of-factly explained that when employers solicit an individual with "good appearance," they are soliciting someone who has a "pretty face," "a small mouth," and "who isn't very *moreno* or . . . very black."

The concept of good presentation manifested organically in my conversation with Alfredo, a fifty-six-year-old fisherman with dark-brown skin. In discussing inequality in the job market, Alfredo told me: "Regularly [whites] have the best positions . . . It is easier for them to find work than the *moreno* and black . . . . In [jobs] . . . they want someone who has [good] presentation." When I responded, "Good presentation meaning . . . ?" Alfredo clarified: "To be white in color and have straight hair." Alfredo's spontaneous reference to presentation during our conversation about whites illustrates the tight conceptual link between these terms. Finally, Lili, the light-skinned upper-class homemaker, articulated what she perceives as the multiple connotations surrounding the idea of good presentation. She believes it implies that, "the lighter, the thinner, and the taller you are, the better." Like Veracruz race-color dynamics, Lili frames various attributes as functioning on a continuum of desirability.

Although it is much more common to hear about good presentation, Mía, the nurse who is forty-seven-years old and who has medium-brown skin, employed the phrase "bad presentation" as a synonym for dark skin. She did so in the context of talking about those who control the movement of merchandise in and out of the port, explaining that they are reluctant to hire people with bad presentation. When I asked Mía what she meant by bad presentation, she swiftly decoded the term: "Very *moreno.*" Taken as a whole, these examples illustrate how seemingly nonracial phrases such as presentation and appearance can become vehicles for racial discrimination.

How individuals interpret terms such as good presentation has real-life consequences. For example, Daniela, a thirty-two-year-old working-class homemaker with dark-brown skin, avoids applying for jobs that solicit individuals with good presentation because she believes they are just seeking white people. According to Daniela, if she applied for these jobs, employers would reject her based on her race-color. Therefore, the notion of good presentation is not just an abstract concept in Daniela's mind; it conveys a clear message that, as a person with brown skin, she need not apply.

Daniela's interpretation of employers' encoded preferences is not a figment of her imagination. Bernardo, the university professor with dark-brown skin, confirms Daniela's read of the situation, when addressing the employer side of the equation. At Bernardo's university there is an employment center that serves the Veracruz business community. Companies often request that the university help locate potential employees. Bernardo has witnessed employers specifically requesting candidates who are white and have straight hair. That being said, Bernardo's behind-the-scenes experience with hiring dynamics is atypical. Most Veracruzanos are forced to rely on their racial common sense to decipher the racially coded messages hiding behind linguistic fronts such as good presentation.

Conclusion

In this chapter I attempted to present a systematic yet nuanced account of the multiple discourses, terms, and meanings that surround Veracruz race-color terminology. This discussion provides the groundwork for understanding the language and concepts used throughout the book. Moreover, it broadens our understanding of the various ways race-color terminology and related classification systems manifest and operate in Latin America. In particular, my identification of the discourse of relativity contributes to current understandings of race-color discourses in the region. Additionally, I demonstrated that, by adopting a methodological approach that incorporates the concepts of both race and color, we are better positioned to capture and analyze popular understandings of these terms. With this approach I was able to detect, for example, how Veracruzanos' use of color talk (as opposed to race talk) escapes charges of racism and evades a conflict with the ideological pillar of nonracism. In the remainder of the book I document how race-color terms and related dynamics relate to identity formation, race mixture, racial discrimination, constructions of blackness, and Mexican national ideology.

3 | Beneath the Surface of Mixed-Race Identities

A S MENTIONED IN CHAPTER 1, ideologies and practices of race mixture have a long history in Mexico, extending back to the colonial era. The *mestizaje* concept played a central role in the country's post-revolutionary ideology. During this time, Mexican elites not only proclaimed hybridity to be a demographic reality but also touted it as a national asset—a quality of which all Mexicans could and should be proud. Elites showcased the mestizo as the national prototype. The construction of this prototype involved not only ancestral components (European and indigenous heritage) but also physical characteristics (brown skin and mixed European and indigenous features); these ancestral and physical traits were soon regarded as markers of Mexicanness.[1] In other words, Mexican national subjects became racialized. At the same time Mexican elites were lauding the mestizo, however, they were also demonstrating a clear preference for whiteness, a dynamic that continues to this day. One wonders how mixed-race individuals of varying hues construct their identities within this context.

The racialization of the Mexican citizenry, coupled with the simultaneous valuation of *mestizaje* and whiteness, creates dilemmas of authenticity regarding Mexicans' race-color and national identities.[2] These dilemmas differ based on phenotype.[3] Light-skinned Mexicans are sometimes viewed as marginal to the Mexican community, as their phenotype contrasts with the prototypical brown-skinned Mexican. Consequently, they need to assert and authenticate their national identities when engaging in race-color identity work. At the same time, however, their phenotype is highly prized in Mexico; lightness and European features signal beauty, status, and financial well-being, as shown in the previous chapter. However, flaunting one's whiteness is seen as pretentious in many parts of Mexican society and violates social norms. Therefore, light-skinned Mexicans are forced to navigate their race-color and national identities amid conflicting images of whiteness. In contrast, the phenotype of brown-skinned individuals of mixed European and indigenous descent[4] clearly positions them within the boundaries of normative representations of Mexicanness. Thus, the national identity of brown-skinned Mexicans of mixed indigenous and European heritage is generally not subject to question. However, these individuals face the stigma of having brown skin and indigenous features in a society that privileges lightness and European ancestry.

In this chapter, I show how both light- and brown-skinned Veracruzanos manage the dilemmas that surface around the intersection of their race-color and national identities. Specifically, I demonstrate how white-identified Veracruzanos navigate social norms and their national status by engaging in various strategies such as exhibiting humility, downplaying their whiteness, evoking others' classifications of them, and asserting their loyalty to Mexico. These strategies allow them to claim a white identity and European ancestry in a socially appropriate manner and in a way that does not threaten their national identities. I also demonstrate how brown-identified Veracruzanos attempt to minimize the stigma of their phenotype through the use of strategies such as highlighting any known European origins. Based on these findings, I argue that we need to recognize the role that color plays in the way that mixed-race individuals understand, conceptualize, and construct their race-color and national identities. Finally, I detail how Veracruzanos of all hues co-opt the national ideology of *mestizaje* to inform and construct their personal identities as mixed and to infuse an indigenous element into their constructions of ancestry, thereby illustrating how individuals selectively and creatively draw upon national narratives in the identity construction process.

Race-Color as *an* Identity

Unlike the United States, Mexico does not have a strong "culture of race." Mexicans' worldviews do not give prominence to race as a basis of group categorization and action. According to Cornell and Hartmann (1998), different cultures give rise to distinct categories of ascription—"the broad bases used by the culture at large to conceptualize and talk about groups" (p. 175). In Mexico, the major categories of ascription revolve around the themes of class and nation, not race. This was evident in Veracruz, where individuals lack a sense of groupness surrounding their race-color identities. For instance, although many Veracruzanos identify as *moreno*, they do not express a connection or affinity with others who identify similarly. Furthermore, unlike their identities related to class, nation, and gender, Veracruzanos' race-color identities are not strongly tied to understandings of self. I often heard Veracruzanos say things along the lines of, "As a Mexican..."; "Since I am poor..."; and "Being a woman..." These statements signal a sense of group consciousness and illustrate how certain identities serve as interpretive lenses for personal experiences. However, parallel statements such as, "As a *morena*..." or "Being mestizo..." were conspicuously absent from Veracruz discourse, indicating a lack of group consciousness related to race-color.

An illustration of Mexico's weak race culture surfaced when I was observing a high school adult education class. The class was held in a medium-sized building made of concrete blocks. Inside sat a long rectangle table perched on wobbly legs atop cement flooring. There were just enough supplies and furniture to simulate a classroom environment. Twelve students were present, most of whom had medium- to dark-brown skin; they sat on metal fold-up chairs arranged around the table. The instructor described his pupils as "lower class"; in most cases, personal problems had prevented them from following a traditional educational trajectory.

In an attempt to stimulate conversation related to my research, the teacher posed the question "what race are you?" to his students. Immediately, a tension and silence filled the air, punctuated by nervous giggles. The students exchanged questioning glances. The tense climate and lack of student participation was uncharacteristic of other discussions I had witnessed among the students. The teacher repeated his question, directing it to the lightest student, who responded by shaking his head and smiling sheepishly, indicating an inability to answer. At this point, the climate transformed into a joking atmosphere as a student with dark-brown skin turned to a fellow classmate of a similar hue and declared: "You are mulatto!" Stifled giggles ensued. Attempting to refocus the class, the teacher personalized the question by making direct eye contact with each student, asking, "Mestizo or *moreno*?" The first two were unable to produce a response. As the instructor moved down the table, posing the same question to each student, two answered *mestiza* and the next, *moreno*. When the teacher posed the question to the best performing student, she answered with her typical preciseness: "Spanish and indigenous, so we are mestizos." The last student to be questioned timidly reiterated this response. As a way of providing closure to the conversation, the instructor offered a set of mathematical-style formulas, dictating: "Spanish and black is mulatto. Spanish and indigenous is mestizo. Eighty percent of us are mestizos." This anecdote illustrates the absence of a strong popular culture of race in Veracruz. The students were clearly uncomfortable with and unsure about how to articulate their racial identities. In contrast, the teacher was confident and prepared when disseminating information related to official definitions of race such as mestizo. Although the term mestizo is generally known to the populace, many Veracruzanos claim mixed heritage without specifically identifying as mestizo.

Veracruz Mixed-Race Identity Construction: Managing Multiple Dilemmas

There is much that lies beneath the surface of mixed-race identities. Veracruzanos of all hues need to negotiate their claims to a mixed-race status in the context of racial stereotypes, nationalist sentiment, and social norms. However, *how* they do this largely depends on their phenotype. As mentioned previously, light- and brown-skinned Mexicans face different circumstances and thus, distinct dilemmas, related to the interplay between their race-color and national identities. Consequently, they have different goals—light-skinned individuals strive to authenticate their Mexicanness and assert their identity as white without sounding pretentious, while brown-skinned individuals work to overcome the stigma associated with their appearance and their indigenous ancestry. Given such divergent goals, these groups develop different strategies for constructing and asserting their identities.

White Identities: Asserting an Unpretentious Whiteness and an Uncompromised Mexicanness

Light-skinned Veracruzanos generally identify as white but also claim a mixed-race heritage. Thus, consistent with constructions of whiteness in other Latin American contexts,[5] whiteness in Mexico does not imply or require racial purity. This contrasts to the United States, where whiteness presumes the absence of non-European ancestors.[6] In Veracruz, whiteness and racial hybridity are highly compatible; claims to whiteness are not threatened by acknowledgments of mixed-race heritage. Moreover, Veracruzanos who identity as white (henceforth, "white Veracruzanos") have something to gain by asserting a mixed-race identity. Because their status as Mexican is somewhat precarious due to the misalignment between their phenotype and racialized images of Mexicanness, claiming a mixed-race identity affords white Veracruzanos an opportunity to reaffirm their national identities.

In my conversations with white Veracruzanos, they made a point of emphasizing the mixture behind their white façade. For example, in a focus-group discussion, Bella, the forty-eight-year-old light-skinned high school teacher, asserted: "Here in Mexico there are no real whites... we are a mixture. There are those who are light in color but not white like the pure white race." Judy, the thirty-five-year-old light-skinned university professor, echoed these sentiments. Judy teaches the *mestizaje* ideology to her students, informing them: "We are a hybrid people, a people that can't be proud of a pure race..." In my interview with Judy she characterized Mexico as representing the vanguard of race-mixing practices, telling me: "In other countries there was racial mixture but it wasn't as deep of a mixture... here in Mexico it definitely occurred very, very strongly." Judy, like others, narrates Mexican history through a lens of hybridity.

Judy's continual use of "we" signals that she includes herself, a white Veracruzana, in the *mestizaje* national narrative. Personalizing the ideology even further, she shared that, although she looks white, she believes her blood is not one hundred percent European. In our conversation, Judy made a point of emphasizing that her European phenotype belies her mixed-race heritage. In other words, rather than claiming racial purity, Judy not only acknowledges but also takes care to highlight her mixed-race origins. We can think of Judy's claim to non-European heritage as being largely "symbolic" (Gans 1979; Waters 1990). Her whiteness and associated privileges are not compromised by her assertion of mixed-race ancestry. Moreover, by highlighting her mixed-race origins, Judy gains something—the fortification of her status as Mexican.

In addition to asserting a mixed heritage, white Veracruzanos' identity construction also involves self-identification as white, as Mexican, and as being of predominately European descent. However, juggling these different identity components can be challenging, especially given prevailing social norms. In Mexico, whiteness is associated not only with wealth, power, and high status but also with domination, exploitation, and a history of Spanish colonization. Thus, light-skinned Mexicans need to tread carefully when asserting a white identity or European heritage, taking care to avoid the appearance of showcasing or flaunting these attributes. Furthermore, they need to avoid having any claim to these identities be construed as antinationalistic; strongly asserting whiteness or Europeanness could be read by their compatriots as an allegiance to those identities over an indigenous or Mexican heritage. In light of the multiple meanings surrounding whiteness, white Veracruzanos manage their identities in a way that avoids the appearance of arrogance or places their patriotism in question.

Anita, a fifty-year-old light-skinned upper-class homemaker, adeptly navigated these issues during our conversation. She informed me that, in Mexico City (where she used to live), even some fifth-generation Spanish immigrants identify as Spaniards. Anita expressed disgust at this practice, contrasting it to the apathy she feels regarding her Spanish heritage. Anita shared, "I am Mexican. I am Veracruzana. My dad is Spanish and my grandparents are also Spanish but I was born here and I am very Mexican." Anita's modest claim to European ancestry is socially acceptable, especially when situated alongside her expression of loyalty to Mexico. According to Anita, flaunting one's Europeanness is not tolerated in Veracruz. Evoking a case in point, she shared how one of her son's classmates is ridiculed because he identifies as Spanish, even though he was born in Mexico.

Similar to Anita, other adult Veracruzanos managed the white symbolic quagmire by exercising caution when expressing a white identity. They asserted their whiteness discretely and employed various other strategies to mitigate potentially negative impacts of their claim. These strategies included exhibiting humility, downplaying their whiteness, evoking outside classifications, and asserting their Mexicanness. White Veracruzanos also employed discursive cues signaling subtlety, hesitancy, and indirectness to soften their claims to whiteness. For example, when I asked Jessica, a twenty-one-year-old light-skinned university student, about her racial identity, she responded: "Well [laughs], I am, uh, white, the white race with features that are uh... well, European." Jessica is very articulate and does not generally stumble in conversation, suggesting that she was treating this particular issue with care. Also exercising caution was Giovanni, the twenty-eight-year-old light-skinned fisherman. He first referred to himself as white (after pausing) and then playfully downplayed his lightness by referencing his sun-tanned arms, joking that he is not completely white.

Corazón, a fifty-six-year-old light-skinned working-class homemaker, also skirted around the whiteness issue. She described herself as not "overwhelmingly white" but, instead, "more or less white." Corazón then added, "Well, I'm not very white but I am not brown either... a lot of people call me white." She subsequently contested others' classification of her as white, stating: "Who knows why they think I am white because nothing about me is white." Although Corazón is identified as white by her fellow Veracruzanos, she refused to unequivocally accept this label. In our conversation, Corazón engaged in a number of discursive maneuvers to remain tentative in framing her identity as white; she consistently employed discursive cues such as pausing, lowering her voice, and introducing qualifiers such as "more or less." Additionally, she passed the classificatory torch to others, claiming whiteness indirectly through outside classification. In doing so, she was able to establish a link between herself and whiteness while sidestepping accusations of arrogance. Moreover, by evoking outside perceptions of her as white and then challenging these perceptions, Corazón was able to perform humility.

White Veracruzanos commonly relied on the strategy of evoking outside classifications to indirectly assert their whiteness while avoiding the appearance of arrogance. Providing another illustration of this is Javier, the twenty-eight-year-old navy employee with light-brown skin. When I asked Javier about his racial identity, he laughed, and said: "Many people say I'm white and, well, I say 'what part [of me is] white?' ... Maybe it is because I descend from a family of whites. My mom, my grandparents, my aunts and uncles are all white." In his response, Javier did not directly present himself as white but established an implicit connection to whiteness by discussing how he is viewed in society and by referencing his white family members. He also questioned the outside classifications of whiteness and, later in our conversation, expressed indifference toward being labeled white, strategies that further allowed him to evade potential accusations of a white superiority complex.

I witnessed the interplay between outside classification and self-identification surrounding whiteness when in the field. One afternoon Gloria, the forty-eight-year-old retired health-care worker with light-brown skin, and I were chatting together with one of her friends. At one point in our conversation, Gloria referred to herself as *morena*. Her friend immediately corrected her, asserting, "You are white." Gloria said nothing, neither accepting nor rejecting this characterization. Her silence had the effect of letting the white classification stand, allowing her to maintain an association with whiteness without appearing pretentious. On another occasion, I observed a mother and daughter engage in a discussion about the daughter's color. When the mother described her daughter as *trigueña* (wheat-colored), the daughter quickly reminded her that all of her friends call her *güera*, a point her mother then confirmed. In referencing outside classifications, white Veracruzanos are able to establish a link to whiteness in a socially acceptable manner.

The symbolic quagmire surrounding whiteness extends to issues of ancestry construction. When asserting their European heritage, whites take measures to secure and protect their national identities. They adopt national authentication strategies that allow them to simultaneously claim European ancestry without compromising their Mexicanness. For example, when discussing their race-color identities, white Veracruzanos often make a point of expressing their loyalty to Mexico and reasserting their status as Mexican. They provide markers of assurance that, despite being of European descent, they in no way *feel* European.[7] At a symbolic level, this distinction is significant as the issue of loyalty to Spain versus Mexico has important historical antecedents. During colonial times there was a contentious relationship between *peninsulares* (Spanish-born Spaniards) and *criollos* (people of full Spanish descent born in the New World). The *peninsular-criollo* tension played a central role in Mexico's War of Independence. Because of these aspects of history, among others, individuals who embody Spanish heritage are cautious about how they present this background, despite the fact that European ancestry and related phenotypes are privileged in Mexico.

White Veracruzanos delicately balance their assertions of European heritage with expressions of patriotism. Cristina, the twenty-year-old light-skinned university student, performed this balancing act during our interview. When I asked how she identifies racially, she gave an indirect, roundabout answer, explaining, "When I was in Italy, a lot of people thought I was Russian or from Ireland because they are said to be tall and very white. They never thought I was Mexican. I would tell them, 'I am Mexican,' and they would say, 'No, no, you aren't Mexican. You are Russian or something else.'" When I asked Cristina how she felt about this mischaracterization of her nationality, she responded, "It felt bad because I am Mexican…I love Mexico." Notice that Cristina did not negate her whiteness but expressed disgruntlement over others' assumptions that she is something other than Mexican. In responding this way, she effectively accepted the white label but also reaffirmed her Mexicanness. Cristina maintained her position as "Mexican first" throughout our conversation. On the topic of her ancestry, she informed me she is of indigenous, Italian, Portuguese, and Spanish heritage. However, after relaying this information, she added: "I am Mexican, right?…I don't identify with the Spanish or with the Italian or anything like that…Mexican, yes." In forwarding this assertion, she unequivocally positioned her European ancestry as secondary to her identity as Mexican. Like other white Veracruzanos, Cristina diplomatically established a connection to whiteness while displaying national loyalty.

Concha, a forty-three-year-old light-skinned upper-class homemaker, also stressed her Mexicanness when talking about her racial ancestry. She shared, "In my family, the truth is that there are no indians....My mom, well, is the daughter of Spanish and Italians. My dad is the son of a Spaniard and a Mexican but one who was the son of a Spaniard....We are of Spanish descent. But we are Mexicans." Elena, a forty-eight-year-old light-skinned working-class homemaker, framed her ancestry in a similar way while explaining why she identifies as "mixed": "I have family descendants who are completely Mexican, from the mountains....I consider myself to be Mexican because I was born here but I believe that three or four generations back I have a little Spanish blood." She then proclaimed, "I am neither from the Selva Lacandona[8] nor from any other country. I am from Mexico." In saying this, Elena positioned herself as neither indigenous nor foreign but Mexican. Like Concha and Elena, white Veracruzanos often emphasized their Mexican identity when bringing narrations of their ancestral lineage to a close. The decision to mention nationality at the end of these discussions gave their assertions regarding Mexican identity a sense of finality and definitiveness. They make it clear that, despite their phenotype or heritage, they are, above all, Mexican.

My findings from Veracruz inform understandings of whiteness in Latin America. Scholars have traditionally sent a clear message about whiteness in the region—it is highly privileged, valued, and desired.[9] However, the dynamics I observed in Veracruz regarding whiteness were more complex. While whiteness is, in fact, prized, it also symbolizes superiority and marginal Mexicanness; these conflicting images affect processes of identity construction. Therefore, addressing white identities in Latin America may require more attunement to national context. In Mexico, this would include a focus on how individuals manage their white identities without compromising national loyalty or violating social norms. Recently, scholars such as Telles and Flores (2013) have begun to explore the issue of how constructions of whiteness vary across Latin American countries. They argue that, in mestizo American nations such as Mexico, *mestizaje* ideologies minimize the tendency for individuals to identify as white. My findings that Veracruzanos are hesitant to assert an unqualified white identity lend support to this interpretation.

Brown Identities: Asserting Mixed (but especially European) Heritage

Brown-skinned Veracruzanos generally identify as *moreno* in a color sense[10] and assert a mixed-race heritage. Self-identified *morenos* (henceforth "brown Veracruzanos") face a different set of identity-related dilemmas and circumstances than their white counterparts. Because their phenotype closely resembles the Mexican norm, brown-skinned individuals of mixed European–indigenous descent do not carry the burden of needing to defend their Mexicanness. Asserting a brown identity is less problematic, as it does not threaten one's national status in the way that claims to whiteness do. Consequently, brown Veracruzanos typically do not defer to others' classifications when discussing their own identities, nor do they make a point of asserting their Mexicanness. Instead, they matter-of-factly and unapologetically claim a brown and mixed identity.

As with white Veracruzanos, being mixed is a central ingredient in the identity construction of brown Veracruzanos. However, unlike whites, they face the stigma of having brown skin and indigenous features in a society that values whiteness and European ancestry. Therefore, many brown Veracruzanos try to minimize their brownness by highlighting their European background, a pattern also documented in Brazil.[11] For example, Pilar, an eighteen-year-old gas station worker who identifies racially as *mestiza,* explained, "I am mixed because my grandmother's parents were Spanish. I have family that is very white and even has blue and green eyes. And on my grandfather's side, well, they were … well, more indigenous you could say … So I am, more than anything, *mestiza …*" Later in our conversation, Pilar revisited the topic of her white family members, discussing them more in-depth: "My grandma is still alive and she looks very white and she has blue eyes like my great-grandma … and I also have uncles that are white. Only I came out brown because of my dad but my mom is also white." Although Pilar acknowledged her non-European ancestors, she accentuated her European roots. Overall, she allotted more time to, was more detailed about, and expressed more enthusiasm toward her European ancestry.

As is typical of the nuances of discourse, it is not just *what* is said but also the *way* it is said that is important. Like Pilar, many brown Veracruzanos displayed a palpable enthusiasm when referencing a tall, light-skinned, blond, blue- or green-eyed member of their family. In contrast, they did not share detailed information or express similar emotion when talking about their non-European ancestors. These ancestors, when acknowledged, were rarely humanized with a face, name, or story. Therefore, Veracruzanos socially reproduce the race-color hierarchy in the creation and narration of their genealogical histories.

Individuals' sidelining of their non-European ancestry is likely influenced by two dynamics. First, it is likely that brown Veracruzanos emphasize their European background while distancing themselves from their indigenous heritage because European ancestry is prized in Mexico. Such ancestry establishes a connection, albeit tenuous, to the privileged realm of whiteness. A second and related dynamic influencing brown Veracruzanos' tendency to underemphasize their indigenous heritage is the fact that interfamily transmission about non-European ancestry is less frequent and detailed compared with information sharing involving European ancestors. Given these circumstances, Veracruzanos often receive little, if any, information about their non-European ancestors; this helps explain their tendency to accentuate the European angle when discussing heritage. Given the lack of concrete family-based knowledge about indigenous ancestry, individuals oftentimes turn to another information source—national ideology—to fill in knowledge gaps and form assumptions about the indigenous aspect of their ancestral lineage.

Identity Constructions: The National Narrative

National narratives play a key role in the creation of a country's race-color schema.[12] Individuals draw upon these narratives, as well as other cultural resources, to make sense of their lives.[13] Mexico's national ideology of *mestizaje,* which emphasizes Mexico's European and indigenous roots, is an example of a cultural repertoire that Mexicans use to construct their individual-level identities. Veracruzanos of all hues draw on this repertoire to (1) reinforce their identity as mestizo and (2) fill in knowledge gaps about their indigenous ancestry. Regarding the former, they rely on the *mestizaje* narrative to claim a mixed-race status, even in the absence of specific knowledge about personal heritage. The fact that many Veracruzanos identify as mixed without concrete information about the details of their ancestries indicates that a mixed-race identity can be a stand-alone identity. This differs from the U.S. context, where a multiracial identity is typically contingent upon knowledge that certain family members are of distinct races.

Regarding the second dynamic—the use of national ideology to fill in ancestral knowledge gaps—I found that Veracruzanos do not comprehensively adopt and employ Mexican national ideology. Instead, they extract particular strands of official ideological thought, molding these snippets of ideology to fit their personal situations and contexts. In many cases, to supplement the knowledge about European ancestry that is available within the family, individuals lean on the national ideology to surmise that they have indigenous ancestry. Thus, both in regards to claiming a mixed and indigenous-rooted identity, Veracruzanos rely on what they have learned about the *nation's* heritage to deduce their *personal* heritage. The alignment of national and individual identities is possible because of the ideological interconnection between race and nation in Mexico and the national rhetoric of racial homogeneity (i.e., "we are all mestizos").

Illustrating how Veracruzanos graft images of mestizo Mexico onto their individual identities is Belinda, the forty-six-year-old working-class homemaker with dark-brown skin. When I asked Belinda about her racial identity, she told me, "Well, I have heard that we are mixed, right? That the Mexican mixture was made with, I believe, the Spanish and from there they made 'the race.' What race, I don't know." Belinda draws on racialized national messages to create an understanding of herself as mixed, independent of knowledge of her specific ancestors. Antonio, a fifty-five-year-old light-skinned employee of PEMEX, the Mexican state-owned petroleum company, engaged in a similar practice. When I asked him what it means to be Mexican, he told me, "I am proud to be Mexican.... The truth is that I am a product of the mixture of races..." Despite Antonio's self-identification as white and lack of direct knowledge about his ancestors, he adopted an identity as mixed based on his status as Mexican.

Veracruzanos also fuse their national- and individual-level identities to deduce they have indigenous ancestry. Rosa, a thirty-four-year-old working-class homemaker with medium-brown skin, exemplified this, stating: "They say that all of us Mexicans are indigenous, right?...They say there were indians and that we descend from them." Illustrating the same point is Roberto, the twenty-three-year-old university graduate with medium-brown skin. When speaking about his racial identity, he mused, "...Well, we are of indigenous descent. It is what has always been here in Mexico." Roberto concluded our conversation by expressing the sentiment that, as a Mexican, he assumes he has indigenous ancestry. Similarly, Salvador, a twenty-four-year-old laborer with light-brown skin, attested: "I am from Mexico.... I consider myself to have indigenous blood." These cases illustrate the strong conceptual link between Mexicanness and indigenous heritage, a connection Veracruzanos rely upon to construct their identities.

The *mestizaje* ideology is even powerful enough to mold the identifications of those who have no phenotypic markers of indigenous ancestry. For example, Concha, the upper-class homemaker with light skin and European features, speculates about having indigenous heritage, despite her phenotype. She explained, "Regularly people here have some indigenous ancestry, even if it is a great-grandparent, a great-great grandparent or something like that....Perhaps me too." Despite Concha's inability to confirm any non-European ancestry, she finds the possibility that she is of partial indigenous descent to be realistic, given that she is Mexican. These cases reveal how the *mestizaje* ideological pillar serves as an important information source for Veracruzanos' mixed-race identity construction. However, individuals' understandings of indigeneity do not end there.

Veracruzanos not only view indigeneity as a necessary component of a mestizo identity but they also define the mestizo category in contradistinction to the indigenous "other." Therefore, their relationship to indigeneity is multifaceted, as indigeneity is both externally and internally related to mestizoness. On one hand, mixed-race Veracruzanos identify as *partially* indigenous. On the other, as mestizos, they exclude themselves from the indigenous category. Veracruzanos view indians as racially pure, something they perceive to be incompatible with a mestizo identity. Furthermore, while individuals' claiming of *some* indigenous ancestry buttresses their identities as Mexican, identifying as wholly indigenous is seen as undesirable, given the stigma associated with being indigenous in Mexico. Therefore, Veracruzanos avoid identifying as completely indigenous. Here, I outline how Veracruzanos conceptualize and distance themselves from the indigenous "other."

Despite the small size of the indigenous population in the Veracruz metropolitan area, Veracruzanos have clear ideas about the indigenous. Their perceptions, however, often do not come from direct interaction with the local indigenous community but instead are derived from a variety of indigenous-related images and discourses disseminated through popular culture, educational curricula,[14] and government discourse. These sources often present superficial and folkloric representations of the indigenous in Mexico. I witnessed the presentation of such stereotypes while attending a public ceremony for the annual Carnival celebration held in the Port of Veracruz. As I sat in crowded bleachers, I watched the outgoing Carnival queen gracefully walk across a raised platform in the middle of the city's public square. The incoming queen then stepped onto the stage, sporting an elaborate indigenous feather headdress. The evening's host narrated her entrance, referencing her symbolic display of indigeneity by evoking the phrases "the origins of our people" and "part of our culture." This indigenous-related performance was not an isolated event; during my stay I saw countless symbols of indigeneity in a variety of venues.

The well-known, low-budget comedy film series *La India Maria* (The Indian Maria) is a prominent example of mass dissemination of indigenous-related imagery. *La India Maria* was primarily filmed in the 1970s and 1980s but is still viewed throughout Mexico. Each episode centers on the main character, Maria, an indian who is portrayed as being poor, backward, and noble. Maria frequently finds herself in predicaments where she is forced to navigate a modern, urban landscape, a purposeful contrast to the rural environment understood to be indians' "natural" habitat. She commits numerous social blunders and frequently displays bouts of ineptitude, all performed for comedic purposes. When talking about *La India Maria* with Selena, a thirty-five-year-old accountant with light-brown skin, she chuckled at first mention of the character and then proceeded to summarize her interpretation of the films: "Well, the general plot has been that she is of a very low class, dressed with clothes that are, well, indigenous, and she is always trying to survive in the big city, right? That has always been the most humorous [thing] about her. Whatever she has to do with her mule or whatever, trying to survive in the big city." Veracruzanos' avid consumption of these films (as well as other media depicting indians in a similar manner) facilitates the development of stereotypical understandings of the indigenous.

Not surprisingly then, Veracruzanos' conceptualizations of the indigenous closely align with those perpetuated by the media and other sources. Observe how Rodrigo, a thirty-seven-year-old fisherman with dark-brown skin, describes the plight of the indian: "[They are] completely poor, very poor. They are very marginalized....They don't get close to civilization. They always want to be hidden....They live without lights, without water, without medical attention in the mountain zones, so when something happens, they arrive to the city and they are surprised to see houses, cars, and everything that they don't have in their habitat...." Rodrigo, like others, portrays indians as being stuck in the past (by their own volition) and consequently ignorant of modern ways, culture, and civilization. He mobilizes this image to contextualize the difficulties indians putatively confront when navigating urban settings.

Veracruzanos reference a host of stereotypes when talking about the indigenous population. They employ markers related to culture (wearing indigenous dress, practicing indigenous cultural traditions, speaking an indigenous language, or being from an indigenous community), geography (living or being from the highlands or rural settings), class (being poor), education (being illiterate), occupation (selling handicrafts or goods on the street), and physicality (being short, dark-skinned, and having straight hair). Focusing on physical and cultural characteristics, Rosalía, an eighteen-year-old light-skinned university student, described a typical indian as "short, with a round head, and eyes a little bit closed," and told me that they speak a different dialect. Describing indians in a different way, Ana, a forty-four-year-old teacher and independent business owner with dark-brown skin, explained:

> Normally, here, in this zone there are no indians. There are indians in the Oaxaca zone, in the highlands. The people still live in small communities...what are they called?...ethnic groups. They are small communities but they have ancestral traditions, very much from the past, right? But they have stayed that way because they are closed-minded and are not open to our current times.

In this statement, Ana touched upon typical geographic- and culture-based definitions of indigeneity.

Rolando, a fifty-seven-year-old accountant with medium-brown skin, spoke about the economic and cultural aspects of the indian equation, telling me: "I see them as being very poor, right?.... We'll see if they change their life or not.... They are not open [to civilization].... The indians are closed." Rolando discussed indians' socioeconomic position in the same breath as their putatively backward cultural orientation, the implication being that it is *because* of their cultural orientation that they are socioeconomically disadvantaged. Like Rolando, many Veracruzanos possess strong notions about the indigenous, despite their minimal presence in the region.

Another important component of Veracruzanos' construction of what it means to be indigenous revolves around the idea of racial purity, a construction that also exists in Brazil.[15] Veracruzanos view the indigenous, unlike themselves, as biologically and culturally pure. This is largely based on the perception that the indigenous population is preserved in the past and is isolated, both physically and culturally, from modern mestizo Mexico. The association of indigeneity with purity defines and hardens the boundary between indians and mestizos. In my conversation with Reina, a fifty-one-year-old light-skinned upper-class homemaker, the notion of indigenous purity came to the fore after she struggled to define what it means to be indigenous. She began, "Indians are, well, communities of birth but they are not races. No, because...I literally don't know the definition but the indian, I mean indians, are people who are originally from a native place, a place without mixture." Alfredo, the fifty-six-year-old fisherman with dark-brown skin, demonstrates how the association between indians and purity shapes his own identity. When I asked Alfredo how he self-identifies, he reflected, "Well, indian 'no' because...well I already have mixed blood. I cannot be indigenous...rather, I am mestizo." Alfredo disqualifies himself from the indigenous category based on his lack of racial purity. Like Alfredo, other Veracruzanos who claimed some indigenous ancestry rejected an indigenous identity because they are not *solely* of indigenous heritage.

Despite the limited indigenous presence in the urban centers of Veracruz, it is evident that Veracruzanos have strong ideas about who is and who is not indigenous. These conceptions facilitate the demarcation of the indigenous–mestizo boundary since the question of who is indigenous directly relates to who is not indigenous (or, in official parlance, who is mestizo). Therefore, although the indigenous population is not central to local race relations, the indian construct plays an important role in defining who is mestizo. Moreover, indigeneity also plays a role in color dynamics *within* the mestizo population.

Mixed-race Veracruzanos who have cultural or physical attributes that place them near the indigenous pole of the mestizo race-color continuum are susceptible to being called indigenous-related terms. However, this does not mean that these individuals are definitively viewed as indigenous. Instead, labels of *indio* (a derogatory term for indian) or similar references are inconsistently applied to individuals considered to be mestizos. The purpose and function of this labeling practice is not to permanently categorize an individual as indian but instead to highlight his or her perceived indigenous physical or cultural traits. When deployed within the mestizo population, indigenous-related labels are used intermittently and do not have permanent sticking power.[16]

I witnessed this temporary tagging dynamic during a trip I took abroad with a group of Veracruzanos. Upon arrival to our destination, we exchanged currency. As we regrouped, Esperanza, the school teacher in her forties with medium-brown skin, shared how she had handed her money to the exchange agent without inquiring about the exchange rate, describing her actions as characteristic of an *indita*. In doing so, she referenced the well-entrenched stereotype of indian ignorance and naiveté. Although Esperanza referred to herself as indian in this specific context, she identifies as mixed. This tagging dynamic demonstrates how race-color labels that refer to the indigenous can be deployed (temporarily) within the mestizo category. As we can see, Veracruz racial common sense on the topic of indigeneity is nuanced and operates at multiple levels.

Conclusion

We can extract a number of concluding thoughts from this examination of the identity construction process of urban, mixed-raced Veracruzanos. First and foremost, there is much that lies beneath the surface of mixed-race identities. Being mixed or mestizo entails much more than simply not being indian. As I demonstrated, Veracruzanos of varying hues engage in a rich and complex process of managing various aspects of their identities. In the identity construction process, they need to negotiate issues related to racial ideology, constructions of nation, and societal norms. Additionally, consistent with one of the main foci of this book, I detailed how individuals' color plays a significant role in the identity formation process—light-skinned Veracruzanos face different dilemmas when navigating societal and national ideological messages compared with their brown-skinned counterparts. Consequently, these two groups adopt distinct strategies for developing and asserting their race-color and national identities. Light-skinned Veracruzanos claim whiteness in a way that weds them to the nation and that also dodges perceptions that they have a superiority complex. Brown-skinned Veracruzanos, on the other hand, often choose to emphasize their European ancestry, situating themselves closer to whiteness.

Veracruzanos of all hues co-opt national ideology and the interconnection between race and nation to inform and construct their personal identities; in the absence of direct ancestral knowledge, they stake a claim to a mixed-race identity and partial indigenous ancestry based on the *mestizaje* ideological pillar. The fact that individuals draw upon select components of ideological thought in particular contexts exposes a nuanced relationship between ideology and racial common sense, one that goes beyond the dichotomy of citizens either fully accepting or wholly challenging national ideology. As seen throughout the chapter, Veracruzanos are adept at adopting specific strands of official thought to conveniently fill in blanks regarding their personal identities. Employing situational creativity, they draw on the national ideology as a cultural toolkit, sifting through and extracting particular snippets of information and molding them to fit their circumstances. The findings presented in this chapter contribute to our overall understanding of what it means to be mixed-race in Veracruz, supplying an important piece of the Mexican racial puzzle. Taken as a whole, the dynamics identified in this chapter illustrate how myriad factors interact to form mestizo identities in the land of the cosmic race. In the next chapter, I examine the *mestizaje* ideological pillar from a different angle, focusing on mestizos' attitudes on race mixture.

4 | Mestizos' Attitudes on Race Mixture

With my color, my wife's color is "cleaning the race" a little bit, right? And the children of my children, well, they will be white. They will not be my color.

—*José, a Veracruz taco vendor who has dark-brown skin*

Whites look to marry other whites to continue producing white children.

—*Carolina, a light-skinned Veracruz homemaker*

A S MENTIONED PREVIOUSLY, the race mixture theme became a fortified pillar of Mexican national ideology in the early twentieth century when elites such as José Vasconcelos glorified and encouraged *mestizaje*. Race mixture was supported, in part, because elites viewed it as a mechanism to whiten the country through the dilution and eventual elimination of the country's black and indigenous populations. Given a national ideology that continues to concurrently privilege race mixture and whitening and asserts the nation is free from racism, one wonders how mixed-race Mexicans form and articulate their thoughts and attitudes on *mestizaje* (the intimate crossing of race-color boundaries)[1] within this contradictory ideological context.

The preceding epigraphs exemplify the dominant themes that run through Veracruzanos' racial common sense on *mestizaje*—while race mixture is viewed as advantageous when used as a vehicle to lighten the phenotype of future generations, it is simultaneously shunned among light-skinned individuals who seek to maintain their whiteness and the whiteness of their family line. Thus, Veracruzanos embrace race mixture in some capacities yet do not embrace it unconditionally. In particular, they are not keen on the idea of relationships involving individuals who are darker. Taken as a whole, this common sense, like its elite counterpart, houses the internal contradiction of simultaneously valuing race mixture and whiteness. It also possesses sentiments that are inconsistent with the national ideological pillar of nonracism. Veracruzanos are thus confronted with the complicated task of managing their attitudes toward race mixture amid a culture that prizes whiteness and a national ideology that lauds *mestizaje* and asserts the nonexistence of racism.

In this chapter I delineate Veracruzanos' strategies for managing their attitudes toward interracial relationships in light of such complexities. Specifically, I describe how Veracruzanos express a qualified openness to *mestizaje* yet reject the idea of interracial marriage with members of select groups. They also adopt the language of "preference" to frame objections to interracial marriage in a way that minimizes conflict with the national ideology. I also show how individuals justify their preference for lighter-skinned partners from the perspective of wanting to lighten their children, the next generation. Finally, I demonstrate how Veracruzanos manage the blatant contradiction with the ideological pillars of *mestizaje* and non-racism that arises when light-skinned Veracruzanos object to interracial marriage. Before detailing these findings, I show how Veracruzanos view anti-*mestizaje* attitudes as symptomatic of racism.

Linking *Mestizaje* with Antiracism at the Popular Level

Consistent with post-revolutionary ideology, Veracruzanos equate the practice of *mestizaje* with antiracism and thus reproduce the interconnection between the *mestizaje* and nonracism prongs of official Mexican ideology. Demonstrating this in a succinct fashion is Fernando, a nineteen-year-old light-skinned car washer. He informed me that "race mixture means that racism does not exist." Felipe, an eighteen-year-old light-skinned university student, displayed a similar sentiment, albeit less directly, when he jumped to the topic of racism in response to a question I posed about interracial relationships and his dating preferences, stating: "For me, racism does not exist here.... If you fall in love with a person, status and color are not important." Felipe's response demonstrates that he interpreted my question about interracial relationships as being fundamentally about racism. The same interconnection between *mestizaje* and nonracism surfaced during a high school class discussion about racism in Mexico, a conversation prompted by the teacher in an attempt to facilitate my research. At one point a student confidently asserted: "There cannot be racism because we are not pure," a comment that elicited nods and murmurs of agreement from fellow students.

Veracruzanos use the philosophy that race mixture implies a lack of racism as an interpretive lens for understanding the attitudes and behaviors of others. More specifically, they view individuals' refusal to date or marry someone of a different race or color as suspect and as a possible sign of racism. For example, Adán, the thirty-five-year-old painter with medium-brown skin, made the serious accusation that a male acquaintance of his is racist, based on his acquaintance's assertion that he would never marry a black or *morena* woman. Arturo, a dark-brown-skinned country club worker in his sixties, applied the same logic. He informed me that in Mexico there is no racial discrimination because people do not say things such as, "I won't dance with a person because she is black. I won't marry her." For Arturo, the assumed absence of blatant anti-miscegenation sentiment proves that Mexico is free of racism.

The fact that anti-miscegenation attitudes are viewed as racist poses a dilemma for the many Veracruzanos who are hesitant or opposed to the idea of marrying blacks, indians, or someone darker than themselves and who generally prefer lighter partners.[2] Veracruzanos with such views are not only faced with needing to evade charges of racism but are also confronted with the task of reconciling these attitudes with the official line of societal openness to *mestizaje,* the belief that Mexico is a nonracist country, and the emphasis on whitening. Veracruzanos navigate this complex and contradictory ideological terrain in the best way they can—by deploying discourses framing their attitudes on the topic in a way that saves as much personal and national face as possible.

Attitudes on *Mestizaje:* Thoughts on Potential Partners

To open my discussion of attitudes on interracial relationships, I will share a conversation that took place during a baby shower, with attendees representing the middle and upper-middle classes. As I arrived, I greeted the hostess and took a seat at one of the many round tables scattered across a ballroom rented for the occasion. My tablemates were a group of seven women, none of whom I had previously met. As we awaited a meal of chicken and mole, one of my tablemates, a woman in her forties with a large build, light-brown skin, thick layers of makeup, and voluminous hair, sparked up a conversation. Her boisterous voice, exaggerated facial expressions, and flamboyant demeanor immediately captivated our attention. Moreover, she initiated a provocative line of conversation, complaining that sex with her husband was unsatisfactory. After detailing the terms of her dissatisfaction, she turned the conversation outward, asking if any of us knew men who might interest her. Two women immediately jumped to her aid, naming a mutual acquaintance of theirs. They circulated his name to see if others at the table knew him, while describing him physically—"green eyes, brown skin...." The woman who had requested suggestions immediately halted the discussion, loudly asserting, "I don't want someone brown." Another joked, "She wants a white guy." The woman who had initially volunteered the man's name quickly clarified, "But he is *light* brown." However, she did not pursue the issue further as the woman soliciting potential partners maintained the disgruntled expression that had surfaced at the first mention of the man's brown skin tone.

This incident shares both similarities to and differences with the general attitudes and discursive patterns surrounding race mixture that I observed in Veracruz. Although preference for partners with light skin is common, most Veracruzanos are subtler when expressing these preferences compared with my tablemate. Furthermore, Veracruzanos are typically more careful to frame their preferences for whiteness in a way that minimizes possible accusations of racism. To finesse their attitudes on *mestizaje* in light of the national ideology, they assert a qualified openness to interracial relationships, engage in selective rejections based on the group in question, and deploy a language of preference.

Expressing a Qualified Openness to Interracial Relationships

During my conversations with Veracruzanos, many expressed a sentiment of qualified openness toward interracial marriage—they were open to the possibility *if* particular conditions were met. When discussing the topic, they frequently erected a series of barriers and forwarded a set of contingencies that made interracial marriage hypothetically possible but practically unrealistic. In response to my question about their willingness to marry someone of another race or color, individuals would oftentimes deliver a qualified "yes" but then proceed to outline the qualifications necessary for them to engage in such relationships. These requisites were applied when discussing potential black, indigenous, or dark-skinned partners. For example, some respondents mentioned that they would consider marrying a black or a dark-brown-skinned person if he or she were extremely attractive or an indigenous person if he or she were highly educated and cultured. However, setting the preconditions of an attractive black or dark-brown-skinned individual or a highly educated indigenous person is extremely restrictive in a society that equates beauty with whiteness and indigeneity with illiteracy. Nevertheless, by adopting the language of beauty, education, and culture when creating a series of inter-racial marriage contingencies, Veracruzanos are able to convey the message that they are open to interracial relationships while minimizing the practical possibility of such relationships.

Simón, a seventy-six-year-old light-skinned, middle-class retiree, engaged in the discourse of qualified openness. He told me, "Color doesn't have anything to do with my choice [of spouse]," explaining that his decision about whether he would marry a black woman would depend on her "education, cultural grade, behavior, and her morals." However, understandings of education, culture, and morals are highly racialized in Veracruz; blacks are frequently perceived as lacking these qualities. Therefore, Simón's response, while nonracial on the surface, carries covert racial undertones. It makes the possibility of involvement with a black woman highly unlikely while not removing it entirely from the realm of possibility. Gloria, the forty-eight-year-old middle-class retired health worker with light-brown skin, used a similar discursive strategy during our conversation about interracial marriage. When I asked if she would con-sider marrying an indigenous individual she hesitated and then replied, "If he had a heart of gold, perhaps." Gloria displayed similar reservations with regards to marrying a black person, telling me, "I don't like [blacks], but if it is a noble man with principles and he thinks like I do and has a similar life project as I do and I love him, then perhaps." By framing her com-ments as such, Gloria is able to maintain an image of openness to inter-racial marriage, thereby disqualifying herself as racist while at the same making interracial marriage an unrealistic possibility given her stringent preconditions. Expressions of qualified openness allow Veracruzanos to both distance themselves from an anti-*mestizaje* stance and escape direct conflict with the national ideology of nonracism.

Selective Rejections Regarding Interracial Marriage: "Oh, You Meant Any Race?"

As we saw with the discourse of qualified openness, Veracruzanos make an effort to avoid rejecting the idea of interracial marriage outright. In fact, most Veracruzanos initially expressed openness to race mixture when I asked them a question about interracial marriage in broad terms—"Would you marry someone of another race?" Because this question does not spec-ify particular racial groups, individuals are free to conjure up scenarios of their own choosing, which likely facilitates positive responses. However, when I then inquired about particular groups, the discourse of openness melted away as respondents realized, "Oh, you meant *any* race?" Under these conditions, objections began to surface, especially regarding relationships with blacks and indians and, to a lesser degree, brown-skinned mestizos. We can see this shift taking place in my conversation with Selena, the thirty-five-year-old middle-class accountant with light-brown skin.

> cs: If you were single, would you marry someone of another race?
> SELENA: Yes.
> cs: An indigenous man, a white man, a black man?
> SELENA: Well, I feel like...perhaps not the indian...in my case it isn't because I consider myself to be beautiful...but because the indigenous people have very little education. They are very illiterate people. We wouldn't match, right? I don't have a lot of education but more or less. Those people don't know how to read or how to speak Spanish.

As we can see, Selena reconsidered her previously stated position on race mixture when discussing the indigenous. However, she framed her objections as due to educational and cultural but not racial factors.

The "oh, you meant any race" realization also occurred during my conversation with Jessica, the twenty-one-year-old light-skinned university student:

> cs: Would you marry someone of another race?
> JESSICA: Maybe, because I am thinking about going to study in Spain and well, we will see what presents itself....I am open to any possibility.
> cs: What about a man from here? An indigenous Mexican?
> JESSICA: No.
> cs: Why?
> JESSICA: Because I don't like them. I mean, I am clearly not racist but deep down, truthfully, I would not marry an indigenous person.

When confronting the initial, unspecified question, Jessica tailored it to her vision of future travel to Spain, expressing openness and even excitement at the prospect of an interracial relationship. However, when I provided her with an alternate vision—marrying an indigenous Mexican—she quickly adjusted her stance, revealing that someone indigenous was not what she had in mind when she asserted she was amenable to the idea of marrying someone of another race. In light of her objections to marrying an indigenous man, Jessica, like Selena, worked to present herself as not racist.

In a final example, Omar, the forty-four-year-old journalist with medium-brown skin, also initially positioned himself as being open to race mixture, albeit more tentatively. However, his initial hesitancy foreshadowed a subsequent objection to marrying members of certain groups.

CS: If you were single, would you marry someone of another race?

OMAR: Uh … yes.

CS: Any race?

OMAR: Well, no. No. I am going to tell you why. I have much respect for the pigmentation of all skin types but sometimes there are skins which have certain characteristics of smell that are not pleasing to me.

CS: Like which ones are you referring to?

OMAR: Well, brown skin, right?

CS: Brown like you?

OMAR: No, browner. … Let's say the black race. It is not for the color. It is not for the color. It is for the smell of the skin. … It is not pleasing to me.

Omar's attempt at a diplomatic explanation does not dilute his bottom line—he would not marry a black person because he doesn't like how blacks supposedly smell. This perspective was also shared by Sandra, the high school teacher who is forty-eight years old and has light-brown skin. Sandra justified her lack of attraction to blacks as being due to their putative odor. To make her point, she referenced a male colleague of hers as an example of how blacks smell, wrinkling her nose for effect. Returning to the case of Omar, notice how he (twice) affirmed that his objection had nothing to do with color. According to Omar, it is an odor, not skin color or black people per se, that is the source of his distaste. From Omar's perspective, this framing deracializes his comments, thus avoiding a direct conflict with the ideologies of *mestizaje* and nonracism.

As we have seen, Veracruzanos' reservations about interracial relationships focus on mixture involving individuals at the dark end of the race-color continuum. Veracruzanos commonly frame indians as unsuitable partners based on issues related to culture, socioeconomic status, and education. In contrast, they generally deem blacks to be undesirable partners based on physical traits. In chapter 1, I briefly mentioned that Silvia, the fifty-four-year-old day care worker with dark-brown skin, objected to marrying an indigenous individual for cultural reasons. To provide more detail, she told me that she would rather remain single than marry an indigenous man because he would surely take her to his ranch and she is afraid of snakes. She also objected to what she perceives as indigenous patriarchal customs, asserting, "They don't like women to work or leave the house. They do not like women to have freedom. They are chauvinistic. The woman has to do what he says."[3] For Silvia, marrying an indigenous individual would entail a shift in cultural and lifestyle conditions, something that would be unacceptable to her. In contrast, Marisa, a twenty-five-year-old English teacher with medium-brown skin, balks at the idea of marrying a black person because of physical traits that she associates with blacks and that she finds unattractive—"hard features, flat noses, and thick lips." Regardless of whether Veracruzanos are expressing objections to marrying indigenous individuals or blacks, they frequently attempt to portray their attitudes as nonracist and often frame their objections as motivated by individual preference as opposed to racist sentiment.

Adopting the Language of Preference—"Personally, I Am Just Not Attracted to Blacks"

One evening I was having dinner with a Veracruz family of middle-class status. The atmosphere was jovial, and the conversation was punctuated by jokes and laughter. At one point, the father, Jorge, the dentist who is fifty-years old and has dark-brown skin, began telling a story about a friend of his who lived in the United States without documentation. He explained that his friend had two options for gaining legal status—marry a prostitute or marry a black woman with two children. The friend purportedly solicited Jorge's advice about this difficult dilemma. Jorge told the group that he suggested his friend marry the black woman but his friend protested, "But she is really fat!" At this point in the story, Jorge could barely contain his laughter. Nevertheless, he managed to deliver the punch line: he advised his friend, "Then it is better if you return to Mexico!" At this, everyone burst into fits of laughter. In this narrative, Jorge equates the symbolic package of a black, overweight, single mother with the image of a prostitute. Jorge's story underscores a salient aspect of Veracruz racial common sense that I touched upon in the previous section—the expressed undesirability of blacks as marital partners.

Strong objection to marrying blacks does not mesh with the image of Mexicans' presumed openness to race mixture and absence of racial prejudice. Consequently, Veracruzanos manage their distaste for these relationships in a way that circumvents a conflict with the national ideology—they couch their objections in a language of personal preference, deracializing the meaning behind their objections. They frame objections as a matter of personal taste as opposed to a manifestation of racism. This dynamic is similar to that documented by Roth (2008) in her study of Dominicans. In the case of Veracruz, the personal preference frame operates freely and unchallenged because individuals do not perceive these kinds of personal preferences as representing racism.

Illustrating the use of this discursive strategy is Pepe, the forty-seven-year-old high school teacher with light-brown skin. In our conversation he made a point of drawing a clear distinction between his objections to marrying blacks or "dark" individuals and racial prejudice. He explained, "The dark color is not attractive to me. I am not racist. . . . It is just not my taste." In another example, Alejandra, the nineteen-year-old light-skinned law student, differentiated between issues of physical attraction and racism. When I asked if she would marry someone darker than herself, she paused, contemplating the question, and then responded: "Yes. But, I mean, I can tell you that blacks are not attractive to me, and *morenos*, more or less—but not much either. I mean, it is not like racism because I have absolutely nothing against them, but physically they are not attractive to me."

Individualistic discourses of preference regarding a partner place race and color on the same symbolic plane as other physical traits; Veracruzanos treat their distaste for dark skin as the symbolic equivalent of not liking people with crooked teeth or prominent noses. To provide a case in point, Concha, the forty-three-year-old light-skinned upper-class homemaker, listed whiteness as a desirable physical trait in a partner: "I like white men. Normally I like blonds . . . and I like [them] muscular, a little bit fat, tall. . . ." By presenting her race-color preferences alongside other kinds of physical attributes and by couching them in the language of personal taste, Concha's race-color preferences appear benign. The personal preference frame is compelling because it dovetails with notions of individual freedom of choice. However, when viewed collectively, the preferences of individual Veracruzanos are not randomly distributed but instead consistently align to privilege whiteness. This alignment, however, is not recognized by Veracruzanos. Instead, they maintain that their objection to marrying members of certain groups is nothing more than their own personal preference.

Attitudes on *Mestizaje*: Employing the Discourse of "Consider the Children"

A significant component of Veracruz racial common sense regarding *mestizaje* involves concerns over the race-color of the next generation. In the United States, concerns for the well-being of the offspring of interracial relationships surface as a means of justifying opposition to interracial marriage.[4] It is sometimes assumed that the children of such relationships may be maladjusted or marginalized in U.S. society, which has historically embraced a system of monoraciality.[5] In Veracruz, the concern over the children plays out much differently. The fear is not that mixed-race children will be marginalized since being mestizo is central to the image of the Mexican national community. Instead, there is concern that interracial relationships run the "risk" of producing children who embody the genes of the darker parent. Therefore, concern about how the children will "come out" phenotypically strongly contextualizes Veracruzanos' attitudes on *mestizaje*.

Veracruzanos generally frame their concern as a matter of aesthetics—family members hope for light-skinned children with European features because they see them as being more beautiful, a dynamic documented in other Latin American contexts.[6] The aesthetic-centered nature of the discourse about the children has important consequences regarding the relationship between this aspect of Veracruz racial common sense and the ideology of nonracism. Since Veracruzanos do not include aesthetic preference for whiteness in their definitions of racism, the discourse regarding the phenotype of future children is viewed as unproblematic. Consequently, Veracruzanos are freed from the burden of needing to manage this particular discourse in light of the national ideology of nonracism. Compared with the attitudes covered in previous sections, Veracruzanos more openly discuss their preference for lighter partners when couching these preferences in a discussion about the next generation; they more freely express wanting light-skinned partners with the goal of producing light-skinned children with blue or green eyes, as there is little threat that these preferences will be read as racist.

Not surprisingly, individuals' concerns and preferences about the next generation oftentimes reveal themselves within the context of pregnancy and birth. Such contexts elicit feelings of hope and anticipation. They hold an element of surprise regarding how babies will "come out" physically. This atmosphere facilitates the expression of family members' desires and expectations regarding the new family member, which oftentimes include preferences about race and color, a dynamic also observed in Brazil.[7] In Veracruz, individuals frequently express a strong desire for babies to be born light, or as light as possible given the genetic composition of family members. They also emphasize eye color, vocalizing preferences for blue or green eyes.[8] Sofía, the university employee in her twenties who has medium-brown skin, has witnessed this on various birth-related occasions. She has noticed that, once a baby's good health has been established, "the criticism begins." She has heard statements such as, "Well, it is a brown baby…" or, much more enthusiastically, "Oh the baby is very good-looking, very white with blue eyes and a pretty nose." Simón, the light-skinned middle-class retiree, also spoke of the societal hypersensitivity surrounding babies' color as well as his own preferences. He explained: "Almost all of the children at birth are pink or red. But soon after, one can tell if the child is going to be white because there are reds that are going to be brown…and after that the color of their skin changes completely. But I really like white children who have blue or green eyes." In addition to unabashedly revealing his preference for white babies, Simón exposes the degree of Veracruzanos' attunement to the nuances of skin and eye color.

Anticipation about a baby's color is most intense within families where members are of noticeably different colors. Under these circumstances, individuals perceive a wide range of possible outcomes for newborns in the game of genetic roulette. When a birth occurs, parents, relatives, friends, and neighbors often gather around a newborn to see how the baby "came out." If the baby is light-skinned, there are frequently comments about how light and beautiful the baby is. Observers quickly spread the happy news. I witnessed this while visiting the home of a local family. A baby girl had just arrived from the hospital, born to a father with light-skin and blue eyes and a mother with dark-brown skin and brown eyes. Given their color differences, there was much discussion about whose traits the baby would inherit. Although the baby could barely open her eyes, within a few minutes of arrival, her aunt, cradling the newborn in her arms, announced triumphantly: "She is going to have blue eyes!"

Marco, the fifty-one-year-old painter with dark-brown skin who was involved with a white woman, spoke of his own feelings of anticipation before their child was born. He desperately hoped that the cards would be stacked in favor of her genes, explaining: "I wouldn't have cared if she was ugly like me, but I wanted her to have green eyes…like her mother or be light like her mother. But she came out ugly like me." When I asked Marco what he meant by "ugly," he clarified, "Like this, like me.

An ugly *moreno*." When I spoke with Esteban, the twenty-nine-year-old light-skinned computer technician, he was able to talk about his feelings pre-birth, as he was expecting a child with his dark-brown skinned partner at the time of our conversation. Esteban shared, "Well, I am wishing that he will have green eyes, right?.... I am not as interested in the skin color as I am in the eye color." Both Marco and Esteban (representing the darker and lighter partners, respectively) expressed hope that European genes would shine through in their children. Like other Veracruzanos, they shared these views without worry of being accused of exhibiting racial prejudice.

The discourse about the children is two-sided. Not only is there a strong preference for whiteness, but also there is a corresponding concern about brownness. Sandra, the high school teacher with light-brown skin, spoke of the dual nature of this discourse: "Many people want the baby to come out white.... If it is brown, they don't like that very much." Sandra's perception of the situation was supported by my observations in the field. I overheard remarks to the effect of, "I hope [the baby] doesn't come out brown" or "Too bad s/he came out brown." Amanda, a twenty-five-year-old working-class homemaker with light-brown skin, shared with me that her mother had made it absolutely clear that she did not want Amanda to have any "very brown" children. In another example, a mother refused to accept her daughter's dark-brown-skinned boyfriend because it opened up the possibility that she could have dark-brown-skinned grandchildren. As exemplified in this latter example, Veracruzanos' concern for the children or grandchildren often influences their attitudes regarding potential partners.

How Concern for the Children Dictates Partner Choice

Veracruzanos frequently view dating, even among young people, through the lens of future offspring. Esteban, the light-skinned computer technician, shared that when he was an adolescent he had dated a girl of African descent, someone with "curly, curly, curly hair." He remembers others making remarks about what their children would look like, predicting they would be the color of coffee with milk. Aracely, the forty-eight-year-old working-class homemaker with light-brown skin, was also socialized to think about potential offspring when choosing a partner. When she was a young girl, someone warned her not to marry a black person because her children would come out black. Aracely was too young to recall who the person was, but her recollection of the "threat" of black children has followed her into adulthood.

Two societal notions—"bettering the race" and "staying white"—serve to link concerns regarding children's phenotype to attitudes toward interracial marriage. "Bettering the race," a common colloquial phrase heard not only in Mexico but also throughout Latin America,[9] refers to the practice of seeking out lighter-skinned partners in hopes of lightening the next generation. The concept of "staying white" refers to light-skinned individuals' rejection of interracial marriage for the purpose of preserving a generational pattern of whiteness. Both of these philosophies contextualize Veracruzanos' thoughts on *mestizaje*. However, whereas "bettering the race" promotes an engagement with partners of another race or color, abiding by the idea of "staying white" necessitates a rejection of interracial relationships. Therefore, the "bettering the race" and "staying white" philosophies have different implications with respect to the *mestizaje* ideology.

"Bettering the Race"

Marisa, the English teacher with dark-brown skin and very curly hair, demonstrates how the idea of "bettering the race" influences her thoughts regarding a future marriage partner. Defending her stance that she would like to marry someone lighter, she explained, "If one is a descendent from dark people, and one marries a person who is dark, the children aren't going to come out very attractive, shall we say. They are going to come out with very flat noses, or in other words, be very unrefined." The connection between a concern for the children and choice of partner also surfaced amid a light-hearted focus group discussion.[10] Observe how the "bettering the race" notion undergirds the ensuing exchange.

> KAREN: Many *morenos* fell in love with me. Good-looking ones...I said, "*Morenos* no because how are my [children] going to come out?"..."Me *morena* and him *moreno*..." So I said "No, I want a white person." And a white person appeared. And it wasn't just him, there were various white men...when one is young they come without looking for them.
>
> PATRICIA: But [your children] came out like you...not [your husband] because he is white.
>
> KAREN: No, all of them were born white....My daughters were born white. Not one was born *morena* like me. My son is browner right now...because of the sun...but he was white, with slightly blond hair....I had my conditions [for a partner]. Straight hair, white, tall, stocky legs....

ELVA: Here that happens a lot...my grandma, being *morena*, looked for a white person. It happens a lot within us. We discriminate against ourselves.

KAREN: Yes.

PATRICIA: Yes.

ELVA: We ourselves do it because if we are *moreno*, we want whites...so they [the children] come out whiter....

Both Karen and Elva are vocal about how the question of the next generation weighs heavily in the assessment of potential partners. The bluntness with which Karen shared her decision to actively seek out and marry a white man with the goal of producing white children and her open articulation of this view in front of fellow Veracruzanos suggests a lack of concern that her perspective and behaviors will be perceived as racist. The "bettering the race" philosophy justifies the seeking out of lighter partners while dodging a conflict with the *mestizaje* ideology (because it encourages interracial relationships) and the nonracism ideology (because it is framed as being motivated by an aesthetic-driven consideration of potential offspring).

"Staying White"

The notion of light-skinned individuals trying to "stay white" involves the reproduction of whiteness and explicitly rejects interracial relationships, and thus conflicts with the *mestizaje* and nonracism ideological pillars. Therefore, reconciling "staying white" practices with the national ideology requires more complex management strategies. Carolina, the fifty-year-old light-skinned upper-class homemaker, referenced the common nature of whites attempting to remain white in the following statement: "Here there are many Spanish people.... [They] have children who married, perhaps Veracruzanos, but also the children of Spaniards—maybe not Spaniards but people with white skin. They had children and well, those children are white." Carolina's comments suggest that the most important factor in whites' marital preferences is race or color; whiteness is a primary concern, whereas nationality and ethnic heritage are secondary. Judy, the thirty-five-year-old light-skinned university professor, also emphasized that "staying white" philosophies and practices are alive and well in Veracruz. Exuding confidence, she informed me, "Those that are white look to marry other whites to continue to produce white children." Interestingly, Carolina and Judy both have partners with dark-brown skin and were among the few light-skinned individuals who spoke so directly about the "staying white" dynamic. Their social trespass of marrying someone significantly darker may have rendered interracial marriage norms particularly visible.

More commonly, it was brown-skinned Veracruzanos who mentioned the "staying white" dynamic. Although one might imagine that they would frown on this practice, brown-skinned individuals were generally not critical of whites seeking out other whites as partners. In fact, Abril, a middle-class homemaker in her sixties with dark-brown skin, and her husband who is of a comparable skin tone, were sympathetic when relaying their thoughts on this tradition. Abril mused: "I think that a white person will always look for a partner of the same color... because later they will have very beautiful children... with green eyes and faces that look like dolls." Abril's husband chimed in with enthusiastic agreement. Abril and her husband not only condone the "staying white" practice but actually embrace the end result—what they perceive to be beautiful, doll-like children. The "staying white" dynamic appears to escape criticism due to the overwhelming societal support for the production of "beauty."

Equally generous in his interpretation of whites' rejection of interracial marriage was Roberto, the university graduate with medium-brown skin. Speaking about one of the wealthiest families in Veracruz, he informed me: "I believe they are the descendants of Spaniards....All of them have white skin. They are white and they have blue or green eyes. They marry other men and women who are the same—with blue or green eyes and white skin, right? It isn't to discriminate but they have always probably believed that is the way things should be and that is best." Not only is Roberto uncritical of whites who engage in this practice, but he also frames their behavior in a way that does not implicate racism. However, the "staying white" dynamic becomes susceptible to conflict with the national ideology of nonracism when it is removed from the perspective of concern over the children, a point I address in the next section. Before turning to this, I want to make note of the implications that my findings potentially hold for scholars of interracial marriage and multiracial families. In particular, there is evidence to suggest that the "unit" of importance in marriage markets may not involve just the individual but also the family. In other words, considerations that surround the choice of a spouse may not be confined to an individual's race-color but may also include the race-color of family members. This may especially be true in societies such as Mexico, where multiracial heritage is common and where concerns about interracial marriage revolve around family genetics and preoccupations regarding the children.

An exchange I had with Sandra, the high school teacher with light-brown skin, elucidates this point. One morning a friend of Sandra's stopped by the house for a quick visit. After she left, Sandra mentioned that, even though her friend is white, her friend's dad is "very, very, very black." Sandra told me that her friend's husband did not find this out until after they were married. Sandra assured me that if he had had knowledge of this, he never would have married her. According to Sandra, once her friend's husband discovered the father was black, he told his wife that he did not want to have any more children for fear they would inherit her father's genes. Another example of how the racial background of a potential partner's family can be meaningful comes from Marisa, the English instructor with medium brown-skin. From the perspective of being single, Marisa articulated her thoughts regarding attributes of a potential spouse. She contemplated, "If I was going to marry a man who has rough features, but his mom has a fine nose and not very thick lips, well, I would have it made because my son or daughter is going to come out like the grandparents, right?.... So you have to look at that, too." Comments such as these suggest that scholars of interracial marriage may want to consider how race-related marriage market dynamics are affected by considerations of the race-color of the potential spouse's family members in addition to the race-color of the potential spouse.

"Staying White" and Saving National Face

Veracruzanos of all hues adopt strategies to save national face in light of whites' attempts to maintain whiteness. They commonly frame the "staying white" dynamic as an isolated phenomenon, not generalizable to the broader population. In doing so, they draw upon the marginal national status of light-skinned Mexicans, distinguishing their behavior from that of the broader national community. Not surprisingly, this strategy is primarily evoked by brown-skinned Veracruzanos. For example, Ramón, a forty-four-year-old high school employee with dark-brown skin, informed me that Veracruzanos with "status" do not mix, stating: "I have lived here in Veracruz for twenty-four years, and I have always seen that they look to marry people more or less at their level, as much economic [level] as skin color." Although Ramón clearly perceives a "staying white" (and wealthy) dynamic operating in society, he attributes this behavior to a particular segment of the population. Similarly, Lorena, a thirty-nine-year-old working-class homemaker with medium-brown skin, argues that only rich whites are opposed to interracial marriage and that the middle-classes "don't differentiate by color." As we can see, brown-skinned Veracruzanos work to save national face by relegating the "staying white" practice to a fairly small segment of the Mexican population.

Unlike brown-skinned Veracruzanos, light-skinned Veracruzanos do not isolate their behavior from broader Mexican dynamics, as doing so would deny their own Mexicanness. Instead, they avoid a conflict with the *mestizaje* and nonracism ideological pillars by decentering the importance of color in white-only relationships. For example, Julieta, the light-skinned university student in her twenties, forwarded a nonracial explanation to justify her behavior of only dating white men, emphasizing random, inexplicable forces of attraction. When I asked Julieta why she has had only white partners, she giggled and said: "I don't know. The love. The chemistry." She told me that color is not important to her when choosing a partner. However, according to Julieta, her social circle is about 30 percent white and 70 percent brown. Despite her frequent interactions with brown-skinned men, Julieta attributes her gravitation to whites as being due to the abstract and intangible forces of love and chemistry, not color. This framing dismisses an anti-miscegenation explanation, thereby evading the potential for ideological conflict.

As part of the Veracruz working class, Elena, the forty-eight-year-old light-skinned homemaker with green eyes, interacts with mostly brown-skinned individuals. Despite this, Elena has dated only light-skinned men, something she revealed during an extensive discussion we had one evening. As we sat in a small room that Elena's neighbor had lent us for privacy, we talked about her relationships. Elena shared that she has never dated a person darker than herself; all of her partners have been white. When I asked her to reflect on the reasons for this, she told me, "Well, maybe because we identified with each other because of our age, or with what one has lived, or with what one is in that moment or simply...physical attraction or friendship." When I asked Elena if she has ever identified with or been attracted to a brown-skinned man, she replied "No." She then elaborated: "I believe that color is not important. What is important is the friendship and heart of a person." Although Elena's neighborhood and social networks are dominated by brown-skinned people, she framed her selection of exclusively white partners as determined by nonracial factors such as age and bonds of friendship.

Pilar, the eighteen-year-old light-skinned gas station worker, has also dated only white individuals. When I asked Pilar why she has never dated someone darker than herself, she replied:

PILAR: I don't know. I mean...It is probably more than anything that the *morenos* I knew were somewhat rude...they would start making sexual jokes and later they were just too rude for me and sometimes the white guys were not like that...So I liked them more because they were more reserved...

CS: And why do you think the *morenos* were ruder than the whites?

PILAR: Well, I think it is not so much about color as the education and the respect that they have for women, right?

Our extended conversation on this topic was periodically punctuated by Pilar's uncomfortable laughter as she tried to justify why all of her former partners have been white. In this excerpt she draws a correlation between brownness and rudeness to rationalize her avoidance of *morenos*, implying that her disinterest is about their behavior, not their color. Like Pilar, light-skinned Veracruzanos who date only white partners in a predominately brown society reconcile their behavior with an ideology that touts *mestizaje* and the absence of racism by decentering color when discussing partner choice.

Conclusion

Do Veracruzanos reproduce the national ideological pillars of *mestizaje* and nonracism in their racial common sense regarding race mixture? The answer defies a simple yes or no. On one hand, those who reject the idea of marrying black and indigenous individuals or who focus on maintaining whiteness express sentiments that contradict the *mestizaje* and nonracism components of Mexican national ideology. On the other hand, individuals' attempts to lighten the next generation, as encapsulated in the notion of "bettering the race," requires the crossing of race-color boundaries, a position highly compatible with the ideology of *mestizaje*. However, the quest to "better the race" does not signify a wholehearted endorsement of race mixture; many individuals support *mestizaje* primarily as a vehicle for achieving whiteness, a goal that aligns with the whitening undercurrent of Mexican national ideology. As Wright (1990) describes for the case of Venezuela, there is a national acceptance of being a *café con leche* (coffee with milk) people, but there is still a desire to have as much *leche* and as little *café* as possible. In Veracruz, the quest for more *leche* has inconsistent implications for Mexican national ideology, as it can foster both an opposition to and openness toward race mixture, depending on the situation and context.

When their attitudes on *mestizaje* conflict with the national ideology, Veracruzanos attempt to smooth over these contradictions. However, this is not an easy task given the tensions and contradictions that surround Mexican ideology and society. As I have continually emphasized, elite ideology itself houses internal contradictions. In formulating attitudes toward interracial marriage, individuals are forced to contend with the coexistence of various forces—official ideology that promotes race mixture and asserts a lack of racism in the country and an indirect ideology and culture that privileges whiteness. Under these circumstances, Veracruzanos do the best they can to navigate this uneven ideological terrain, working to save as much personal and national face as possible when expressing attitudes on *mestizaje* that could potentially threaten the national stance. In striving to save national face, Veracruzanos work not only to preserve a sense of dignity for the Mexican nation but also to reassert their own national identities. As Basave Benítez (1992) astutely points out, "The tendency to tie race mixture to Mexicanness essentially corresponds to a search for national identity. In this sense, the current mestizofile is inscribed in the context of nationalism" (p. 14). In other words, when Mexicans manage their racial attitudes on *mestizaje*, they are also managing their national identities as Mexican.

Mexicans are not alone with respect to the need to negotiate their racial common sense under conflicting ideological conditions and nationalist contexts. Similar ideological inconsistencies plague national ideologies throughout Latin America. As Wade (1993) notes, the presence of the dual themes of race mixture and discrimination has resulted in a coexistence of "two variants on the nationalist theme: on one hand, the democratic, inclusive ideology of '*todos somos* mestizos—everyone is mestizo'...on the other hand, discriminatory ideology points out that some are lighter mestizos than others, prefers the whiter to the darker, and sees the consolidation of nationality in a process of whitening" (p. 11). In the case of Mexico, Stepan (1991) argues that the myth of *mestizaje* is too often taken at face value and is interpreted to mean there is a general acceptance of all races; in other words, only one variant on the nationalist theme (that of racial inclusiveness) is recognized. In this chapter, I have addressed both variants, illustrating the process through which individuals reproduce both inclusionary and discriminatory sentiments regarding interracial relationships in their racial common sense. Veracruzanos' equation of *mestizaje* with antiracism and their willingness to cross race-color boundaries under certain circumstances demonstrates some degree of racial inclusivity. However, the emphasis on whitening and staying white reproduces the discriminatory undercurrents embedded in the original development of the *mestizaje* ideology. The next chapter continues to explore the theme of *mestizaje*, honing in on the experience of members of mixed-color families and those engaged in intercolor relationships.

5 | Intercolor Couples and Mixed-Color Families in a Mixed-Race Society

What is going to emerge out there is the definitive race, the synthetical race, the integral race, made up of the genius and the blood of all peoples and, for that reason, more capable of true brotherhood and of a truly universal vision.
—*Mexican intellectual José Vasconcelos, [1925] 1997*

Our historical experience and the makeup of the Mexican population, which is 90 percent mixed race as a result of the mixing of Spaniards and indigenous inhabitants, have given rise to one indisputable fact, namely, that there is no negation of one or another racial origin in our country.
—*Mexican government official, 1994*

Our community is uniquely situated to confront these issues [of race and interethnic relations] because of the special experiences and understanding we acquire in the intimacy of our families, our own personalities, and our friends.
—*U.S. Association of Multiethnic Americans*[1]

[Due to cultural and biological mixing] by the middle of the twenty-first century, America will have problems aplenty, but no racial problems whatsoever.
—*U.S. scholar Orlando Patterson, 2000*

FIRST MET SANDRA, the forty-eight-year-old high-school teacher, in 2004 when inquiring about a room to rent in Veracruz. When I moved into her home, Sandra was initially guarded and only cautiously friendly. However, over time we formed a very close friendship. It was in this context that I began to witness and understand the subtle and complex dynamics operating within her mixed-color family,[2] dynamics that are not clearly evident on the surface. Like many Veracruz families, Sandra's family represents a wide range of phenotypes. Sandra's mother has dark-brown skin, and her father was light-skinned. Sandra herself has light-brown skin, whereas her fraternal twin is a shade lighter. Her brother is medium-brown in color, as are many of her nieces and nephews. Pepe, Sandra's husband, has light-brown skin like Sandra, but their two daughters embody the family's color variation—the oldest is light, and the youngest is medium brown. Completing their nuclear family is Sandra's light-skinned, blue-eyed son from a previous relationship. Sandra's family gets together often. The atmosphere at these gatherings is typically jovial, full of laughter and relaxation. Observing their mixed-color family in action, an onlooker would likely conclude that race or color is not an issue.

Sandra and I informally spoke about race and color on a number of occasions. However, it was not until I interviewed her that she shared her thoughts in greater detail. During this conversation, I asked Sandra her perspective about the role of race and color in mixed-color families. Consistent with Sandra's usual matter-of-fact demeanor, she did not waste time giving lip service to the idea that race and color do not matter. Instead, she told me that mixed-color families oftentimes hope to produce white babies, even if this goal belies their own racial backgrounds. She offered details of a specific case involving an acquaintance, a new grandmother, who loudly complained that her grandson was born with brown skin, a skin tone similar to that of other family members. Throughout this discussion, Sandra kept the topic of her own family at a safe distance.

Later in our conversation, I moved to bring Sandra's family into the discussion. I began with Sandra, asking if she would consider marrying someone of a different race or color. Her response was swift: "I don't like blacks." She then stumbled while attempting to provide a justification: "Because I don't like—perhaps this is normal, right? Physically, well, it is not the same, I mean....A black person is always more—I don't know...." Her voice trailed off. When she continued, she vocalized what she had previously left unsaid. "Generally the black person is not very good-looking. I would not marry a black person." However, Sandra made sure that I understood that she allows her feelings about blacks to guide only *her* choice of partner. She would not object if one of her daughters had a black boyfriend. But when pausing to reflect on this statement, she waivered, adding, "But who knows?...If the person was a very good person, there would not be a problem but sometimes we have the idea that blacks are...bad people."

Although our conversation about Sandra's daughters' relationships was hypothetical, her son's partner does, in fact, have dark-brown skin. However, it was only months later that Sandra spoke about this directly, a conversation she initiated one afternoon as I accompanied her to work. As we pulled out of her driveway, Sandra began to express concern about her son's alcohol use. He had been staying out late, causing his girlfriend to worry. The mention of his girlfriend sparked a new line of conversation. Sandra began: "Look...I like my son's girlfriend. She is a good girl but...she is *morena*. Not very *morena* but inside I feel bothered that he is with her since he is very white...." In sharing this, Sandra confirmed what I had come to suspect—her opposition to darker partners extended to her children. Additionally, she revealed that her concerns are not limited to blacks; she also includes individuals who are *moreno* in color.

Sandra exposes the contradictions and ironies that surround mixed-color families and intercolor relationships. She is uncomfortable with her son's involvement in an intercolor relationship despite the fact that her own family is mixed and that her son's girlfriend is similar in phenotype to many members of Sandra's family, including Sandra's own mother and daughter. However, the irony of the situation does not end with Sandra. When Sandra's son spoke to me about his girlfriend, he shared that he would have preferred to have a partner who is white with green eyes. He recognizes that his girlfriend does not conform to this ideal, but he still hopes that their children will inherit his blue eyes rather than her brown eyes.

The thoughts expressed by Sandra and her son are not unique in Veracruz. Similar perspectives and dynamics exist within many mixed-color families as well as among individuals involved in intercolor relationships. The widespread existence of such sentiments directly contradicts the messages conveyed in the epigraphs presented at the beginning of this chapter, taken from statements made by Mexican and U.S. academics, a Mexican government official, and a U.S. multiethnic movement leader—that the intimate crossing of race-color boundaries is an antidote to racism. In this chapter I go to the heart of the cross-regional claim that interracial couples and multiracial families are sites of decreased racism by systematically examining the dynamics that occur within intercolor relationships and mixed-color families in Veracruz. I begin by showing how Veracruzanos view intercolor relationships through the lens of status exchange, signaling that race mixture is not embraced in and of itself in Veracruz society. I then detail the collective gatekeeping that occurs both in white and mixed-color families, including the strategic efforts they undertake to block the entrance of brown-skinned individuals into their family networks. I also outline how individuals conceptualize their involvement in intercolor relationships, showing how darker partners express a sense of "brown inferiority" and focus on putting the philosophy of "bettering the race" into practice, while lighter partners hold onto the ideal of a white partner and make efforts to conceptually lighten their partners' race-color classification.

Regarding mixed-color family dynamics, I demonstrate how distinction-making practices and differential treatment occur within these families and how these dynamics produce negative social and psychological consequences for the darkest members of the family. Furthermore, I show that, despite the ideology of *mestizaje*, families are often forced to provide an explanation for any significant phenotypic variation between family members. I conclude the chapter by arguing that, contrary to claims made in the literature, race and color *do* matter in intercolor relationships and mixed-color families; in fact, they matter a great deal. Before illustrating this, however, I provide an overview of the relevant literature and discuss societal and familial reactions to intercolor relationships in Veracruz.

Interracial Couples and Multiracial Families: The Vanguard of Antiracism?

As mentioned previously, in Mexican national ideology, the *mestizaje* and nonracism ideological pillars are intricately intertwined. Mexican elites assert that, because of Mexico's hybrid nature, the country is free of racism. The perceived incompatibility between race mixture and racism is not only embedded in Mexican official ideology but is also well established in academic thought. Elites and intellectuals alike have proffered interracial relationships and multiracial families as explicit sites of antiracism, viewing individuals in these situations as pioneers on the antiracist frontier.

Throughout the twentieth century, scholars of Latin America theorized a link between the region's high degree of race mixture and racial inclusivity.[3] They credited race mixture with blurred racial boundaries and decreased racial polarization.[4] In particular, Harris (1964) argued that race mixture results in the inability to clearly distinguish people by race, thereby reducing the possibility for systematic discrimination. The association between race mixture and a lack of racism has also been asserted in the U.S. context, representing a rare ideological convergence on philosophies of race between these two regions.

In the U.S. literature, there is also well-established theorizing regarding the assumed correlation between an increase in interracial marriage and a decrease in racism. Sociologists, in particular, have defined interracial marriage as the final stage of assimilation—a symbol of the ultimate erosion of racial boundaries.[5] Reacting to the recent surge in U.S. interracial marriage rates and multiracial identification, some scholars are boldly predicting that racism will become a thing of the past.[6] In *The End of Racism*, D'Souza (1995) asserts that "the country is entering a new era in which old racial categories are rapidly becoming obsolete, mostly because of intermarriage" (p. 552). Others, such as Nakashima (1992), posit that multiracial people and their families pose a threat to the U.S. racial system, which depends on discrete racial categories for political, social, economic, and psychological organization. Finally, Susanne Heine, a guest editor for *Interracial Voice*, a newsletter promoting global multiracial advocacy, describes multiraciality as a tool equipped to dismantle the racial hierarchy. She asserts that "with each new wave of immigrants who cause new mixes to arise, 'Black America' and 'White America' will continue to fade into each other, atrophying and losing their steam..." (Heine 2006, pp. 3–4). As we can see, scholars in both Latin America and the United States have designated racial mixing as a marker of the decreased salience of race. Given this, I dedicate the rest of the chapter to exploring this theme, beginning with a look at Veracruzanos' reactions to intercolor relationships.

Societal Reactions to Intercolor Relationships: The Common Sense of Status Exchange

In the mixed-race nation of Mexico, where national narratives highlight the historic mixture between indians and Spaniards and where contemporary Mexicans claim multiple ancestries, one might expect that intercolor partnerships—unions where individuals are more than a color shade or two apart—would not engender much interest. However, in Veracruz, even though such relationships are fairly common, intercolor couples often draw attention, suggesting that such alliances are not, in fact, viewed as a societal norm. Individuals in these relationships characterize outside reactions to their relationships in various ways—some perceive their relationship as accepted, while others feel criticized. Criticism is particularly intense when onlookers find no compelling rationale for the perceived imbalance in the relationship.

I saw this dynamic in operation when Sandra shared her thoughts regarding our mutual friend Mike, an African American living in Veracruz, and his relationship with Lupe, a woman with medium-brown skin. One afternoon, when I was attending a baseball game with Sandra, we unexpectedly ran into Mike and Lupe before the game and spent a short time chatting. As we took our seats and parted ways, Sandra, apparently suspecting that Lupe was jealous of our friendship with Mike, turned to me and said: "She is stupid to think that someone would take him away from her, as ugly as he is. I don't like blacks. I wouldn't marry a black person." Later she told me that Lupe must be with Mike for his money because she clearly is not with him for his looks. On another occasion, Lupe herself shared with me that people often make comments suggesting that she is with Mike for financial reasons. These assumptions are illustrative of a broader societal perception—that, in intercolor relationships the darker individual needs to somehow "compensate" for his or her darker skin tone. In other words, Veracruzanos view intercolor relationships through the lens of status exchange.[7]

The theory of status exchange posits that interracial marriage is not a random phenomenon but instead represents a situation in which individuals exchange factors such as economic status, power, beauty, or race to make a relationship more equal or balanced.[8] Positive traits, as defined in Veracruz society, include being well educated, having high economic status, and having light skin; the inverse of these qualities are viewed as negative traits. When individuals with dark skin, a perceived negative trait, marry someone lighter, there is an implicit expectation that they will compensate for their color by contributing a "positive" attribute such as higher socioeconomic status. This example applies to the case of Lupe and Mike—Mike is seen as exchanging his higher socioeconomic status for Lupe's lighter skin color.

Veracruzanos often use the status exchange philosophy to judge the acceptability of intercolor relationships. For example, the light-skinned daughter of Concha, the forty-three-year-old upper-class homemaker with light skin, had previously dated someone with dark-brown skin. Surprised at herself for having allowed the relationship, Concha admitted that she had, in fact, accepted him. I asked Concha to reflect on why she felt okay with this particular relationship, given that she had made clear that she does not want her children to be with someone darker. She mused:

Well, I don't know. I knew his family and knew he was a well-mannered person.... He was also very cultured. He had already studied in good universities, he lived in Boston, he spoke very good English, he had finished his degree.... He was already manager of one of his father's businesses and everything ... so yes [I accepted him], even though he is *moreno*.

Upon saying this, Concha quickly clarified that he does not have a "mulatto's face" but is "just brown." I then asked: "If he had been black, do you feel you would have accepted him?" To this, Concha gave an unequivocal no. Through her comments, Concha made it clear that having brown skin is not a desirable trait but is something that can be overlooked under certain circumstances. In the case of her daughter's ex-boyfriend, certain attributes compensated for his dark skin, making him an acceptable suitor. However, Concha was equally clear that education and family background will go only so far—no amount of money, status, or good education would make it allowable for her daughter to date a black man.

Another important component of the status exchange dynamic is gender. In Veracruz, it is much more common and acceptable for men to marry women who are lighter compared with darker women marrying lighter men, a pattern also documented in Brazil and Colombia.[9] The most common intercolor pairing I encountered in Veracruz involved brown-skinned males of fairly good socioeconomic standing in relationships with light-skinned females. This combination is not surprising given the popular belief that men are more likely to privilege beauty (which is equated with whiteness) in a partner, whereas women are more likely to focus on financial stability. This dynamic was mentioned by Jessica, the twenty-one-year-old light-skinned student from the upper-middle class. She explained that her white girlfriends will date men with brown skin only if they are members of the upper class.

The power of the status-exchange perspective becomes exposed when individuals cannot identify an obvious status exchange in a particular intercolor pairing or if a couple does not conform to traditional intercolor gender norms. For example, Abram, the forty-year-old car washer with medium-brown skin and hazel eyes, violated traditional gender and intermarriage norms when he married a woman from Oaxaca who is not only darker than he but who has no obvious attributes to compensate for her darker skin. Based on the perceived illogic of their relationship, Abram is criticized. His friends and coworkers point out how he is taller and lighter than she is. They remind him, "You have options with other ladies." Abram defends his choice of spouse by citing her talent in the kitchen. In responding to critics in this way, Abram ends up reifying the status-exchange logic and the race-color hierarchy; he provides information to help others understand why he would "settle" for someone darker.

Adán, the thirty-five-year-old painter with medium-brown skin, was previously involved with a woman who he described as "dark brown" in color. When they were together, his friends gave him a hard time. Since women are expected to offer beauty, they attacked her looks, referring to her as an "ugly *negra*." However, Adán's brother was his harshest critic, continually asking Adán: "How did it occur to you to marry that ugly black woman?" Adán's response: "I am not married" and "That is my problem." Like others in similar situations, Adán did nothing to challenge the underlying popular expectations regarding intercolor relationships. Instead, he engaged his brother's criticism by focusing on a technicality (that he is not married) and by adopting an "it's none of your business" stance and evading the substance of the critique. As with Abram, Adán's response leaves intact the underlying assumption that people with brown skin are less desirable partners.

Marisa, the twenty-five-year-old English teacher with medium-brown skin, feels burdened by having to constantly explain and justify her parent's relationship. Her light-skinned mother comes from a higher socioeconomic and educational background than her dark-skinned father, a deviation from traditional intercolor gender norms and a situation that leaves the family subject to questions and criticism. Marisa shared how she is confronted with questions such as, "How is it that your mom, who is white, married your father?" and "Why did your mom, being who she is, marry him?" During our conversation, I was struck by Marisa's ability to effortlessly regurgitate the arsenal of questions she receives on the topic, suggesting she encounters such questions frequently.

Cristina, the twenty-year-old university student with light skin and blond hair, was also questioned regarding her relationship with an ex-boyfriend who she described as "very dark" in color. According to Cristina, people would "always, always" make comments about him. They would ask, "How is it that you are with that black guy?" The comments went beyond mere curiosity; they were made in a way that "put him down," Cristina lamented. For example, people would tell her, "You are white. Look for someone better." Summoning the logic of status exchange to defend her relationship, Cristina would respond by pointing out that he is "super good looking" and he "has money." However, this reasoning did not convince her parents who remained unsupportive of the relationship. "It could've been worse though," Cristina reflected. If he had been black, her parents would have "killed her." Articulating the cut-off line of acceptability according to her parents' standards, Cristina explained, "If he is *moreno* to the point where his lips look purple, then it is not okay."

In cases where individuals cross national as well as race-color boundaries, societal receptions can be even more intense. This was the case with Amelia and Héctor. Amelia is a forty-one-year-old middle-class homemaker with light-brown skin. Héctor is a thirty-eight-year-old middle-class Afro-Cuban who coaches youth sports. In my conversation with Amelia, when speaking in the abstract, she informed me that inter-color relationships are accepted in Veracruz. Her stance shifted, however, when we began to discuss her relationship with Héctor. They receive a variety of reactions to their relationship. Sometimes the tone is one of "curiosity"—people look at them as if they are "strange or weird" because, according to Amelia, "they are not used to seeing a white person with a black person." Other times the reception is more clearly negative.

Criticism most frequently comes from Amelia's family and friends. Amelia explained, "In my family, the fact that he is black, [makes them ask me] 'what do you see in him?'" However, the reactions extend beyond questions and comments. Amelia had always been invited to family get-togethers, but now that she is with Héctor she is excluded. Her sister has been very explicit about the reason for her disapproval of Amelia's choice of partner—he is black and Cuban. Even Amelia's daughter from a previous relationship initially rejected Héctor, although she now affec-tionately refers to him as "my chocolate." Amelia is not only confronted by these issues within her family but also is forced to deal with her friends who make remarks such as, "What were you thinking? Why were you in such a hurry to date whomever?" "Whomever," Amelia explained, means a black person. Amelia generally adopts a nonconfrontational approach to these comments, figuring it isn't worth getting into an argument. Although Amelia presents herself as having "thick skin," she worries about how these comments impact Héctor. She notices that he never gets angry but instead becomes sad when such criticisms surface. She shared, "Sometimes they make my partner feel bad but I tell him that, as long as I love him. . . ." She ended the conversation without completing her thoughts.

My separate in-depth discussion with Héctor revealed many of the same themes that surfaced in my conversation with Amelia, although Héctor expressed them differently. Whereas Amelia became fired up and incensed when describing how they are treated in society, Héctor appeared resigned when discussing the same topic. When I asked if he felt margin-alized due to his color, he calmly replied, "Yes, of course." Héctor has resided in Veracruz for three years in accordance with a sports exchange program. He self-identifies as a black Cuban but is sometimes mistaken for being Puerto Rican or African American. Héctor tells me that 70 per-cent of Veracruzanos are "pleasant, friendly, and affectionate" toward him, although he feels it is harder to be black in Mexico than in Cuba. When I asked about intercolor couples in Mexico, he described them as "accepted" but then qualified this generalization: "Sometimes people don't look at you with 'good eyes'....They say 'Ah, look at that lady with that guy'....It looks like she has money and she is with that *negro*." After a moment of reflection, Héctor then offered a more conservative estimate—that 50 percent of Veracruzanos accept intercolor relationships. He included Amelia's family as part of the unaccepting half, stating, matter-of-factly, "They do not accept me because I am black, because I am Cuban, and because I don't have money."

Family Reactions to Intercolor Relationships: Gatekeeping Dynamics

As we have seen, negative reactions to intercolor relationships come not only from society at large but also from family members, a dynamic similar to that seen in Brazil.[10] In Veracruz, criticism most frequently surfaces within light-skinned families, a behavior consistent with the "staying white" philosophy covered in chapter 4. For example, Adriana, the fifty-two-year-old light-skinned upper-class homemaker whose husband is darker than she, explained how her husband's aunt, who is white, "freaked out" when one of her cousins married a person who Adriana described as "brown, but not black." In another case, Rosalía, the eighteen-year-old light-skinned university student, spoke of a close friend who had to hide her relationship with a young man "of color" because her parents prohibited her from dating him. Rosalía assured me this is not an isolated incident; she described white families in Veracruz as wanting to engage in relationships only with other whites.

Also facing parental rejection of an intercolor relationship was Gloria, the forty-eight-year-old retired health-care worker with light-brown skin. She recalled having to confront her father's distaste for blacks when she was dating. During a trip to Canada, Gloria met a "really, really black... but handsome" man who fell in love with her. Gloria was attracted to him but dismissed the possibility of having him as a boyfriend, explaining: "My father always told us that he did not want us to bring blacks home.... He didn't want us to mix with a black person." Gloria learned of her father's thoughts on the matter at an early age when they lived in a house near the Veracruz nautical school. In this context, her father observed white North American female tourists visiting Veracruz with African American boyfriends. When he saw these couples, he would call Gloria and her siblings to his side to express his disapproval, characterizing such relationships as "aberrations." In sharing this history, Gloria tried to avoid vilifying her father. She softly added, "He had reasons to think like that because his father had inculcated it in him....They disowned him because his first marriage was to a black woman." Ironically, then, Gloria's father reproduced the same prejudice within his own family, despite the fact that he had challenged his own father's antiblack sentiments by marrying a black woman.

The recipients of prejudice—the darker-skinned partners—also spoke of family objections to their intercolor relationships. Daniela, the thirty-two-year-old working-class homemaker with dark-brown skin and dark wavy hair who is married to a white man, is a case in point. Early in our conversation, Daniela boldly charged her mother-in-law with racism, explaining that her mother-in-law is not pleased that her white son has chosen to be with Daniela. Narrating her experience with the in-laws, Daniela recalled, "Three years ago he took me to his mother's house and his mother wanted another class of person for her son.... [She wanted to know] why he took an interest in me, someone with brown skin." I asked Daniela about her current relationship with her mother-in-law, to which she responded: "To this day she still doesn't speak to me...because I am darker than him." These stories, representative of many, illustrate a form of gatekeeping in which light-skinned families mobilize to block the entry of brown-skinned individuals into their family networks.

This form of gatekeeping may not be too surprising given the entrenched privileging of whiteness in Mexico. However, even in mixed-color families, I found that family members criticize and marginalize darker-skinned boyfriends, girlfriends, sons-in-law, and daughters-in-law. Lighter-skinned individuals, in contrast, are often enthusiastically welcomed into the family. Although the discriminatory dynamics in mixed-color families are similar to those occurring in white families, the fact that these dynamics exist in mixed-color families holds an additional layer of irony—mixed-color families discriminate against people whose brown phenotype is similar to that of members of their own family. Osuji (2011) refers to the rejection of interracial marriage by individuals who are themselves racially mixed as the "irony of opposition."

Judy, the thirty-five-year-old light-skinned university professor, provides an example of how race and color matter when outsiders are integrated into a mixed-color family. She told me of two brothers, one with a white, green-eyed girlfriend and the other with a dark-brown-skinned girlfriend. Judy went to school with the darker girlfriend and recalled her complaining that her boyfriend's family liked the other girlfriend but not her. She explained that when visitors came to the house the mother would proudly introduce only the white girlfriend, leaving her feeling "rejected" and "marginalized." According to Judy, her classmate was "absolutely convinced" that this differential treatment was due to their color difference.

Judy had her own story to tell. Bernardo, her partner of seven years, has dark-brown skin and tightly curled hair that noticeably contrasts to Judy's pale skin and straight blond hair. Bernardo is from a mixed-color family. His family adores Judy. She is cognizant that her whiteness is a "plus" in his family's eyes, emphasizing: "Since I am white—since the time I met him, that is what [his mom] liked about me." Bernardo, however, is received quite differently by Judy's mixed-color family. He is not rejected outright, Judy explained, but is subjected to frequent ridicule. Her mom, in particular, makes fun of Bernardo and expresses concern about their relationship. Judy shared, "My mom is very, uh...particular about these issues. My mom likes white children...so, for my mom, yes it has been a complicated process, right?....For my mom, it has been hard [to accept him]." The situation is further complicated by the fact that many people taunt her mother with the hypothetical scenario of future grandchildren with dark skin and curly hair. These examples give us just a taste of the race-color dynamics that exist within mixed-color families, a theme I return to later in the chapter.

A Look Inside Intercolor Pairings: How Individuals Conceptualize Their Relationships

Now that I have addressed societal and familial reactions to intercolor relationships, I will turn the lens inward, presenting the stories of those involved with someone of a different color. This inside view is important since it is these individuals who are purportedly challenging racism. Here, I focus on the *meaning* of such relationships to those involved in them, detailing the discourses that the darker and lighter partners use to contextualize their relationships.

Discourses of the Darker Partners: Privileging Whiteness

Given Veracruzanos' preference for light skin and their focus on whitening the next generation, it is not difficult to imagine that people involved with someone lighter would reproduce these perspectives in their relationships. In particular, darker partners in intercolor relationships evoke discourses that revolve around the themes of "bettering the race" and "brown inferiority." Recall the discussion in chapter 4 regarding how the notion of "bettering the race"—seeking out lighter-skinned partners so that one's children will be born lighter—influences Veracruzanos' attitudes on race mixture. Here, I show how Veracruzanos put this philosophy into practice beginning with Roberto, the twenty-three-year-old university graduate with medium-brown skin. Roberto's parents are members of the Veracruz upper class, a factor that has increased Roberto's opportunities in the Veracruz dating and marriage market. In fact, Roberto has dated only light-skinned women. Roberto shared his thoughts on his relationships: "I believe that when we look for a partner, up to a certain point we focus on the physical, right? So when you find yourself in a situation that your partner...is white with blue or green eyes...we call it 'bettering the race,' even though it is poorly put because, in one way or another, it means discriminating against oneself." Roberto, unlike most, articulated the irony surrounding the discourse and practice of "bettering the race"—that, for people with brown skin, a focus on "bettering the race" is self-discriminatory. However, despite any internal qualms Roberto may have about this philosophy, in behavioral terms he embraces the practice.

José, a sixty-three-year-old taco vender with dark-brown skin, also takes the idea of "bettering the race" very seriously, wholeheartedly embracing the whitening ideal by putting it into practice. He is married to a light-skinned woman and openly expressed his preference for white women. Elaborating on and personalizing his position, he explained, "With my color, my wife's color is cleaning the race a little bit, right? And the children of my children, well, they will be white. They will not be my color." I asked José if this bothered him, to which he replied, "No, of course not. No, no, no," in a tone that implied that my question was rather ridiculous. José's thinking has been adopted by his children who "jokingly" tell him: "You refined your race because mom is white with a delicate nose." José's daughter, Vanesa, a thirty-year-old working-class homemaker with medium-brown skin, also spoke openly about her desire to "better the race." She explained, "You have to clean the race, right? You need to lighten a little bit. Because of that, my partners have always been white." Nevertheless, Vanesa confides that she "runs the risk" of having children who inherit her father's features.

Tomás, a seventy-nine-year-old retired military officer with light-brown skin, who is married to a light-skinned woman, was also not shy about expressing how his wife's color influenced his decision to become involved with her. He told me that the first time he saw her, he noticed how pretty she was and decided to marry her to "better the race." My findings regarding Veracruzanos' unabashed admittance of their desire to "better the race" contrast with what Osuji (2011) found in Brazil, where it is not socially acceptable for Brazilian interracial couples to say they are in their relationships for the purposes of whitening. She attributes the stigma associated with whitening to the increasing valorization of blackness in Brazil. In contrast, in Veracruz, as we have seen, there is no stigma attached to the idea of whitening nor, as I demonstrate in the next chapter, is there a parallel valorization of blackness. In fact, darker-skinned individuals in intercolor relationships in Veracruz sometimes express a sentiment of inferiority regarding their color.

Catalina, a thirty-eight-year-old working-class homemaker with light-brown skin, touched upon the topic of "brown inferiority" during our conversation. She believes that her husband, who is a few shades darker than she, is uncomfortable with his color in relation to hers. According to Catalina, this concern has been present since the beginning of their relationship. She shared, "When we were dating, [he said] he felt bad for being dark because I was light." She has continually attempted to assuage his concerns and insecurities by telling him, "Don't feel bad. We are equal." Nevertheless, she perceives that her husband has an internalized sense of inferiority, a sentiment that lives within their intercolor relationship. These feelings of inferiority, connected to the societal valorization of light skin, can create social and psychological dilemmas and produce power inequalities within intercolor couples.

Belinda, the forty-six-year-old working-class homemaker with dark-brown skin, spoke about this issue. Unlike the others presented in this section, Belinda has never been in an intercolor relationship. Representing an unusual case, Belinda has actively avoided dating individuals who are lighter. She told me she would not feel comfortable alongside a white man. Belinda shared a situation from her past—a white man with green eyes had wanted to be her boyfriend. She liked him, she confessed, but ultimately rejected his proposal out of worry that "one day he would tell me that he was leaving me due to my color." She explained, "I have never wanted anything to do with white people....I don't want them to play around and then, in a short while, hurt me." Belinda's explanation reveals how, in her mind, intercolor relationships are not devoid of race-color inequalities. Based on what I learned about the experiences of those involved in intercolor relationships, Belinda's assumption that such relationships house internal power dynamics related to color appears to be accurate. Her concerns certainly do not appear to represent unfounded fears divorced from reality.

Discourses of the Lighter Partners: Maintaining a White Ideal

Given the ideology of whitening in Veracruz, one may wonder how individuals who engage in relationships with people who are darker think through or justify their choice of partner. As an introduction to this topic, I present an in-depth look at the case of Carla, a fifty-seven-year-old light-skinned middle-class homemaker. When I spoke with Carla, she struggled to classify herself racially, musing: "Well, I have light skin, not arriving at an Anglo-Saxon, but yes, I am very light." Carla's husband, in contrast, has dark-brown skin and features that reflect his partial African ancestry. People clearly notice the contrast between Carla and her husband, referring to her as "day" and him as "night." Carla is amused by these characterizations, which she assured me are only jokes.

Carla described her husband as "dark brown" in color and as having "Cuban, Spanish, and Mexican blood." She reminisced that it was his hard work ethic, simplicity, and honesty that she initially found attractive. She has never regretted marrying him because he is darker. Although Carla feels that people generally accept their relationship, she believes that their color difference has affected their children, especially their second son. According to Carla, their firstborn came out with "polished, white skin." However, his brother was born "a little bit brown." Carla shared with me how a neighbor made "hurtful" comments about her second son's color. Carla retaliated, telling her neighbor: "I can buy my son pretty clothes that look good with his skin to resolve the problem." Despite the fact that Carla is in an intercolor relationship, her response reifies the idea that brown skin is an undesirable trait; it fails to challenge the assumption that her son's skin color is a "problem" that needs to be solved.

Like many Mexican women, especially those of older generations, Carla was not very comfortable discussing her relationships prior to marriage. However, she did share that all of her ex-boyfriends had light skin; her husband is the only man with dark-brown skin that she ever dated. Carla was more at ease discussing hypothetical scenarios and abstract notions of attractiveness. She unapologetically told me that she finds light-skinned men attractive. When I asked her directly about the darker end of the race-color continuum, she responded, albeit with a good dose of hesitancy, that she would marry a man who is indigenous or black. However, she introduced the following qualification: "I don't like Cubans.... I am not interested in that race.... In reality, I don't like the black race." Carla's antiblack prejudice extends beyond the realm of marriage. At one point in our conversation, she referred to black people as "orangutans."

I asked Carla if she would support her children if they decided to marry someone darker. She responded, "It appears as if there is going to be a wedding like that here....My son's girlfriend is very brown....I don't reject them, nor do I support them. They do their will....It is like when I made my choice. Perhaps my parents didn't like it but they stayed quiet. They didn't get involved." This comment, coupled with other statements of a similar nature, suggests that Carla is not happy with her son's choice but is determined to respect it. Confirming my suspicions, at one point she confessed that she prefer he marry someone lighter.

Like many individuals in intercolor relationships whose partners are darker than themselves, Carla socially reproduces notions that privilege lightness and denigrate darkness via her attitudes, discursive framings, and interpretations of her relationship. She does this despite her involvement in a relationship that, for some, represents an undermining of racist ideologies. In Carla's narrative we see a number of the discourses that lighter-skinned Veracruzanos typically use to contextualize their intercolor relationships. First, she demonstrates a preference for lighter-skinned partners for both herself and her children. She also displays a general prejudice toward dark-skinned individuals. Finally, she deploys discursive tactics to conceptually "lighten" her partner's color, distinguishing her husband from "Cubans" and "blacks," whom she finds distasteful. Taken as a whole, Carla, like others, engages in an intercolor relationship without disrupting a system that privileges whiteness.

Many individuals involved with darker partners maintain an ideal of dating or marrying lighter individuals, despite their behaviors to the contrary. For example, although Jessica, the light-skinned university student with blond hair and green eyes, has dated darker men, she still defines beauty in the following manner: "A person with refined features...with blue or green eyes, white skin, tall, and with a nice body." She characterizes the incongruence between her ideals and some of her dating behaviors as "curious." Attempting to reconcile this seeming contradiction, she asserted: "There are good-looking people with brown skin who have refined characteristics because of the mixture that has taken place."

Displaying a similar attitude-behavior discrepancy is Adriana, the light-skinned upper-class homemaker. Adriana was forthcoming about the fact that she did not want a partner of her husband's color (which is darker than hers), recalling: "When I was a young girl, I liked white people...but I married someone with light-brown skin." Living a similar contradiction is Rosa, the thirty-four-year-old working-class homemaker with medium-brown skin. Her husband has dark-brown skin. As a child she was adamant that she would not marry a black person. She wanted to marry lighter. She told me how she would look at white people and they would "catch her attention." Attempting to reconcile her preference for whiteness and her choice of spouse, she said: "When I met my husband, he was a guy who was thin, well-dressed, and well-behaved...." Rosa implies that these qualities compensated for her husband's less-than-ideal brown skin.

Alejandra, the nineteen-year-old law student with light skin, is currently in a relationship with a brown-skinned man who she has been dating for six months. However, she also has a preference for light-skinned individuals. According to Alejandra, she has always dated white men, with her current boyfriend being the only exception to this pattern. Despite her current involvement with a brown-skinned individual, Alejandra insists that she would never marry an indigenous man. She further shares: "Black people are not physically attractive to me and brown-skinned people, more or less—well, not much either." Managing her response in a way that does not reflect poorly on her, she clarified, "It is not racism because I have absolutely nothing against them. It is just that physically I don't find them attractive."

In discussing her relationship, Alejandra uses another common discursive strategy employed by lighter partners in intercolor relationships—she conceptually "lightens" her partner's color. According to Alejandra, when she began dating her boyfriend, her parents and brother were bothered by the situation. They made comments such as, "Don't you see that he has brown skin?" Alejandra felt their rejection was unwarranted, arguing, "I don't think he is *that* brown." Reinforcing her position, she told me: "I can tell you that—physically, I don't like people with brown skin. I am not attracted to them." Thus, like others in relationships with darker partners, Alejandra lightens her partner in an attempt to reconcile her preference for whites and her involvement with someone darker.

The "lightening the partner" dynamic also surfaced in my conversation with Judy, the university professor, about her relationship with Bernardo. As you may recall, Judy is light-skinned with blond hair, and Bernardo has dark-brown skin and African-origin features. When I asked Judy about Bernardo's color in the context of their relationship, she replied:

For me, if he was green or had purple hair, I wouldn't care.... I don't like him because he is a certain color. I mean, that is not important to me. I have never liked men with dark skin. I have never seen a person who is of the black race that I can say "I like him. I am attracted to him." Never. Out of all the partners I have had, I can tell you that the majority have had light skin, dark hair, and dark eyes because that is what I like. Well, I also had a boyfriend with green eyes, but that isn't important.

In this statement Judy expresses her preference for light-skinned individuals and shows how her behavior aligns with this preference by citing her dating history. At the same time, she reveals her distaste for blacks and men with dark skin. However, she frames her relationship with Bernardo as not being about color, thereby employing a colorblind framing despite her color-centered comments about partner preferences.

After Judy made the previous remark, I felt that there was an unresolved tension surrounding her comments. I had known Bernardo for a while and knew he self-identifies as black and is considered black by his friends and coworkers. However, in her comments, Judy expressed a clear distaste for black men. In this context, I asked Judy how she classified Bernardo racially. Her response:

He comes from a family that—it is a Mexican family. His brothers are light brown, a little bit lighter than him since he studied in military school and he was doing I don't know how many things, but obviously he is more suntanned than all of the rest of his family, right? But I know his family and well, it is not a family of blacks, to put it like that.

Judy's characterization of Bernado clearly diverges from his self-identification and how others view him. In effect, she lightens his race-color classification, which, given her stated preferences, helps to justify her relationship. From these examples, we see how, unlike claims made in the literature, intercolor relationships are neither devoid of race-color dynamics nor are they sites of antiracism. To the contrary, individuals in these relationships demonstrate a clear orientation to race and color. Moreover, many individuals involved in intercolor relationships perpetuate societal notions that value whiteness. I will dedicate the remainder of the chapter to an analysis of dynamics that occur in the other hypothesized site of antiracism—the mixed-color family.

Within Mixed-Color Families: Stories of Differentiation and Marginalization

I first met Lili, the forty-seven-year-old light-skinned upper-class homemaker, after being invited to her home, located in the "Coast of Gold," the wealthiest neighborhood in the Veracruz metropolitan region. Lili is from a mixed-color family. She self-identifies as mixed-race but as white in color. She was told that one of her grandfathers was French, although she cannot confirm this. According to Lili, her other grandfather had "Spanish characteristics" and her grandmother was "a little bit more Mexican. More native...brown." More recent generations in her family also vary in color. Lili provided an example: "My dad was brown but one of his brothers was very white. The other, in between." On her mother's side, there are whites and *morenos*. Throughout our conversation, Lili continually underscored the mixed-color nature of her family.

Within Lili's family, comments are frequently made about the darkest family members. Lili shared an example: "I have a niece who is very brown. She stands out among the other nieces and nephews....They call her 'the *morenita*.' She is the least attractive." A cousin of Lili's is also called out for being the darkest among her siblings. Lili described her relationship with this cousin as "close"; they spent a lot of time together when they were young. Lili recalled, "She was 'the *negra*,' and her brothers bothered her about this her whole life." According to Lili, her cousin would drink milk and put on powder, hoping to become white. Lili explained, "She heard herself being called *negra*, and she wanted to be like the rest." Even an uncle of theirs, who Lili described as "very very *moreno*, but not black," ridiculed and criticized Lili's darker-skinned cousin. According to Lili, "He himself couldn't stand people with brown skin." Pointing to the irony of the situation, Lili mocked her uncle's hypocritical behavior, saying, "As if he was blond with blue eyes."

The tone with which Lili narrated the plight of her brown-skinned cousin was one of sympathy. Nevertheless, Lili's own attitudes and behaviors, in many ways, align with those in her family who discriminate against her cousin. On one occasion, she admitted: "Yes, I am a little bit racist." She proceeded to tell me that, when she was young, her mother had a *morena* house servant. Lili refused to go near her. She remembers one time when she wanted a tortilla and the woman offered to heat it up for her, but Lili refused, complaining to her mom: "No, she is going to stain me." This prejudicial thinking persisted into adulthood. At one point Lili vowed to never fall in love with someone with brown skin, a pledge she has kept to this day. Her husband is white, as were all of her former boyfriends. Lili is aware of the hypocrisies surrounding her behavior, noting how her objection to dating individuals who are darker is at odds with the fact that she comes from a family with a range of phenotypes.

However Lili insists that her color prejudices do not affect all of her relationships; she adores her *morena* niece and does not feel prejudiced toward darker-skinned people in general. In these cases, "color isn't important," Lili assured me. However, for people who are "very close" to her, color does matter. Lili supplied the case of her light-skinned daughter whose current boyfriend has brown skin. Lili worries that their children will be brown. In the immediate aftermath of this confession, Lili added: "My husband would almost hit me if [he knew] I said that, but I feel like I am telling you the truth." As if giving voice to an internal struggle, Lili added, "He is a good guy.... [I don't care] that he is brown. Even though...I imagine little brown grandchildren. I do. I am not going to say anything, but yes, I feel something." Despite her reservations, Lili affirmed that his color is not enough of an impediment for her to prohibit them to date. However, when I asked Lili if she would prefer her daughter be with someone lighter, she quickly answered in the affirmative. The case of Lili and her family serves as an illustration of the dynamics that play out in other mixed-color families. For example, within-family comparisons and distinction-making practices, which manifest in the form of insults and jokes, are common. In addition, the darkest members of mixed-color families often experience differential treatment and rejection. Finally, tactics to attempt to lighten oneself are not uncommon among darker-skinned family members.

Various distinction-making practices occur within mixed-color families in Veracruz, a practice found in other parts of Latin America.[11] As I mentioned in chapter 2, it is common for individuals in mixed-color families to receive racialized nicknames. However, labels for those who are darker are frequently deployed as weapons of insult. Pilar, the eighteen-year-old gas station worker with light-brown skin, recounts how her white ex-husband would bestow derogatory nicknames upon his dark-brown sister. Pilar vividly remembers one occasion when her ex-husband's sister was particularly proud of her appearance. According to Pilar, her ex-husband attempted to "put her in her place," saying, "Calm down little lizard.... You are blacker than I am," making reference to the dark skin of lizards in the region. In another mixed-color family, Giovanni, the twenty-eight-year-old light-skinned fisherman, admits calling his darker brother *negro* to irritate him. In yet another family, Eva, a forty-five-year-old working-class homemaker with light-brown skin, recalled that she and her siblings would call their darkest sister *negra* and taunt her, saying, "Nobody loves you because you are black." This sister was nicknamed the "ugly duckling" of the family.

Flor, a thirty-six-year-old working-class homemaker with dark-brown skin, spoke of distinction-making practices in her husband's family as well as her own family. As the darkest person in her family, Flor was the recipient of the label *negra*. However, it was within the context of her husband's family that Flor openly protested these labeling practices. According to Flor, her husband always called his darkest brother a "stinky black." This bothered her. She eventually confronted her husband, telling him: "Don't call him that. It makes me feel bad. It is like you are saying that to be black is to be stinky....What fault does he have for being black?" As we can see, race-color labels can become weapons of insult, attack, and power within mixed-color families.

Within-family comparisons not only surface in the form of nicknames but also manifest in the differential treatment of family members. Rather than embracing their rainbow of color differences, mixed-color families often exclude or isolate those whose phenotype is darker than the family norm. In speaking with members of mixed-color families, I heard many stories of differential treatment, generally revolving around the theme of lighter-skinned children receiving more affection, positive attention, and resources than their darker-skinned counterparts. This is consistent with Brazilian family dynamics, where light-skinned children are provided with special opportunities and more resources compared with their darker-skinned siblings.[12] Speaking candidly yet cautiously about this reality in Veracruz, Rosa, the working-class homemaker with medium-brown skin, lowered her voice before explaining, "Here, there are some people I know who are white and they treat the *moreno* people in their family like less and call them *negros*." Similarly, Mariluz, a fifty-two-year-old teacher with light-brown skin, confided, "Sometimes there are people...of a darker color than others within the same family and sometimes they don't accept these people. They don't love them and they treat them poorly because of their color." Mariluz formed this opinion based on observations of other mixed-color families as well as her own. Speaking about the latter, she told me: "They always reserve a little bit of rejection for the one who is darkest."

Jimena, a forty-two-year-old light-skinned working-class homemaker, has witnessed discrimination occurring within her brother-in-law's mixed-color family. Jimena describes her sister as *morena* and her brother-in-law as white. Referencing the reception her sister has received from the husband's family, Jimena explained: "There has always been this...mmm—I mean...they don't like her because she is *morena*." Despite the varied phenotypes within their own family, Jimena's brother-in-law's family engages in differential treatment. On the topic of the grandchildren, Jimena explained: "Since the first one came out white...they were happy. After that, another child was born. He was a little bit darker. Well, yes,

yes, they loved him but... there has always been a rejection there." At this last statement, Jimena lowered her voice considerably, as if speaking of something that is better left unsaid.

Other Veracruzanos directly referenced race-color dynamics within their own mixed-color families. For example, an eighteen-year-old female survey respondent wrote: "My aunt discriminates against people of color, including her daughter. She is embarrassed by her." Carlos, a fifty-four-year-old high-school teacher with dark-brown skin, also had a story of rejection to tell, a story that circulates in his mixed-color family. It is said that his great-grandmother, who was tall and white with blue eyes, did not love his sister, her great-granddaughter, because she was born black. Finally, Judy, the light-skinned university professor, spoke frankly about what she perceives as the racism running through her own mixed-color family. Judy matter-of-factly told me: "I come from a family that is racist in all forms. I come from a family where the first thing they tell you when a baby is born is if he or she was born white. When one of my little nephews was born *moreno*, his mom was very worried. She said to me, 'Your mom is not going to love him because... he is *moreno*.'" In this case, the mother's fears proved unfounded. According to Judy, her mother loves her grandchildren equally. However, it is clear that Veracruzanos recognize that being from a mixed-color family does not render race and color irrelevant.

Practices of distinction making, nicknaming, marginalization, and rejection within mixed-color families can have significant social and psychological effects on family members, especially on those who are singled out for being the darkest. Burdick (1998) argues that differential treatment of this kind can create particularly deep psychic wounds due to the intense emotional connection that surrounds family bonds. In Veracruz, the emotional ramifications of the aforementioned practices include attempts to lighten oneself and the adoption of an "If I had only..." mentality. Regarding the former, we have already heard about two attempts to lighten—Silva, who put white makeup on before posing for a photograph; and Lili's brown-skinned cousin who drank milk and put powder on her face.

In another case, Alberto, a forty-year-old teacher with light-brown skin, told me a story involving his darker-skinned sister who, at age five, would vigorously scrub her skin, saying that she wanted to be white like their lightest sister. Stressing her young age, Alberto explained that she thought she was dark because her skin was covered in dirt. Alberto shared this story with me during a classroom break. The tone of his remarks was light— Alberto smiled and chuckled at his sister's behavior. A student of Alberto's was listening in on our conversation. Judging by her expression, she was not at all surprised by Alberto's sister's behavior, suggesting that attempts to lighten are not uncommon.

As I spent more time in the field, stories about darker-skinned family members' attempts to lighten mounted. Belinda, the working-class homemaker with dark-brown skin, told me that her older sister suggested that she put Clorox on her skin to whiten. Belinda generalized her sister's prejudicial attitude to all whites, telling me that white people think that people with brown skin are "dirty and don't bathe." Another story came from Adriana, the light-skinned homemaker who is located on the opposite end of the economic spectrum from Belinda. Adriana recalls how her darker-skinned sister would bathe in milk to try to become white. While most Veracruzanos are not able to afford milk baths, the goal of Adriana's sister's more costly tactics was the same as her less financially stable counterparts—to lighten and to escape being branded the darkest member of the family. It is important to note that attempts to lighten are not just about avoiding being "othered" or marked as different. In these same families, the lightest members are also "othered" but in a manner that teaches them that their color is an asset. Therefore, they do not engage in similar attempts to change their appearance for the sake of "fitting in." After talking with Adriana, I had the chance to meet her sister, Anita. Anita confirmed what Adriana had told me and also added that she avoided eating beans and drinking coffee since both are dark in color. Attempts to whiten by drinking milk or avoiding coffee might be considered juvenile reactions to inter-sibling conflict or other dynamics that typically manifest in families. However, as individuals outgrow these particular practices, other social psychological effects of their status as the darkest in the family manifest, including the sentiment, "If I had only...."

The notion of "If I had only...," which encompasses individuals' desire to have been born with a lighter phenotype, is commonly expressed by the darkest individuals in mixed-color families. This philosophy functions in Mexico because having varied ancestries is the Mexican norm. Therefore, within one family there is a wide range of possible phenotypic outcomes, representing a game of genetic roulette. Because of this, darker individuals in mixed-color families often entertain the notion that they could have been born lighter.

I again turn to Belinda to highlight this dynamic. During one of our conversations, she blinked rapidly to fight back tears, as she told me about her experience with being the darkest among her siblings. We were seated on a set of wobbly wooden chairs on the front porch of her neighbor's house located on the outskirts of the city, an area inhabited by some of the poorest members of Veracruz society. A few pigs were fenced in a small enclosure attached to the house. Flies were everywhere and dust from the unpaved dirt roads periodically blew in our faces. Our conversation had turned unusually somber as Belinda told me of her family nickname "lizard," designed to differentiate her from her lighter-skinned siblings. This designation has left a lasting impression on Belinda, and it is evident that she clings to the fact that she could have come out lighter. She told me that she used to cry because she wanted to be white, a wish she retains to this day. She verbalized:

> All of my siblings said that I had been born on a night with no moon and because of that I am black. My older siblings made me cry, even the younger ones, because I am my mom's color.…All of my sisters and brothers were white and I was the only black one. I felt like they paid less attention to me, like they rejected me, and made fun of me because I am this color.

Belinda shared with me a time when her mother intervened, trying to assuage Belinda's concerns about her color:

> One day my mom took me aside. She hugged me and said, "Don't cry daughter. Look, come here. I am going to show you something." And she showed me the Virgin [of Guadalupe]. [She asked], "What color is the Virgin?" "Well mom, she is black." "And who is she?" "Well, the Virgin." "So then, why do you get sad? Why do you cry? Look, she was made by God and God made all of the colors so you should not feel like less. When you are grown, you are going to be a very fortunate woman and have luck and you are going to have children and be happy." I told her, "Yes, you say that so I don't cry but you also get angry because I want to be white." "Well, look at the color that I am and know that it gives me pleasure that you are the only one who got my color." "But I wanted to be like my father. They say I am not my father's daughter." "No, but you are my daughter," she told me. And…it started going away, but my mentality still is…"Why was I not white?"

In a rare critique of the privileging of whiteness, Belinda's mother used the themes of religion and family representation in an attempt to quell Belinda's concerns. However, her efforts were apparently no match for the overwhelmingly negative focus on Belinda's color coming from other family members. Try as she might, Belinda has not been able to shake her desire to have been born lighter. The color of her light-skinned siblings serves as a constant reminder of the color she could have been.

Rosa, the working-class homemaker, has medium-brown skin which represents a logical outcome given her light-skinned mother and her dark-brown-skinned father. Despite this, she had hoped for something different. She explained, "My mom is white. So I wanted to be white." But Rosa acknowledged the impracticality of this wish, stating, "But none of us are white. I have sisters who are lighter than I am, but we are all brown." In another case, Marisa, the English teacher with medium-brown skin and African origin features, also expressed unhappiness over her phenotype. In the forefront of her mind is the fact that her genetic makeup could have produced a different result, given the fact that her mom has light skin. She told me, "I would have liked to have gotten my mom's nose because hers is not very wide." As she said this, Marisa touched her own face as if to reconfigure her nose to be narrower like her mothers. She referred to her wider nose, reflective of her father's genes, as a "manufacturing defect."

It is not only females who entertain ideas of "If I had only. . . ." Alfredo, the fifty-six-year-old fisherman with dark-brown skin and curly hair, images how he could have come out differently based on his family's genetic composition. According to Alfredo, he inherited the features of his father, whom he described as "black, not black-black, but *moreno*." However, he reflects: "I could have come out like my mom—being very light, with straight hair, and having blue or green eyes. But I came out like my dad." Martín, the sixty-year-old navy captain with dark-brown skin, expressed a similar lack of satisfaction regarding the hand he was dealt in the game of genetic roulette. In a voice filled with lament, he told me, "My dad was tall and dark-skinned. My mom was white but short. So I got what I didn't want to get—shortness from my mom and dark skin from my dad. I should have gotten whiteness from my mom and being tall from my dad, right?" According to Martín, he spent years entertaining the idea of an alternate outcome based on the mixed-color status of his family. These examples illustrate the complexity of mixed-color family dynamics. Interestingly, however, the ideology of *mestizaje,* or the belief in a multitude of possible phenotypic outcomes, is not consistently applied to mixed-color families, a point to which I now turn.

Contradictions within a Mixed-Race Nation: Expectations of Sameness

During a focus group session, a male participant shared a story. "They say it is true," he began. He proceeded to tell the group about a black couple, whose children were black except one, who was white. The father obsessed over the white child and even went to church to ask the priest: "How is it possible that my woman is black and I am black and, from us, this white child came? We have ten children and nine of them are black and one is white. This is screwed up." After listening carefully, the Father concurred: "it is screwed up."

Given Mexico's powerful ideology of *mestizaje*, one might anticipate that there would be a lack of surprise regarding the phenotypic outcome of children, especially given the existence of the "If I had only..." sentiment, which is predicated on the possibility of within-family color variation. However, the reactions described in the story are consistent with another aspect of Veracruz racial common sense—the expectation that the color of offspring should resemble that of close relatives, especially the parents.[13] If offspring do not meet societal or familial color expectations, as was the case in the aforementioned example, questions and suspicions arise. In the words of Sara, a sixty-three-year-old secretary with light-brown skin, "if people see a brown child with white parents, the mind flies."

When in the field, I heard a variety of explanations for individuals who are color outliers in their families, including scenarios about undisclosed adoption and hospital birth ward mix-ups. However, the most common suspicion, which was implied in the focus-group story, was that of an affair. The suspicion of an affair is exemplified in the commonly heard phrase "the milkman's baby." Individuals tagged as milkmen's babies typically have physical characteristics that are dissimilar to those of nuclear family members. This label is oftentimes applied in a joking fashion but sometimes the implied accusation of an affair is taken seriously.

In the mestizo nation of Mexico, the existence of the idea of the milkman's baby is rather ironic and demonstrates that, on some level, individuals do not fully embrace the ideology of *mestizaje*. If this ideology were wholeheartedly accepted, surprise or suspicion should not surround within-family color variation; such variation would be understood to reflect the mixed genetic pool of the Mexican population. The irony of the coexistence of the discourses "we are all mixed" and the "milkman's baby" is represented in a popular song, "Sorullo."[14] The song opens with Sorullo and Capullo exchanging wedding vows and then proceeds to tell their story—the couple was "blond like butter" and had nine children. Eight came out blond and one black. Sorullo, the husband, kept quiet for many years, but the silence was eating away at him, and he decided to confront Capullo, his wife. He told her that he loves all of his children equally but wants to talk about the *negrito*. "Is it his child?" She answers: "Listen Sorullo, the *negrito* is the only one that is yours." The song concludes with their marriage ending. Capullo keeps her eight blond children and Sorullo his one black child.

This song, in clever form, exposes the tension between the discourses of *mestizaje* and the milkman's baby; Sorullo was working under the assumption of the latter, believing that the only viable explanation for the black child was that of an affair. However, the surprise at the end of the song—that the black child was indeed their child (and the only one, at that)—employs an ironic twist, relying on the ideology of race mixture to demonstrate that children can be distinct in phenotype from their biological parents. This song has resonance among the mixed-race societies of Latin America, including Mexico.

Veracruzanos sometimes adopt the assumption of Sorullo—that significant color difference in a family signals an affair—thus failing to recognize the range of possible outcomes presented by a mixed-race nation. Ironically then, despite the fact that Veracruzanos reproduce the discourse of a mixed-race nation in the abstract, they simultaneously hold "expectations of sameness"—that children should resemble the color of their parents. Illustrating these expectations is Adán's experience as a man with medium-brown skin married to a woman with dark-brown skin and having a light-skinned daughter. According to Adán, strangers erroneously assume that his wife is not his daughter's biological mother.

Belinda provides an additional example of how "expectations of sameness" operate. As we already know, Belinda has dark-brown skin and comes from a mixed-color family, which could easily explain why her son is light-skinned. Nevertheless, Belinda complains that people do not believe that he is her son. Offering a specific example, Belinda told me of a time when a group of young people approached her at a health clinic to ask if she was her son's mother. According to Belinda, people also comment on the contrast between her color and that of her son. In the case of Catalina, the working-class homemaker with light-brown skin, people remark about the difference between her black husband and his white brother. When people see them together, they do not believe they are brothers because "they are so different," Catalina explained. Sometimes, people inquire about this difference. These questions have conditioned the family to have a response ready—the blackness was inherited from their father's family. These reactions to phenotypic variation are somewhat surprising given the image of Mexico as a mixed-race nation.

As illustrated in the case Catalina, when there is a color outlier in the family, Veracruzanos often seek an explanation. Jennifer, the forty-two-year-old homemaker with light-brown skin, felt compelled to inquire about variations within her own family. She explained, "In the family, there is a very, very brown person. I asked my grandma: 'Why is there a *moreno* in the family?' She said 'Your great-grandfather was Cuban, one of those Cubans that they call *negros*.'" Jennifer was satisfied with her grandmother's explanation for what she had originally perceived to be an inexplicable anomaly.

In another case, the siblings of Flor, the working-class homemaker with dark-brown skin, invented a story to explain Flor's color. Individuals from Flor's father's side of the family are "white and tall," as are her siblings. Flor, however, is what she terms "indian black," meaning she has indigenous features and very dark-brown skin. According to Flor, her siblings have always teased her, concocting scenarios in which she is not a blood relative. Sharing one of their theories surrounding her lineage, Flor explained, "Where my parents were raised, there were indians who sold bread. So [my siblings] always told me that a bread maker had given me to my mom. [They'd say]: 'An indian bread maker left you with mom and that is why you are black.'" Flor recalls one of her brothers putting his white hand alongside hers and saying: "I am white and you are black. They gave you to my mom." These comments have had a lasting impact on Flor, who admitted, "I came to believe that I had been given to my parents," a belief she still holds to this day.

Embedded in the milkman's baby and related discourses is an obvious gender dynamic—because the suspicion of an affair falls on the mother, so does the burden of an explanation for color outliers. Alfredo, the fisherman with dark-brown skin, shared how this burden manifested in the family dynamics of his ex-girlfriend. The mother was "very very black" and the father *moreno*. The first child was born "blond with blue eyes." Alfredo explained, "They separated because [the father] thought...." His voice trailed off, wanting to avoid an explicit reference to an affair. However, he continued, explaining that the mother then produced photographs of her French grandfather, thus "proving" it was "in her blood" to give birth to a white child. The couple reunited and is happy now, according to Alfredo. Even though photographic evidence saved the marriage, the couple continues to be subjected to doubts about the child's parentage. As Alfredo explained, "Anyone would think that [the mom] stole [the child]."

Veracruzanos' reactions, comments, and general behavior toward significant within-family color variation demonstrate that the national ideology of *mestizaje* does not have enough symbolic weight to explain significant color variations. In the case of Alfredo's ex-girlfriend's family, hard proof was required to confirm the mother's European lineage. This is ironic when juxtaposed against Veracruzanos' strong embracement of the *mestizaje* ideology, which contends that Mexicans are a racially mixed and phenotypically varied population. Veracruzanos' expectations of sameness reveal the inconsistencies embedded in their racial common sense and further demonstrate that the notion of the cosmic race goes only so far.

Conclusion

The central concern of this chapter has been to interrogate the claim that interracial partnerships and multiracial families are spheres of antiracism and sites where race is less salient. I have investigated this assumption in the context of Mexico, a country that touts an open and progressive approach to race mixture, both in ideology and practice. In this chapter we heard from members of mixed-color families and individuals in inter-color relationships. Their stories expose a clear reality—prejudice and discrimination comfortably operate within these social units.[15] However, Veracruzanos' stories imply more than a simple challenge to the idea that such relationships and networks are sites of antiracism. They demonstrate that intercolor relationships and mixed-color families can actually be sites of *increased* race-color salience where whiteness is hyper-valorized and practices of distinction making and discrimination abound.

In this chapter we saw the collective gatekeeping that occurs to block the entry of brown-skinned individuals into both white and mixed-color families. In the case of the latter, we saw the "irony of opposition" in operation—some individuals, themselves products of mixed-color families, oppose intercolor relationships, oftentimes shunning family members engaged in such relationships and making potential family members who are dark, feel rejected and invisible. We also saw that when a family member is involved in a relationship with someone darker, parents and siblings are often plagued by fears of the prospect of dark-skinned grandchildren, nieces, or nephews.

Dynamics existing within intercolor pairings are no less tame. We heard individuals who have darker partners openly equate beauty with whiteness and state that they would prefer being with someone lighter. Others insisted that their partners are dark only because of sun exposure and not because of "black" lineage. We also saw that an absence of prejudice is not a requisite for marriage to a dark-brown-skinned person; in one case, the lighter-skinned partner even referred to blacks as orangutans. On the flip side, darker partners in intercolor relationships were vocal about the "benefits" of having a lighter counterpart—if they were lucky, their children would not inherit their dark genes but instead inherit the European genes of their partner.

Stories of marginalization and rejection surround the mixed-color family experience. Darker family members become the butt of jokes, the target of insults, and the "black sheep" of their families, while lighter members receive compliments, resources, and extra love. The darkest sibling is frequently "othered," relegated to the margins of (or even outside) the family unit. I illustrated the social and psychological consequences of these dynamics, particularly for the darkest family members. There was evidence of deep psych wounds and their consequences—individuals being driven to bathe in milk, shun coffee, and scrub their skin in a desperate attempt to change their color. Additionally, many darker individuals continue to dwell on the possibility that they could have been born lighter. Taken as a whole, the stories presented in this chapter demonstrate that, far from being free of racism, intercolor couples and mixed-color families can become prime breeding grounds for an extremely vicious and intimate form of racism.

6 | Situating Blackness in a Mestizo Nation

We have very few blacks, and a large part of them is already becoming a mulatto population.

—*Mexican intellectual José Vasconcelos, [1925] 1997*

I believe that there are no blacks here...but in the United States, they are really black....If you compare the blacks of the United States to the blacks here, we are less black.

—*Roberto, a Veracruz college graduate who has medium-brown skin*

I N MAY 2005, during a speech about immigrant rights, former Mexican president Vicente Fox said, "There is no doubt that Mexicans, full of dignity, purpose and the capacity to work, are doing the work that not even the blacks want to do there in the United States." Prominent African Americans and members of the U.S. government pounced on Fox's words, deeming them unfair characterizations of the African American community. However, critics on both sides of the border overlooked a significant implication of Fox's comment—the insinuation that the categories "black" and "Mexican" are mutually exclusive. This detail was recognized by Eduardo Añorve Zapata, a journalist from the Mexican state of Guerrero, who furnished the following response in a prominent Mexico City newspaper:

President Fox:

Do you know that José Maria Morelos, Vicente Guerrero, Juan Álvarez, Lázaro Cárdenas and Emiliano Zapata (heroes of the nation) were blacks? Did you know that one of the constituent roots of Mexicans is heritage from black African slaves, whose work and lives contributed to forming this nation?.... Did you know, in fact, that in the Costa Chica of Guerrero,

Acapulco, and Oaxaca the majority of the population is black?....I am sure that if you responded "yes" to these questions, you would realize that a large part of the immigrant population that goes to the United States to work on difficult tasks is Mexican blacks. I don't know if you should ask forgiveness from the African Americans; I know that, apparently, we black Mexicans continue to be invisible.[1]

Zapata's eloquent challenge to the popular assumption that the term "black Mexican" is an oxymoron was highly unusual. Few Mexicans questioned this aspect of Fox's statement, further perpetuating the nonblackness pillar of the country's national ideology, which marginalizes or negates Mexico's African heritage and implies that there are no black Mexicans in contemporary Mexico.

In some regions of Mexico, however, messages about blackness are more complex. For example, despite Mexico's national ideology of nonblackness, in Veracruz, some local narratives recognize the region's history of African slavery and highlight its connection to the Caribbean, particularly Cuba. Furthermore, in the national consciousness, Veracruz is sometimes viewed as a "black-influenced" state.[2] Therefore, when developing a racial common sense related to blackness, Veracruzanos are forced to reconcile the reality of the state's multifaceted connection to blackness with the national narrative, which minimizes and sometimes even erases blackness from the image of the Mexican nation; in other words, they need to situate and explain their experiences with blackness in Veracruz without disturbing the national ideological pillar of nonblackness.

In this chapter, I assess the complex relationship between Mexican national ideology related to blackness and Veracruz racial common sense on the topic. In doing so, I explore the multiple contradictions surrounding blackness in Veracruz, addressing questions such as the following: How do individuals of African descent,[3] whose phenotype deviates from the image of the prototypical Mexican, think about and manage their race-color and national identities? How do Veracruzanos of all ancestries understand and frame their state's association with blackness given Mexico's national ideology of nonblackness? Additionally, how do they construct the black category in this context? I show how Veracruzanos mobilize a series of discourses that manage the dilemmas highlighted in these questions in a way that generally maintains a consistency with the national belief system. However, I also highlight the difficulties involved in this process; socially reproducing the national stance that asserts an absence of blackness is not an easy task when local histories, cultural symbols, and even individuals' physical characteristics betray it.

Consistent with the sentiments expressed in the epigraphs presented at the chapter's opening, I demonstrate how Veracruzanos' discourses and actions effectively downplay the country's blackness. I detail how at the individual level Veracruzanos of African descent project an unstable black identity, allowing them to maintain some truth to themselves and their histories without challenging the national ideological stance or jeopardizing their identity as Mexican. At the regional level, I illustrate how Veracruzanos of all hues attempt to distance their state from its black connotation by transporting blackness to other regions of Mexico and constructing blackness as foreign.

Veracruzanos import racialized images of others, mainly African Americans and Afro-Cubans, to represent authentic blackness. Ironically, Veracruzanos have also co-opted recent efforts to draw attention to Veracruz's African root to achieve their goals of distancing themselves and their state from blackness. Taken as a whole, my findings reveal how the black category is simultaneously fixed and fluid in the Veracruz context. Based on these findings, I encourage scholars to become more attuned to how globalized notions of race may be affecting local racial terrains. Before delving into these findings, however, I discuss how blackness is marginalized in Mexican narratives at both the national and local levels.

The Marginalization of Blackness in Mexico

As discussed in chapter 1, early twentieth-century Mexican ideology played an important role in the national-level marginalization of blackness. Elites of the time promoted Mexico's mixed-race character, deliberately highlighting the indigenous-European composition of the national mixture while excluding the African component. This narrative fueled the contention that blackness is not part of the Mexican racial landscape, an assumption that continues to this day. Here, I provide just a few examples of how this assumption is perpetuated by contemporary forms of minimization that exist at both the national and Veracruz state level.

At the national level, textbooks included in the national curriculum expose all fourth-grade public school students in Mexico to a one-paragraph discussion of African slavery. This paragraph explains that, due to the high death rate of the indigenous population, Spanish officials brought thousands of African slaves to work in the mines, sugar fields, and textile mills and as domestic servants. They also learn that some of these slaves fled in pursuit of freedom and formed small towns. Slavery, or more precisely its abolition, is mentioned in another section of the same textbook: "During the Viceroyship, in all of America there were slaves. In Valladolid, Miguel Hidalgo ordered that they be set free. Later, in December of 1810, in Guadalajara, he promulgated a ban on slavery. In the United States, slavery was suppressed as late as 1863." The fourth-grade curriculum, the most extensive treatment of the topic of slavery in the national curriculum, not only devotes little attention to the subject but also minimizes Mexico's involvement with slavery via comparison with U.S. slavery.[4]

From the aforementioned textbook references, Mexican children learn that Mexico participated in slavery but that such participation was typical of norms at the time. They also learn that Mexico was more progressive than the United States in its call for abolition. What they do not learn, however, is that between the early sixteenth and mid-seventeenth centuries no other region in the Americas received more slaves than New Spain and that up until the mid-eighteenth century blacks outnumbered whites in Mexico.[5] Furthermore, they do not learn that Mexican slavery collapsed for economic reasons rather than progressive morals.[6]

At the Veracruz local level, the historic role of Africans in the country is also minimized. I witnessed this on one occasion when taking part in a tour of San Juan de Ulúa, a prominent fortress in the Port of Veracruz, which has served as a military post, a warehouse for goods during the colonial era, and a prison. The fort was built under Spanish rule, largely by slave labor. As a major historic landmark, it continues to draw large numbers of tourists. As with most tourism hotspots, guided tours are available. I participated in one of these tours, along with approximately ten other visitors. Our guide (whose accent suggested she was a Veracruz native) carefully described the labor-intensive nature of building the fort, which included the retrieval of large chunks of coral from the sea floor. She did not mention who actually performed this labor but continually described the fort as a European construction. At one point she mentioned that the Veracruz population included a mixture of the indigenous, Spanish, and black races. Anticipating surprise regarding her reference to Veracruz's black root, she posed the rhetorical question, "Why blacks?" and then responded: "Because the Spanish brought them from the Caribbean Islands." This was her only mention of blacks during the entire tour. After the tour ended, I approached her and asked who actually built the fort. Without missing a beat, she responded, "Indians and African slaves." Although she was clearly aware of this fact, it was omitted from her prepared spiel.

Minimization even surrounds explicit symbols of blackness in Veracruz. For example, within the state of Veracruz lies the town of Yanga. The town is named after Gaspar Yanga, an African prince who was captured and brought to Mexico in the late 1500s. As a slave, he led a successful rebellion in Veracruz; the revolt is said to represent the first of its kind on the continent.[7] During the uprising, the slaves escaped to the mountains and built a free slave colony, surviving on goods stolen from passing caravans and nearby haciendas.[8] In 1609, the Spanish sent troops to squelch the growing community.[9] After years of conflict, with casualties on both sides, a deal was brokered between Yanga and the Spanish, who agreed to Yanga's request for territorial autonomy in return for the community's allegiance during times of war.[10] In 1630, the town was established as an official community and named "San Lorenzo de los Negros." Today, the town is simply known as "Yanga." At the entrance a banner reads: "Welcome to Yanga—the first free town of America." A park houses an impressive statue of Yanga, a lean muscular figure with one arm raised, machete in hand. In his other hand is a stick; a broken chain dangles from his previously shackled wrist. Despite the potential for Yanga to represent a major focal point of blackness in the local and even the national consciousness, the individual and the town, as well as what they stand for, are known to few, other than some locals and passersby. The story of Yanga has failed to become a major rallying point for commemorating the country's African heritage and slave past, despite its rather remarkable role in history. Instead, when recognized, it is relegated to the extreme margins of Mexican national narratives.

In the following sections, I discuss how Veracruzanos manage their understandings of blackness in light of national- and local-level minimizations of Mexico's African heritage. I show how they conceptualize blackness within a black-influenced state and within the context of a mestizo nation—a nation in which mestizo is recognized as representing the mixture of indians and Europeans but not Africans. I begin by explicating how Veracruzanos of African descent, in particular, think about their ancestries and identities in this complicated ideological environment.

The Social Construction of Ancestry: Weak African Ancestral Claims

As living contradictions of the nonblackness pillar, Veracruzanos of African descent are faced with the task of needing to situate *themselves* in the mestizo nation of Mexico. In my interviews with Veracruzanos of African descent, they generally asserted a mixed-race heritage, with most acknowledging some form of African ancestry. They typically described this ancestry as "black," rarely voicing a direct connection to Africa, which is consistent with Martínez Montiel's (1993) claim that in Veracruz, "the black exists but the African does not" (p. 157); similar negations of African ancestry by self-identified blacks have been noted in Peru and Brazil.[11] Another way Veracruzanos referred to their African ancestry is through the use of the descriptor "Cuban," a term that often functions as a euphemism for blackness. However, individuals typically mentioned the African/black/Cuban part of their heritage only after I probed extensively into their ancestral knowledge base; it was not something they generally volunteered. Instead, when a possible association with blackness surfaced, they often moved to downplay it.

In many cases, individuals appeared to lack concrete information about the African side of their heritage, most likely because these lineages, like indigenous roots, are oftentimes marginalized or neglected in family discussions of ancestry. This was the case with José, the sixty-three-year-old taco vendor who describes his dark-brown skin as *cobrizo* (copper-colored). He told me that he understands his ancestors to be African but that he cannot verify this because his family never talked to him about his predecessors. Recently, he became curious about his heritage and looked into the origins of his surname. José concluded that he probably descends from Africans but provided no details of his findings. Although José was motivated to seek out this information, during our conversation he gave the impression of disinterest, merely shrugging while sharing his discovery.

In contrast, Alfredo, the fifty-six-year-old fisherman with dark-brown skin who identifies as mestizo, responded to my questions about his ancestry with subtle yet powerful feeling; my inquiries obviously triggered emotion-laden sensitivities. With apprehension in his voice, as if approaching a forbidden subject, Alfredo shared how he has respected his family's silence regarding their African heritage:

ALFREDO: I believe that we are descended from the slaves, including myself. I believe that probably, I descend from the slave race.
CS: From Africans?
ALFREDO: I imagine so...I never asked my dad about race—I don't know, out of embarrassment or respect, I don't know.
CS: You haven't asked him?

ALFREDO: Nor do I ask him about color, my father [long pause] because he was black...Not very, very black. No. He was very, very, very black, African black. I don't know what. Really big. The black race.

CS: But you never talked about it?

ALFREDO: No, he never told us.

Alfredo intuits he is of African origin but his suspicions remain unconfirmed. However, like others, Alfredo does not need it spelled out for him; he realizes that his phenotype is evidence of his family's African heritage, even if it is not explicitly verbalized.

When interviewing Carla, the fifty-seven-year-old light-skinned middle-class homemaker, and her daughter, Marisa, the twenty-five-year-old English teacher with medium-brown skin, I was able to locate the point of rupture in their family's generational transmission of African ancestral knowledge. Carla's husband (Marisa's father) is of African descent. Marisa described her own features as resembling those of her father—"a flat nose, big eyes and curly hair." As we conversed, it became evident that Marisa was largely unaware of Mexico's slave history and did not know much about her ancestors. This surprised me since, in previous interactions, Carla always made a point of conveying how educated, knowledgeable, and cultured Marisa is.

When Marisa's ignorance about Mexican slavery became evident during our conversation, Carla became noticeably uncomfortable and quickly intervened. Attempting to rectify her daughter's gaps in knowledge, she began to explain to Marisa that, long ago, there were African slaves in Veracruz. She then paused, as if she had spoken prematurely, not having thought through the implications of the conversation; her facial expression suggested a realization that she was about to tread on a sensitive topic. Carla cautiously continued: "This is why some people have unrefined features such as wide noses and thick lips." In an effort to give the topic the gentle handling it deserved, Carla then told her daughter: "Don't be angry but you have a nose like that." Marisa reacted instantly, placing her hand over her nose as if to hide it.

Later in our conversation, we revisited the issue when I asked both Marisa and Carla how they would describe Marisa's physical features. The following conversation ensued:

MARISA: Cuban.

CARLA: Well, there is mixture, in reality, not very, very Cuban.

MARISA: No, because Cuban women are very ugly.

CARLA: [She has] some characteristics.
MARISA: Uh-huh.
CARLA: For example, her hair is very curly—
MARISA: Curly.
CARLA: It is curly and her nose, her lips....

Over the course of our conversation, Carla and Marisa began to piece together information regarding Marisa's African heritage, information that had apparently escaped the generational transmission process up until that point. They accomplished this sharing of knowledge in a roundabout way, drawing parallels between African slaves, Marisa's physical appearance, and "Cuban" features. Carla then supplied some crucial details previously unknown to Marisa–that her father is of partial African ancestry. As a result of this conversation, the generational gap in knowledge began to close. However, I do not know if Marisa will pass this information on to the next generation, a decision that will determine the fate of the information about her African heritage that she now possesses.

As I demonstrated in chapter 3, not all ancestries are treated equally with respect to the generational transfer of ancestral knowledge. Consistent with this notion, when Veracruzanos with African ancestry discussed their European heritage, the social silence surrounding ancestry lifted, and the tone of the conversation dramatically changed. In sharp contrast with their reluctance or inability to share information about African predecessors, discussions of their European background flowed freely and surfaced unexpectedly. Not only would conversations about European ancestry emerge spontaneously, but oftentimes my inquiries about non-European ancestors were derailed and rerouted to the topic of European heritage. For example, immediately after the awkward conversation with Carla and Marisa about Marisa's African roots, Marisa launched into a discussion about her white, blue-eyed maternal grandparents. Veracruzanos' claims to African/black/Cuban heritage were both fleeting and superficial, especially compared with their assertions of European heritage. However, more volatile still were their claims to a black identity.

The Social Construction of Identity: Unstable Black Identities

During my first visit to the field, I was confronted with the slippery nature of black identities in Veracruz. Under time pressure to collect preliminary data, I prioritized the identification of individuals considered to be black in the local context so I could interview them. The process I went through in pursuit of this goal is best described as a wild goose chase. It began when Sandra and Pepe, my main informants, arranged for me to speak with Ramón, a man whom they assured me was definitely black. In the course of my conversation with Ramón, he informed me that he is not black. However, wanting to be helpful, he suggested that I talk to Ociel, a black friend of his. I then spoke with Ociel, only to be told that he too is not black but not to worry; he knew someone who is black with whom I could speak. This cycle occurred again and again throughout my time in the field. I eventually abandoned all attempts to locate a black subject and, instead, turned my attention to the moving target phenomenon.

The metaphor of blackness as a moving target captures how black identities manifest inconsistently in Veracruz. I illustrate this point by introducing a series of cases that draw attention to various aspects of the identity construction process of individuals of African descent. I begin with Rodrigo, the thirty-seven-year-old fisherman with dark-brown skin and black curly hair. I first met Rodrigo, the informal leader of the fishermen, on a trip to the docks, a visit inspired by remarks made to me by other Veracruzanos—that the local fishermen are black. Indeed, fellow fishermen also described Rodrigo as black. Rodrigo, however, identifies as *moreno* and reports having ancestors from the "dark" race. When we spoke, Rodrigo made sure that I understood that he is *not* black. Despite his insistence on this point, comments he made throughout our conversation seemed to undermine his disassociation from blackness. For example, at one point, Rodrigo shared with me his love for music and then proceeded to justify this affinity:

> The instinct, the instinct—do you know that the black race invented the music? The slaves and all of that, right? On some occasions there are songs that have a message about the slavery of the past....Well, more or less, we [my family] identify like that and we consider ourselves to have some mixture or something in the blood of that black race that existed before and continues to exist.

Rodrigo quickly clarified, however, that his family is not "really black" but a mixture of races.

As part of my wild goose chase, Sandra and Pepe introduced me to Carlos, the fifty-four-year-old high school teacher with dark-brown skin and tightly curled hair. After some initial exchanges, I was confident that

I had finally secured my first interview with a black Veracruzano. Then we spoke at length and it became evident that Carlos too was ambivalent about his blackness. As I broached the topic of racial identification, Carlos, like others, insisted that racial categories do not exist in Veracruz, thereby evading my question on racial identity. However, when he talked about his family, the topic resurfaced:

> In my house, they have called me *negro* since I was born....My mom was white like you, or even more so, and my dad was *moreno*. But well, I am black and I have a brother who is whiter, and that is that....Lots of mixture....My white sisters have blond hair, which is natural, not dyed, and green eyes."

Every time Carlos took one step toward the boundary of blackness, he took a half step back; he would identify as black but then qualify his identification. In the previous excerpt, this qualification manifested in him emphasizing the whiteness, not the blackness, of his family. At another point in our conversation, Carlos self-identified as black in terms of color but mestizo in terms of race. His reluctance to racially identify as black again suggests a retreat from the racialized black category. He further hastened this retreat by explaining that his dark skin merely reflects a high degree of sun exposure.

Other individuals of African descent also deployed the "sun discourse" to justify their skin tone in a way that does not implicate African heritage. One of these individuals was Ramón, the forty-four-year-old high-school employee with dark-brown skin and very curly hair, one of the initial players in my wild goose chase. When I asked Ramón what color he considers himself, he hesitated, before responding: "Mmm, *moreno*....Normal because, well, blacks—there are some who are blacker than I am. My original color would be—look, what happens is that I am out in the sun a lot when I am fishing. I am always out in the sun. Too much sun." Not only does Ramón use the sun discourse, but he also compares himself with others to lighten his color.

The story of how I met Paula, the center of my next case study, is a bit more circuitous. It begins with Flor, the thirty-six-year-old working-class homemaker with dark-brown skin, whom I met while attending a Marco Antonio Solís concert. "El Buki," as he is called, is a well-known Mexican singer; most Veracruzanos are unable to afford tickets for his regular performances so the demand for seating at this free event far exceeded the supply. Those of us who successfully secured space on the bleachers collectively joined hips to allow as many people as possible a seat. Because the demand for stage viewing was sure to be high, both Flor and I had arrived very early. In the hours that we waited, amid tight quarters, we became good friends. Within the week she had invited me into her home and introduced me to her family and neighbors. Flor was my entrée into the ring of poor communities lying on the outskirts of the city. It was in this context that I met Paula, Flor's neighbor.

Paula is a forty-two-year-old working-class homemaker with dark-brown skin and very curly jet-black hair. Flor had mentioned Paula's hair in previous discussions when describing Paula as her black neighbor. Paula is soft-spoken. She is also careful to conform to her husband's requests. He wants her to be in the house when he arrives from work, although his schedule is irregular. During our interview, she continuously glanced across the street to ensure that she was not in violation of this mandate. She assured me she could get back home in time if she saw him coming. Despite the situation, Paula was generous with her time and diligently answered my numerous questions. "I am mestiza," she told me, "descended from mestizos." In terms of color, Paula explained that she thinks of herself as *morena*, although, she added, others may think of her as black. She laughed before elaborating:

> In regards to my color, they say I am black—to say it like that, right? But there are people who come from Africa, let's say, who come and visit us, and one notices that there are people much more *morena* than oneself. So I—it doesn't matter to me if they say I am black or I am *morena*. For me it is the same. If a white person pejoratively tells me that I am black, I'd rub my arm on him or her and, if my color washes off, then we are the same. Because he passed his color to me and I passed mine to him. Do you understand?

I did understand. Color is only skin-deep. We are all humans. That was Paula's message. I frequently encountered these discourses as well as Ramón and Paula's perspective on the relativity of blackness. According to their logic, they are not black because, on the race-color continuum, there is someone blacker than they are. This comparative framework allows Veracruzanos to evade or distance themselves from the black category and thus a black identity. In the case of Paula, however, she did not evade a black identity entirely, as she evoked outside classifications of her as black and did not directly challenge them.

The blackness-as-a-moving-target phenomenon disarms the potential for the formation of a stable black identity or a group consciousness around blackness. In Veracruz, there is no in-group feeling or sentiment among individuals of African descent that they are a group distinct from others in society, a perspective that often facilitates the formation of racial groups.[12] Veracruzanos of African descent do not express an affinity for or a sense of shared understanding with others of similar heritage or phenotype. That being said, as the previous examples illustrate, neither do they wholly negate or evade a black identity.

Through vacillation and displays of a fleeting connection to blackness, Veracruzanos avoid a direct confrontation with the national belief that there are no Mexican blacks. If Veracruzanos of African descent were to stake an unequivocal claim to blackness, they would be relegating themselves to the margins of the Mexican nation; in other words, asserting a strong black identity would place their national identity in jeopardy. The interconnection between ideas of race and nation in Mexico creates strong incentives for Veracruzanos of African descent to manage their race-color identities in a way that does not conflict with their Mexican identity.

By distancing themselves from a fixed, concrete, and stable black identity while not completely cutting their ties to blackness, Veracruzanos of African descent navigate the sea of contradictions that their bodies, histories, and nationalities represent. They walk a fine line, striving to avoid direct contradictions with the nonblackness ideological pillar without completely denying their own experience—they may know of black ancestors, but they don't tell their children; some of their ancestors may be dark, but others are light; they may have black "blood," but this doesn't mean they are black; they may look black, but others look blacker. Through these discursive framings, Veracruzanos of African descent manage the contradictions surrounding their identities, experiences, and society's ideologies.

In contrast, the Afro-Cuban immigrants I spoke to talked about their blackness very openly. These individuals, all born and raised in Cuba, asserted strong, unequivocal, black identities. My first contact with the Afro-Cuban community was with thirty-eight-year-old Gonzalo. I knew him as a dance instructor, but he is also a singer, performer, and music composer. I enrolled in Gonzalo's dance class after learning about it from an acquaintance. The class was marketed as being taught by an authentic Cuban instructor; this strategy was effective as Veracruzanos attribute almost supernatural dancing and musical skills to Cubans, particularly Afro-Cubans. When Gonzalo entered the room on the first day of class, he greeted us, flashing a ready-made smile. He was impressive, tall in stature. The effect was exaggerated by the way he carried himself. Gonzalo exuded confidence but not arrogance. He appeared secure in himself and his abilities. His presence was captivating as he is a skilled performer. Gonzalo's dream is to become famous.

As I got to know Gonzalo, I realized this presentation was a cover disguising a much more contemplative, troubled, and conflicted personality. This side of Gonzalo and the stories associated with it were strikingly familiar; they reminded me of the experiences of many non-European immigrants living in the United States who have to balance their pride, visions of success, the struggle to fit in, and being marked as racial and national "others." In Gonzalo's case, I directly witnessed the kinds of jokes and unpleasantries that he has to confront related to his racial and national status. One evening a fellow classmate, irritated by Gonzalo's late arrival, called Gonzalo a monkey as he entered the studio. I am sure Gonzalo heard, but he pretended not to. On another occasion, a group of friends and students, including myself, were on a bus trip to Mexico City with Gonzalo. One of our companions couldn't reach her bag so she motioned for help, while joking: "It is the black one, next to the black one" (meaning Gonzalo). Gonzalo smiled stiffly. However, I never heard him complain about these kinds of slights. Like many immigrants, Gonzalo believes that hard work and perseverance will bring success. He once told me, "I am a person that does not faint in front of just any barrier. I am a person who likes to fight. I don't care if, when I am fifty years old, I still have not achieved what I want. I will continue to fight."

Although now a Mexican national, Gonzalo first came to Veracruz in 1993 when he was invited to participate in a musical performance surrounding the inauguration of the new aquarium. He returned to Cuba in accordance with the terms of his visa but married his Mexican girlfriend later that year. In 1995, the Veracruz Cultural Institute offered Gonzalo a contract to teach Afro-Caribbean dance. In addition, Gonzalo began to freelance, teaching salsa classes and recording his own music. He was quite successful, later being chosen to participate in a Mexican talent show competition, comparable to the U.S.-based series *American Idol*.

Months after I first met Gonzalo, I approached him for an interview. Up to this point, he was unaware of my research. After I explained what I was doing in Veracruz, he agreed to meet me at a local restaurant, a few blocks away from the dance studio. We chose outdoor seating. Gonzalo appeared to be comfortable, but was subdued. He lit a cigarette, leaned back, and waited for me to begin. I started by asking him to tell me about his experience in Veracruz. He has been lucky, he said, very well received. We were then interrupted by a woman who spotted Gonzalo from her car. She waved, pulled over, and came to join us. She looked to be a member of the Veracruz upper-middle to upper class. Her new grandchild had just been born in Italy, and she wanted Gonzalo to know. She pulled out pictures of the baby and jokingly remarked, "She looks like a Mexican indian," referencing her straight hair, which was standing up. After she departed, Gonzalo told me, "She is a good example. She has money and is cool," using the interaction to buttress his statement that he is accepted in Veracruz.

As our conversation progressed, Gonzalo began to contradict himself. When he and his wife (who has medium-brown skin and who Gonzalo describes as mulatto) decided to get married, they did not find support among his wife's family or friends. He attributed their opposition to stereotypes about Cubans—that they steal money and don't want to work. Gonzalo omitted the race connection but didn't need to spell it out. We both knew that, in Veracruz, "Cuban" frequently means "Afro-Cuban."

Gonzalo's experiences in Veracruz cannot solely be attributed to his status as a foreign national. His dark-brown-skinned, Mexican-born sons have not been well received. They have had trouble at school, Gonzalo shared, because of their color. Other kids say things like, "Look at your skin. What you touch, you'll stain." Gonzalo explained, both he and his wife try to encourage them to be proud of being black:

> Maybe there is someone with black features or maybe there are blacks who are not happy with their race. They can exist too, and maybe they are upset [about being black]. But for me, they call me black and … in fact my son is black and I am teaching him that … since there is not much of [the black] race here in Mexico, it is something unusual. [My son] is different. … I have him in a school where there are almost no blacks and he is black. And when the kids are with him, sometimes they tease him and try to upset him. But he has already learned that "I am black. I am black." I have told him: "Look son, you are a person, the same as anyone else, only you have black skin. You have the same rights." So, at the beginning he was a little bit upset, but not anymore.

The experiences of Gonzalo's sons are not unique. I overheard similar comments directed toward other Veracruzanos of African descent. However, not once did I hear the kind of sentiment expressed by Gonzalo coming from a native Veracruzano, encouraging children to embrace a black identity and take pride in their heritage.

Comments directed at Gonzalo's sons should not be dismissed as immature remarks that would be made only by youngsters. Similar comments are made by adults. One evening, Gonzalo brought his sons with him to dance class. His older son, who is quite artistic, was seated at a table in the back of the studio drawing cartoon characters. He ran out of ideas of what to draw, so adults around him began to throw out character names. One of the male class participants began insisting that he draw Memín Pinguín, the black comic book character (see figure 1.1, chapter 1). The man laughed loudly, obviously amused by the parallel that he was trying to establish between Memín and Gonzalo's son. The boy did exactly what his father had done when he was called a monkey—he ignored. The stories of discrimination that were relayed to me and the discriminatory incidents I witnessed did not differ significantly between Afro-Cubans and Veracruzanos of African descent. What did differ, however, was how these two groups responded to discrimination and how they constructed their identities.

Racial Distancing and Constructing the Boundaries of Blackness

As we have seen, Veracruzanos of African descent deploy racial distancing strategies to evade the black label. However, Veracruzanos of all ancestries, not just those of African descent, engage in strategies to distance Veracruz and Mexico from blackness; all state residents are susceptible to being connected with blackness by their regional association with Veracruz, which is seen as the most "black-influenced" state in the Mexican nation. Effective distancing, however, requires the creation of something concrete, something stable, against which they can measure and therefore distance themselves. Blackness needs to be projected onto others for evasion to be successful. In other words, Veracruzanos cannot simply produce a discourse about what blackness *is not*; they need to identify what blackness *is*. Therefore, their approach to blackness is two-pronged: they distance themselves from definitive blackness and simultaneously construct a new target of blackness. We have already seen how this works at the individual level of racial ancestral and identity construction. Here, we learn how Veracruzanos of all ancestries implement this strategy at the level of the state and the nation.

Distancing Veracruz from Blackness

Veracruzanos' efforts to maintain a safe distance from blackness are complicated by racialized images of the region. Whereas northern Mexican ideology asserts a purer European ancestry compared with the rest of the country and southern Mexico evokes images of dark-skinned mestizos and indigenous individuals,[13] in the national mind Veracruz is oftentimes considered to be the most black-influenced state. Residents of the Port of Veracruz or surrounding towns are known as *Jarochos*. During certain time periods, the term Jarocho held strong racial connotations, which included a reference to Veracruz's African root. This past is resurrected in a plaque that hangs on the wall of a local museum:

> In the caste society of the 18th century, in particular in the coastal region of the central Gulf, *Jarocho* was an offensive term for the people of indian and black mixture....Towards the end of the 18th and in the 19th century, it stopped being an offensive term and was used for the mestizos of the Veracruz countryside of European, African and indigenous roots, with predominately black features. The *Jarocho* began to be recognized for his/her happy and festive personality.

In the mid-twentieth century, the relationship between the *Jarocho* stereotype and blackness began to be erased through the remaking and popularizing of a whitened image of the *Jarocho*. The new image was characterized not by African heritage but instead by a particular form of attire.[14] Recently however, select Veracruz cultural institutions have fought back, seeking to resurrect the traditional, African-related meaning of *Jarocho*. I witnessed this during various cultural events. For example, when attending the twenty-fifth anniversary celebration of the folkloric ballet of the University of Veracruz, I listened as the host introduced a *son jarocho* musical piece as representing the "indians and blacks that populated this area." Despite his mention of blacks in association with the Veracruz region, the host still relegated their existence to the past.

The symbolic tug-of-war that exists between a whitened and blackened image of Veracruz and its population has created conflicts in popular understandings. The whitening of this stereotype has, in some cases, been effective. For example, Anita, the fifty-year-old upper-class homemaker with light-brown skin, even as a Veracruz native, did not associate Veracruz with blackness for most of her life. However, a friend of hers "made her realize" that people in the city have "black features." Sharing this revelation, she told me: "Here there are a lot of people with curly hair, a lot. Their bodies have a lot of hip. This is from the black race." Whereas Anita, like many others, grew up with a de-blackened sense of Veracruz, others are familiar with the *Jarocho* image before it was whitened. For example, Adán, the thirty-five-year-old painter with medium-brown skin, maintains this image through a personal connection. He explains that his mother-in-law's father was "one of those old people from before, from here…the blacks, the pure ones…the ones that used to live here." In Adán's mind, there is a strong connection between Veracruz and blackness, albeit one rooted in the past.

This connection also surfaced while I was driving across the country with two individuals, one a Veracruz native and the other a Veracruz resident originally from Oaxaca. As we approached a security checkpoint, my travel companions began discussing among themselves if I could pass as Mexican. Their hope was to avoid introducing me as a U.S. citizen since that would likely lead to a car search and extensive delay. Yes, I look Mexican, they agreed, but a *Jarocha*? They were skeptical. "Her skin is too light," I heard them say. "Let's say she is a *Chilanga* [from Mexico City]. She looks like a *Chilanga*." We presented my regional alias to the officials, and we rolled on through.

Even among those who are familiar with the original meaning of *Jarocho,* maintaining this regional image is difficult, especially outside protected realms such as Veracruz cultural institutions. Many people are not receptive to hearing about Veracruz's connection to blackness. Carla, the light-skinned middle-class homemaker, flagged the socially unacceptable nature of this topic during one exchange by moving close to me and lowering her voice to narrate her understanding of local history:

> Look, the *Jarocho* is a mixture of African [hushed tone]….I am speaking of the past….The mixed roots of Spaniards and blacks stayed here because— and indians, because here the Spanish left a lot of slaves….A lot of slaves came. So they brought them and they also mixed with the Spanish and the Mexican indigenous, African with indigenous, Spanish with African—that is why we have that blood.

Carla was noticeably unsettled during this conversation. This is not a popular subject, something of which she is fully aware.

Alberto, the forty-year-old school teacher with light-brown skin, who is originally from Oaxaca, is more naïve about the social consequences involved in directly discussing Veracruz's connection with blackness, or at least he used to be. Alberto has always adored history and is excited to impart his knowledge, something I consistently noticed when observing his interactions with his high school students. During a class break following a lesson on Mexican history, Alberto took a seat next to me, proudly showing me pictures of former students. He pointed to a female student with dark-brown skin and curly hair and said, "See. She looks like she has African features." I interpreted this as a reference to a comment he had made about Mexican slavery during class. When looking at the picture, Alberto vocally reminisced about a time when, in an attempt to connect students' understanding of Mexican history to the present, he had approached this student, pointing out how her phenotype resembles that of the slaves brought to Veracruz. Alberto remembered how she vehemently denied the connection and became very upset with him. He then understood why she always put so much white powder on her skin. A wave of sadness crossed Alberto's face as he retold this story. It was through this interaction that Alberto learned that the topic of Veracruz's blackness is something most people do not want to discuss.

Most Veracruzanos I spoke with attempted to challenge, in one way or another, the image of Veracruz as the "black state" of Mexico. Even those who did not completely negate the state's affiliation with blackness frequently downplayed the connection. For example, Omar, the forty-four-year-old journalist with medium-brown skin, begrudgingly said: "I think that we are the blackest [state]…but we aren't that black," and then laughed nervously. Veracruzanos of all hues expressed discomfort around the idea that their state is sometimes thought of as the blackest part of Mexico. They mobilized discursive tactics to deny, contest, or revise this regional stereotype and went to great lengths to anchor blackness elsewhere. Godreau (2006) refers to the dynamic of rejecting a black label and applying it to others as the "spatial distancing of blackness" or the "displacement of blackness." This terminology nicely describes the strategies of Veracruzanos—they root blackness in other regions and then distance themselves from those regions.

Displacing blackness, however, is not easily executed in the Mexican context since Mexico does not have many regions that are likely candidates for the black label. This became evident when I asked Veracruzanos, "If not Veracruz, which region of Mexico merits the designation as being the black region of Mexico?" Many were unsure how to respond. For example, Rodrigo, the leader of the fishermen with dark-brown skin, struggled to produce an alternate option to Veracruz:

Acapulco also has a lot of blacks…Cancun, well, no.…In every state of the Republic, all along the coast, from…Tamaulipas, it is all black people. Tamaulipas, all of the ports, all of the Caribbean, from the side of Quintana Roo to the Pacific side, Puerto Escondido, Acapulco. All of the places where there is a coast and where there is a port, there are blacks.

In contemplating possible rivals for the title of blackest, Rodrigo attempts to weaken the Veracruz–blackness association by framing Veracruz as not uniquely black.

Veracruzanos also mobilized the "sun discourse" to account for the darker skin seen throughout the region while pursuing an agenda to distance the state from racialized notions of blackness. In adopting this discourse, individuals conveniently centralized skin tone in their discussions and dismissed other phenotypic markers (e.g., hair and facial features). In other words, they treated blackness in a color sense as opposed to a racial sense. Veracruzanos frequently characterized the darker skin tone of many in the region as a testament to the local climate, explaining that the sun, not African heritage, is responsible for the local phenotype. Any Mexican living in Veracruz would look the same, they argue.

Ana and Laura, brown-skinned sisters in their forties, were in agreement on this point. Ana informed me that, on the coasts, there are *morenos* and blacks. She then corrected herself: "Better said—on the coast there are *morenos*." Justifying her terminological waffling, she continued: "Yes, there are more blacks, but because of the sun.... I mean even though oftentimes we are white, normally there is always sun and one is always in the sun, and so the skin always gets a little bit darker." The two sisters then worked in tandem to address my question about blacks in Mexico:

ANA: Where are there more blacks?... It would be in... [pause]. We have traveled to many parts of the republic...
LAURA: In Mexico City.
ANA: Here in... only in Mexico City, right? In the federal district, yes.
LAURA: There are all kinds of people.
ANA: There are more blacks than here, yes. Here there are none. Here there are *morenos* but no blacks.
CS: Would you say that there are *morenos oscuros* [dark-brown-skinned people] here?
ANA: Mmm, *morenos*—
LAURA: Claros. [Light]
ANA: *Morenos claros* [light-brown-skinned people].
LAURA: And blacks because of the sun.

Although rocky in the delivery, Laura and Ana displace blackness to other regions of Mexico while simultaneously applying the sun discourse to explain Veracruzanos' darker hue. In a smoother fashion, César, Laura's eighteen-year-old medium-brown-skinned son, loyal to his mother's perspective, informed me that there are more blacks in Veracruz because of the intense heat, which results in "burned" skin.

Despite the assumptions embedded in the sun discourse, being black in Veracruz is oftentimes much more than a matter of skin tone. Although other physical markers such as hair and facial features play an important role in how people are classified racially, Veracruzanos draw attention to these markers only under certain circumstances. They sideline physical features unrelated to skin tone when employing the sun discourse because accounting for them would not serve the purpose of this particular strand of racial common sense—to minimize evidence of an African root within the Veracruz population. Acknowledging these other features would make Veracruzanos' task of ideological management more difficult. That being said, Veracruzanos do recognize a broader range of phenotypic features when conceptualizing blackness outside the boundaries of the nation.

Distancing Mexico from Blackness

Although Veracruzanos struggled in their attempts to relocate blackness to other regions within Mexico, they had no difficulty whatsoever exporting blackness beyond Mexico's borders. There was resounding agreement among Veracruzanos that blackness is largely foreign to Mexico, a discourse also heard on Mexico's Pacific Coast[15] and a position that mimics Mexican national ideology of nonblackness. Veracruzanos' charge that blackness is foreign is much more powerful, consistent, and unequivocal compared with the weaker and more poorly formulated discourses related to blackness that we have seen thus far. It is firmly rooted in their racial common sense.

In my conversations with Veracruzanos, they steadfastly maintained the stance of "black is foreign," despite its contradiction with the presence of Veracruzanos of African descent. Managing this contradiction in their everyday environment, I was frequently told that individuals of African descent in Veracruz were "not from around here"—a message whispered into my ear more than once upon encountering someone of African descent. One time, Sandra, the forty-eight-year-old high school teacher with light-brown skin, didn't even bother to whisper. We had gone to play bingo, a favorite pastime of hers. As we entered the casino, we greeted other regulars and made our way through the smoke-filled room. Sandra was always in search of signs of luck; sometimes she identified particular tables as lucky. This time, she selected a table where a woman we did not know was seated, so we proceeded with introductions. As I scanned the room, I saw a man of African origin at another table. I asked Sandra if she knew him. She did not but confidently asserted that he is not a local but may be Cuban. She loudly asked the woman at our table: "Where would that *moreno* be from?" The woman looked over her shoulder and swiveled back to face us, saying: "Not from here, probably Cuba."

When I inquired about individuals of African origin, Veracruzanos repeatedly responded in two forms, saying either they are foreigners or their parents are. Miguel, the twenty-five-year-old university student with medium-brown skin and African-origin features, exemplifies this frame of thought in the following excerpt from our conversation:

CS: Are there black people here?
MIGUEL: Yes, yes there are. Cuban people live here, tourists live here, tourists come here.
CS: Are there people that you have seen that are Mexican who you identify as being from the black race?
MIGUEL: That are Mexican?
CS: Yes, that are Mexican.
MIGUEL: Yes, yes there are. If they have descendants from Cuba, Puerto Rico, Panama, Africa, Colombia. Yes, yes there are. Including from North America—children of North American parents or grandchildren of North Americans. Or the English.

Miguel equates blackness with foreignness despite the fact that he himself has African heritage.

Corazón, the fifty-six-year-old working-class homemaker who has light skin and no apparent African heritage, draws similar conclusions:

CS: Do you know any Mexicans who are black?
CORAZÓN: Yes…That are really black…We say that they are probably from—well that they are not from around here. People say that….A lot of people left their countries and I imagine that they, or one of their family members, ended up here. Because they are really black with very curly hair.
CS: But they are Mexican?
CORAZÓN: Supposedly now they are Mexican.

Corazón may reluctantly recognize the status of black Mexicans as co-nationals, but she still views them as different—as foreigners or the children or grandchildren of foreigners.

Is Veracruzanos' system of identifying persons of African descent as foreigners accurate? Although it was not always possible to ascertain an answer, I learned that sometimes they were correct and sometimes not. Pepe, the forty-seven-year-old high-school teacher with light-brown skin, provides an example of a case of false identification:

> PEPE: I just met a person. I don't have a friendship with him. He is a friend of a friend here at the house. He caught my attention and I said "this guy is a foreigner," because he is a guy of color like a Haitian-type or like that....
>
> CS: He is black?
>
> PEPE: Yes, very black....I saw him in the park and I asked Toño [a friend]: "What about that guy?" Toño said, "He is a coworker." I said, "But he is a foreigner." And he said, "No. He is more Mexican than the cactus."[16]

As Pepe relayed the story, I got the sense that he still does not fully accept that he was wrong and continues to wonder if the guy is really Mexican.

The discourse of foreignness allows Veracruzanos to powerfully and consistently reproduce the national ideology of nonblackness. It also assists them in reconciling the existence of "black-looking" people in Veracruz with the national stance. However, in adopting this discourse, they betray other kinds of knowledge. For example, approximately 70 percent of the individuals I interviewed were aware, at least to some degree, of Mexico's history of African slavery. In anchoring blackness elsewhere, they contradict their own understandings of this history.

Bernardo, the forty-three-year-old psychology professor of African heritage, also reinforced the belief that blacks do not exist in Mexico. However, his stance is even more ironic given his personal experience of exclusion from a Mexican identity based on his phenotype. Bernardo was stopped by immigration officers at the airport in Mexico City. They insisted he produce credentials "proving" he was Mexican. Bernardo blames his "Afro" hairstyle of the time for his mistaken nationality. Despite this experience, Bernardo, along with others, upholds the belief that blackness is foreign to Mexico, even though it contradicts everything he is and knows. Bernardo is of African descent, he is Mexican, he self-identifies as black,[17] he is aware of Mexico's slave history, and he was irritated when Mexican immigration officials questioned his national status. Yet Bernardo informed me that if he sees a person who is "very black," he knows the person is not Mexican and assumes he or she is Cuban, Central American, or from Africa, ironically mirroring the assumptions that immigration officials made about him. Bernardo's perspective underscores the finding that Veracruzanos of all phenotypes participate in maintaining the view that blackness is incompatible with Mexicanness.

State actors, such as police and immigration officials, also reproduce the association between blackness and foreignness, in some cases allowing it to dictate their actions. We already heard what happened to Bernardo at the airport. Another individual of African heritage I spoke with also had his nationality challenged. Upon a return trip from Cuba, despite producing valid documentation of his Mexican nationality, he had trouble getting back into Mexico because immigration officials thought he did not look Mexican. Cruz Carretero (n.d.) encountered similar stories in her research in Mata Clara, Veracruz. She found that some police officers operate under the assumption that "there are no blacks in Mexico" when attempting to identify illegal immigrants. She described a situation involving a group of individuals of African descent from Mata Clara who were incarcerated by Mexico City police and charged with residing illegally in the country. The police justified their actions in the following manner: "We were confused, because there are no blacks in Mexico" (p. 4). Officials from Mata Clara needed to convince the police from Mexico's capital city that there are indeed blacks in their jurisdiction. As the incident concluded, the president of the municipality stated, "When Blacks travel out of town they should carry their I.D." (p. 4). Reports of similar incidents have surfaced recently in the Mexican media.[18]

Cross-national variation in understandings of blackness can also produce confusion and frustration, when, for example, Veracruzanos travel to places such as the United States and are forced to abide by different racial rules. Juan, an eighty-two-year-old retired electric company worker with medium-brown skin, described a past visit to the then Jim Crow segregated U.S. South. On one occasion he went to the movies with a friend, a fellow Mexican who Juan described as having "large lips and curly hair." Juan told me in no uncertain terms that his friend is *not* black. However, a movie theater attendant classified the friend as black and, in the spirit of racial segregation, directed Juan's friend to the back entrance. They argued with the attendant, pulling out their Mexican identification, certain this would prove that Juan's friend could not be black. Their efforts were unsuccessful. Juan, still upset by what had occurred decades earlier, bitterly told me, "In the United States, even if you are not black, but you have curly hair...that is enough." Ultimately, Juan was distressed because local understandings that disassociate Mexicans from blackness were not recognized in the U.S. context.

Harris (1952) describes the black individual in Brazil as an ideal type to which no specific individual corresponds. This resonates with my wild goose chase and moving target metaphors. However, Veracruzanos do have a fixed target of blackness; they map blackness onto specific locations and certain groups of people. As remarks made by Bernardo, Sandra, and the woman at the bingo table exemplify, Veracruzanos anchor blackness primarily in the bodies of Cubans and North Americans.

As mentioned in chapter 2, in Veracruz there is a cognitive overlap between the terms black and Cuban since Cubanness is frequently equated with blackness.[19] Despite their relatively small numbers, Afro-Cubans were highly visible in the urban ballroom settings of Veracruz (and Mexico City) in the 1940s and 1950s[20]—this visibility likely influenced the racialization of Cubans. The conceptual link between blackness and Cubanness provides an important backdrop for contemporary Veracruzanos' popular understandings of blackness. Furthermore, because of their consistent exposure to the United States and U.S. culture, African Americans also serve as a prominent image of blackness in the Veracruz mind.

For Veracruzanos, African Americans and Afro-Cubans represent central symbols of blackness, a standard against which all others are compared. Other Caribbean groups, Central and South Americans, and Africans are also sometimes used as anchors; however, given Veracruz's geographic location and history, of these groups, Cubans and North Americans figure most prominently on Veracruzanos' radar. Illustrating this is Roberto, the medium-brown-skinned college graduate in his twenties: "I believe that there are no blacks here . . . but in the United States, they are really black. They are very black. So, well, if you compare the blacks of the United States to the blacks here, we are less black." You may recall from chapter 2 that Roberto was the darkest individual at his private school. Although not black by typical Veracruz standards, he was labeled black by his classmates according to the discourse of relativity. After making the prior comment, Roberto continued his train of thought, reflecting on why Veracruzanos, including himself, may situationally be labeled black:

I think that here people are called *negro* not because—to give them a name—but I will repeat, people haven't realized that in other places there are really black people, I mean purple. You could say it like that, right? So for me, for example, in school they call me *negro* or whatever, for affection and it does not bother me. . . . But when they see a person who is really really black, they say, "Wow, you are white compared to him." So what we see here are people who are *moreno* who are called *negro*, but they aren't black, they are *moreno*.

For Roberto, relocating blackness is personal. He is more invested than fellow Veracruzanos who escape the *negro* label. His strategy to distance himself and other Veracruzanos from blackness seems convincing and logical. If he can identify someone who is darker and looks blacker than he is, why should he be classified as black? In light of Roberto's remarks, we can better understand why the moving target dynamic exists in Veracruz—labels shift as the terms of comparison change. As I illustrated in chapter 2 when discussing the discourse of relativity, it is the "blackest" person in a given comparison who becomes "it" at that moment or in that context. By expanding the terms of comparison to the global community, Veracruzanos are more readily able to summon a "blacker" individual.

Although Roberto and other brown-skinned Veracruzanos are more personally invested in constructing the terms of comparison in a way that enables them to evade the black label, Veracruzanos who are spared this predicament because of a light skin tone and European features deploy similar discourses. A case in point is Judy, the thirty-five-year-old university professor who described her partner Bernardo as not black and attempted to lighten his race-color classification. When I asked Judy to identify someone she does consider to be black, she referenced residents of the "black neighborhoods" in New Orleans, Louisiana, where she recently traveled. "Those people," she said in dramatic fashion, "when you see them at night, you can only see their eyes shining." That is a black person, she informed me. She then drew a comparison with the governor of Veracruz, Fidel Herrera Beltrán, who is designated by some as black, assuring me that he also is not black to the same degree as the African Americans she saw in New Orleans. By locating Afro-Cubans and African Americans at the black pole of the race-color continuum, Veracruzanos are able to distance themselves from the black category.

The aforementioned dynamics have potential implications for the study of race. Scholars have typically examined racial dynamics within the confines of the local. However, the case of Veracruz illustrates how the concept of the race-color continuum is, in fact, not confined to the Veracruz population. In other words, the race-color continuum is not always limited to the range of phenotypes within the local area; the phenotypes of outside groups are not only fair game but are sometimes even preferred, as in the case of Veracruzanos' constructions of blackness.

Overpowering Local Discourses

The national ideology that attributes a foreign status to blacks is so entrenched that it can overpower local discourses. In recent years, individuals, organizations, and national and local governmental agencies have attempted to promote Veracruz's African root and its relationship to the Caribbean. For example, Mexico's Office of Popular Culture has funded investigations and cultural projects in Veracruz that focus on the "third root" of the population.[21] Also, in 1989, the Port of Veracruz City Museum incorporated an exhibit on slavery. Finally, the late Mexican anthropologist Gonzalo Aguirre Beltrán combined efforts with the Veracruz Cultural Institute, the Veracruz State government, and the National Council for Culture and Art to initiate an annual Afro-Caribbean festival in the Port of Veracruz. The idea for the festival was spawned during a 1989 academic symposium titled "Veracruz is also Caribbean."[22] During the annual festival, participants from the Caribbean, Latin America, and the United States give public music and dance performances. Although the initial festivals were popular and well attended, financial support has waned in recent years. Due to budgetary concerns, there was even a question as to whether the festival would take place in 2005. When the governor of Veracruz was asked about the fate of the 2005 festival, he responded by laying out a series of rhetorical questions: "Does the Afro-Caribbean festival attract visitors?" "Do we identify with one of our own roots which is negritude?" "Will the governor be supporting the festival?" "Of course!"[23]

Although the motivation behind the festival was to awaken a societal affinity between Veracruz, the Caribbean, and the broader African Diaspora, my research suggests that the festival has not achieved these goals. For Veracruzanos, the festival is a symbol of music and dance rather than a connection between Veracruz and blackness. Veracruzanos generally interpret the festival as a display of an outside Caribbean and African culture, disconnected from Veracruz culture and Veracruzanos of African descent. They view the festival as a means to learn about *different* countries, *different* cultures, and the African roots of *other* places. Marisa, the English teacher of African descent, informed me that Afro-Caribbean festivals "show us the Afric—Caribbean culture. How *they* dance, what *they* are like." Arturo, the thirty-five-year-old small business owner who has dark-brown skin and is also of African descent, says he attends the festival to enjoy "the music, the traditional dances of each place, and the way *they* dress." His connection to the festival is no more than that of a detached yet interested spectator.

Why is the festival held in Veracruz? This is the question I posed to Veracruzanos. Gael, a twenty-three-year-old medium-brown-skinned university student of African descent who intermittently identified as black, represents the primary target audience of the festival. Black cultural promoters would undoubtedly view Gael as a potential convert; in sometimes identifying as black, he is already one step closer than the typical Veracruzano to embracing a black consciousness. Despite this, Gael is unsure why the Afro-Caribbean festival is celebrated in Veracruz. He guesses it is because of the Caribbean and the Cuban immigrants that reside in the Port of Veracruz. Unfortunately for its sponsors, the festival clearly does not hold any meaning for Gael regarding his personal identity.

Some locals justified the choice of venue by highlighting Veracruzanos' appreciation for music and dance, positing that they are more lively and festive than other Mexicans. Ironically, in employing this reasoning, Veracruzanos embrace many of the regional stereotypes associated with blackness and Cubanness (e.g., they love celebration, are natural-born dancers, and have an affinity for music). However, in this context, individuals strip these characteristics from their black connotations[24] and reinvent them as simply Veracruz traits. Based on the accounts of Gael and others, it appears as if the state-sponsored messages of "Veracruz is Caribbean" and "Celebrate our black roots" have not successfully penetrated the mind of the general public. Veracruzanos of all ancestries displayed a conceptual disconnect between the festival and the race-color makeup of the Veracruz region.

The ineffectiveness of this particular state-sponsored message cannot be blamed on a lack of publicity or dissemination of information. A likely disappointment to "third-root" promoters, even those who were exposed to the official line about the significance of the festival appeared to dismiss the festival as irrelevant to their own identities and region. This was the case with Vanesa, the thirty-year-old working-class homemaker who has medium-brown skin and is of African descent. When Vanesa was in high school, she took a field trip to the Veracruz Cultural Institute and learned about the Afro-Caribbean festival. However, she confessed, "The truth is, I don't remember, but I think the festival is about the union of races or something like that, right?" For Vanesa, like others, the festival did not translate into new connections with her heritage or her race-color identity.

Two individuals stood out as stark exceptions to the aforementioned pattern of confining the festival's symbolism to foreign "others." Felipe, the eighteen-year-old light-skinned university student who works part-time selling medicinal herbs used for the practice of Santería, an African-based religion, eagerly imparted his knowledge about the region's African heritage: "What I have heard, I have heard in events that the state government has organized, such as the Afro-Caribbean festival. There, they talked to us a lot about the third root in Veracruz. You understand, the blacks. In fact, there are events to remind us that there is also a third root in Veracruz." Felipe explained that he first heard the term "third root" in a radio advertisement encouraging people to attend the Afro-Caribbean festival and identify with Veracruz's African root. Felipe may be more attuned to or interested in the country's African heritage because of his connection to Santería and Santería practitioners.

Rodrigo, the dark-brown skinned fisherman who has a tentative black identity, also deviated from general responses about the festival. He is a regular festival participant and is inspired by the festival's music. He told me, "It connects to something in my blood." For Rodrigo, the festival signifies "a kind of tribute to where the roots of the Afro-Caribbean music were born." Although Rodrigo alludes to the festival's larger significance, later in our conversation, when I asked him why the festival is hosted in Veracruz, he reverted to a more typical response, saying that it is because "Latinos" are fond of music and dance. Apart from statements made by Felipe and Rodrigo, there was minimal to no evidence that the Afro-Caribbean festival, a state-sponsored local endorsement of blackness, has influenced popular understandings of the region's African heritage. This is simply one more testament to the power of national ideology.

Conclusion

Veracruzanos deploy complex strategies to situate blackness in a mestizo nation, often doing so without disturbing the pillar of Mexico's national ideology which holds that Mexico does not have a black population. These strategies play out at different levels. At the individual level, Veracruzanos of African descent downplay their black ancestry and inhibit intergenerational transfer of knowledge regarding African ancestors, thereby allowing this part of family history to slowly erode. These strategies minimize the possibility of current and future conflicts with the national ideology. African-descended Veracruzanos also take an inconsistent and contradictory stance toward their own blackness and avoid asserting a firm and stable black identity. In doing so, they accomplish two things. First, by retaining some connection to blackness, they respect a part of themselves, their histories, and their families. They also maintain a consistency with some local narratives that recognize the region's African root. Second, by constructing a mixed, unstable black identity, they avoid direct conflict with the nonblackness ideological pillar while affirming the *mestizaje* ideology. In collectively adopting these strategies, they manage the delicate balance between their experience as Mexicans of African descent, a national ideology that marginalizes this experience, and local discourse that partially recognizes it. Most importantly, however, their management strategies allow them to protect their national identities; by not presenting themselves as completely black, they can remain part of the Mexican national community.

The identity construction of Veracruzanos of African descent complicates the literature on Latin America, which presents an image of individual denial of black ancestry and the shunning of contemporary blackness.[25] The stories presented in this chapter show that this depiction only captures part of the story. Although they avoid a consistent black identity, blackness does, to some degree, form part of the way Veracruzanos think about their ancestries and identities. As Hoffman (2006) reminds us, individuals of African descent adopt a gamut of strategies ranging from denial, to affirmation, to allusion in an attempt to negotiate the experience of being black in Mexico. The use of multiple strategies and shifting identities results in ambiguity and contradiction, as we saw in the case of Veracruz.

Telles and Paschel (n.d.) propose that Latin American regions identified as black in national narratives are prime sites for the fostering of a strong black identity. Although they found this to be the case for regions portrayed as black in Colombia, Costa Rica, and the Dominican Republic, this is not currently the case for Veracruz, the representative black state of Mexico. Veracruzanos work to undermine the state's association with blackness. They do this regardless of phenotype since all state residents are vulnerable to being linked to blackness through regional association. Therefore, as a regional-level strategy, Veracruzanos of all hues collectively mobilize to combat the image of Veracruz as the "black-influenced state." They transport blackness to other regions of Mexico and locate the source of the dark skin of many Veracruzanos in Mother Nature's solar rays. To further unglue the bond between Veracruz and blackness, Veracruzanos go to great lengths to securely fasten blackness to foreign others, particularly Afro-Cubans and African Americans. They have the weight of the national ideology supporting their efforts to displace blackness and the necessary momentum to override local attempts to bring blackness back home to Veracruz. Despite facing ideological contradictions, everyday challenges, discursive inconsistencies, and seemingly irreconcilable paradoxes, Veracruzanos ultimately design a racial common sense that manages potential affronts to the national ideology of nonblackness in a way that ultimately reproduces it.

The juxtaposition of Veracruzanos' understandings of blackness at the individual, local, and national level reveals how, within a particular context, race can be simultaneously fluid and fixed. This revelation is somewhat at odds with characterizations of race in Latin America that describe race as fluid and absent of discrete categories or hard boundaries.[26] Such depictions of race in Latin America, although valid, are seemingly incomplete. In Veracruz, blackness is both a moving target *and* a stable, fixed category. When the Veracruz or Mexican populations are used to determine the parameters of blackness, blackness is a moving target; it is slippery and fluid. However, when the population pool is expanded to include non-Mexicans, the black target becomes fixed and boundaries harden around the Mexican–foreigner distinction. This finding has important and potentially broad implications for studies of the social construction of race. If we confine our interrogations of race to the local level, we potentially miss an important aspect of race-color dynamics. Acknowledging that global dynamics can affect racialization processes in local racial terrains can lead to new conclusions. Adopting this perspective, Candelario (2007) argues that to understand racial dynamics in the Dominican Republic one needs to understand the system of triangulation between the Dominican Republic, Haiti, and the United States. In the case of Veracruz, triangulation is also evident but involves Mexico, Cuba, and the United States.

I end this chapter by discussing a set of counter-discourses that have recently emerged in Mexico—discourses that challenge the nonblackness pillar of Mexican national ideology. Over the past few decades, there has been a small but notable shift occurring in government discourse regarding blacks in Mexico. First, in the 1980s, the national Office of Popular Culture, headed by Guillermo Bonfil Batalla, developed a program called "Our Third Root," with the goal of recovering African contributions to Mexican multiculturalism and providing a space for the study of blackness in Mexico. Additionally, in 2006, in exchanges between the Mexican government and the committee for the UN International Convention on the Elimination of All Forms of Racial Discrimination (CERD), the Mexican representative noted that "Indigenous people and persons of African descent are socially and economically disadvantaged, and particularly vulnerable to discrimination."[27] In 2007, the CERD committee requested more information from Mexico on its communities of African descent.[28] In response, the Mexican government produced a fairly detailed report which included the following points:

1. There are no official statistics on these communities although the National Council for the Prevention of Discrimination (CONAPRED) is attempting to collect information on groups of African descent in Mexico.

2. CONAPRED funded a study on this population aimed at "identifying living conditions and identity-building processes in communities of African descent in three States—Oaxaca, Guerrero, and Veracruz."

3. The National Institute of Geography and Statistics (INEGI) explored the possibility of including a category of persons of African descent on the 2010 census.[29]

4. In 2003, the Ministry of Education launched the Multicultural Mexico Project "with the aim of raising the profile of the groups of African descent." As part of this initiative, a series of television and radio broadcasts dedicated to showcasing diversity in Mexico included a focus on the "Afromestizo" population.[30]

My findings suggest that these recent initiatives and counter-discourses, aimed at highlighting the role of Mexico's African heritage have thus far had little to no effect on Veracruz racial common sense. Judging by Veracruzanos' interpretations of the Afro-Caribbean festival, breaking down the nonblackness pillar of Mexican national ideology will not be an easy task. In fact, exogenous or top-down attempts to create a sense of blackness in Veracruz could backfire. We have already seen evidence of this. In the case of the Afro-Caribbean festival, the endeavor to promote a connection between Veracruz and the Caribbean produced the opposite effect. It provided fuel for the discourse of the exotic black "other." Instead of identifying with the Caribbean and resuscitating their own "third root," Veracruzanos use the festival's presentation of Afro-Caribbeans to anchor authentic blackness within foreign bodies. By placing Afro-Caribbeans at the black pole of the race-color continuum, Veracruzanos escape the black category and further distance themselves from blackness. Given this particular outcome, it may be wise to rethink the common assumption that urbanization, globalization, and increased exposure to an African diaspora automatically leads to a group-based black consciousness.[31] As we have seen, in the Port of Veracruz, an urban setting with important historical and contemporary connections to the African diaspora, a local black identity remains elusive. In the following chapter we will see how globalization, among other things, affects Veracruzanos' understanding of racism.

7 | Silencing and Explaining Away Racial Discrimination

There is no negation of any racial origin in our country.
> —*Mexican government official, 1994*

Racism is never spoken of, nor is color, nor is race. I believe the Mexican is not racist. He never has been and he never will be.
> —*Alfredo, a Veracruz fisherman who has dark-brown skin*

In our Mexico, there is no racism.
> —*Ana, a Veracruz teacher who has dark-brown skin*

A S ILLUSTRATED IN THE FIRST quotation, national ideology contends that racism does not exist in Mexico. This passage comes from a report submitted by the Mexican government to the UN International Convention against the Elimination of Racial Discrimination (CERD). CERD requires member nations to submit reports identifying forms of racial discrimination in their countries and a plan for combating such discrimination. In 1994 the Mexican government asserted a purported absence of racism in Mexico in its report, revealing the strength and endurance of the nonracism ideology at the close of the twentieth century.

The perspective that Mexico is racism-free does not just live in official discourse. It pervades popular thought. Like Alfredo and Ana (quoted above) many Veracruzanos uphold the national stance of nonracism, despite the many realities which contradict it. They support the state-sponsored "legitimizing myth" (Sidanius and Pratto 1999) of nonracism by espousing a racial common sense that justifies the race-color hierarchy. Although some scholars regard similar legitimizing myths as playing a role in reproducing racism throughout Latin America,[1] others argue that these same myths have the potential to create openings to undermine racism.[2] My findings indicate that Mexico's ideology of nonracism has fortified, not de-stabilized, Mexico's race-color hierarchy. This chapter shows the process through which this ideological fortification occurs at the popular level.

Veracruzanos do not simply profess a belief in nonracism—they actively work to maintain the ideology when faced with realities which threaten it. Two aspects of Veracruzanos' reality—the existence of a race-color hierarchy and contemporary racism—pose a potential challenge to the national ideology. In this chapter I detail the complex process through which Veracruzanos manage these contradictions and the social consequences of their management strategies. I pay particular attention to points of ideological rupture—circumstances or events which contradict the national ideology. When confronted with such ruptures, individuals have several choices: they can frame the situation as a non-contradiction, manage the contradiction in a way that reproduces the ideology, or use the contradiction to challenge the ideology's legitimacy. Overwhelmingly, Veracruzanos, independent of color, adopt the first two strategies, often in tandem. In doing so, they foreclose openings to challenge the national ideology, thus perpetuating the race-color hierarchy. They manage contradictions using a variety of discursive strategies—they silence critical discussions of racism, deploy symbolic boundaries vis-à-vis the United States, and adopt discourses of nonracism—to handle incongruities between the national ideology and social realities. Not only do the findings presented in this chapter speak to the broader theme of the book—the relationship between ideology and common sense—but they also address the topic of racial attitudes.

The Comparative Study of Racial Attitudes

The topic of racial attitudes, including perceptions of racism, has received much less attention in Latin America compared to the United States. In the United States, blacks are more likely than whites to perceive racism in society and attribute racial inequality to racism.[3] Those coming from an "interest-based" perspective on racial attitudes would argue that blacks and whites hold divergent views because of their different locations in the racial hierarchy.[4] As the logic goes, since it is in whites' best interest to maintain the status quo (as the racially-privileged group) they develop and articulate attitudes that seek to support the current hierarchy (e.g., by not focusing on racism). In contrast, since maintenance of the status quo is not in racial minorities' best interest, they create and display attitudes that highlight and challenge racism. This perspective undergirds much of the U.S. literature on color blindness.[5] Colorblind discourse—that which downplays or negates race as an explanation for inequality—has been conceptualized as an ideological tool used by *whites* to defend their interests in perpetuating the current hierarchy.[6] While interest-based theories are oftentimes well-suited for explaining U.S. racial dynamics, we know much less about their effectiveness in non-U.S. contexts and about the underlying mechanisms driving the formation of racial attitudes in Latin America.

Recently, Bailey (2002, 2004, 2009) and Roth (2008) tackled this issue. Bailey assessed the applicability of U.S.-based racial attitude theories to the Brazilian case. He found U.S. theories to be ineffective in Brazil as the majority of Brazilians in his survey perceived racism in society, regardless of race. Consequently, he argued that class and education, not race, are the main predictors of racial attitudes in Brazil. Similar to Bailey, Roth found that Puerto Ricans' and Dominicans' perceptions of color discrimination were unrelated to their color. She, however, identified an alternate predictor of racial attitudes—the degree and strength of individuals' connections to the United States and exposure to U.S. culture; the stronger the connection, the more likely they were to perceive colorism. Both Bailey and Roth have made important contributions to cross-national dialogues on racial attitudes. However, we still know little about how racial attitudes function in other contexts such as Mexico.

In this chapter I show how Veracruzanos reproduce the ideology of nonracism, even when it is not in their best material interest to do so. The finding that Veracruzanos, regardless of color and position in the socioeconomic hierarchy, uphold the status quo, suggests that interest-based theories of racial attitudes have minimal explanatory power in Mexico. Furthermore, based on an examination of Veracruzanos' rare use of counter-discourses that challenge the national ideology, I propose that the strength of individuals' ties to non-Mexican contexts may be an important factor influencing their perceptions of racism, lending support to claims made by Roth. I return to these points after outlining the myriad ways in which Veracruzanos uphold the ideology of nonracism via their racial common sense.

An Open Secret: The Social Silence on Race

> [Racism] is something that all of us Mexicans know. An "open secret" as it is called. Few, however, dare to say it in public or recognize it, for fear of being pegged as anti-patriotic.
>
> —CÉSAR FERNANDO ZAPATA, *a Mexican journalist, 2004*

A conspiracy of silence, or an "open secret" in Zapata's words, is a social phenomenon where "a group of people tacitly agree to publicly ignore something of which they are all personally aware."[7] Silence is an important component of Mexican racial common sense and a crucial mechanism for the reproduction of Mexico's legitimizing myth of nonracism. I was repeatedly told by Veracruzanos that they do not talk about racism with family members or friends, in church, in school settings, or in political discussions. My observations supported these statements; I rarely overheard critical discussions of race in the public or private spheres, a dynamic documented in other Latin American contexts.[8]

In Veracruz, this silence is institutionalized. I witnessed this first hand when Pepe, who has light-brown skin, informed his high-school students about my research and opened the floor for remarks on racism. Sensing a teacher-approved rupture in the social silence on the topic, a few students began to share their experiences with racism in Mexico. However, Pepe quickly intervened, assuring them that he had already explained to me that there is no racism in Mexico. Asserting his authority on the topic, he went on to say that, having lived longer he is able to realize this fact. Pepe then continued, in lecture style, to educate his students: racism does not exist in Mexico but in the United States it is present "one hundred percent." He then re-opened the topic for discussion. The class was silent. It had become clear that the invitation to discuss racism was a mirage, a smoke screen devised to create the appearance of an open conversation. Eventually, a light-skinned student, in a final attempt to treat her teacher's request as authentic, raised her hand. Pepe called on her. She described how a friend of hers with dark-brown skin was not served in a restaurant. "They said he was dirty," she shared. Pepe quickly clarified, "Here in Veracruz?" She nodded. His response was swift: "One case out there." No more comments were made. Like Pepe, many Veracruzanos uphold the national ideology by closing openings to challenge the official view, by comparing Mexico to the United States, and by framing contradictory occurrences as isolated incidents.

Only rarely did I witness individuals break the socially-imposed silence by initiating or participating in critical discussions of racism.

When this occurred, conversations became ripe with tension, discomfort, and insecurity. My conversation with Camila, a sixty-three-year-old working-class homemaker with light skin, provides a case in point. Camila and I were sitting at her kitchen table. Her husband, who has dark-brown skin, was in the next room. Only the outline of a door frame separated us. Up to this point, Camila had responded to each of my questions in a calm, relaxed manner. However, when I introduced the topic of racism, her demeanor instantly changed. Her body tensed and she leaned towards me, in an apparent attempt to decrease the audible range of our conversation. When I asked if she had witnessed any specific instances of racism, she resorted to fervent eye signals and hand motions to convey to me that her husband suffers from discrimination. She refused to verbalize her thoughts beyond a quick whisper of "they look down on him because of his color."

As the next story illustrates, Veracruzanos are not blind to realities of racism. Instead, they work to render these realities invisible when they become exposed; the silencing work that Veracruzanos perform around race is necessary precisely because race is *not* invisible. When Mexico's claim to nonracism is challenged or contradicted, Veracruzanos actively work to re-conceal the issue of racism in society. Carla, the fifty-seven-year-old middle-class homemaker with light skin, did this when her son, who is a few shades darker than she, was subjected to discrimination when applying for a job at a local McDonalds. He was dejected, she recalled. They didn't give him the job. They didn't want him; they were only hiring those who were "very light with blue or green eyes." Carla told me she reacted "as a mom": "I told him to not pay much attention, that maybe it was not the job that he deserved...I calmed him down and invited him out to eat and it passed. And ever since, I haven't liked to bring it up because I feel that he was hurt, right? I continued on as usual and he forgot about it." According to Carla, they have never revisited what happened that day. In a tone of defiance, she explained, "When I saw that they hurt him, I was quiet and never again said anything." In the absence of discussions of racism, Carla's son and others are left to interpret their experiences as isolated, personal matters, and to deal with them in the solitude of silence.

A handful of people defied the norm of silence. Jessica, the twenty-one-year-old university student, is a host on a local TV program. Her light skin, green eyes, long blond hair, and slim figure provide aesthetic appeal. Women like Jessica are staples of Mexican media. I was introduced to Jessica by Judy, her university professor. I had shared with Judy that I was interested in meeting light-skinned Veracruzanos or members of the Veracruz upper class. In response to my request Judy told me she had a couple of "pretty, white, rich girls" in her class. Jessica was one of them. I later realized that Jessica only kept up an appearance of being part of the upper class; she is in a more financially precarious position than most in her social circle. She is only "upper-middle" class, she confessed. Jessica is also more than a pretty face. She is intelligent, articulate, and frank. "Do you really want to know about racism in Mexico?" she asked during one of our conversations. Responding to my nod, she proceeded to tell me. "First things first, people don't talk about it." She explained, "It is like a topic that does not exist, as if it did not exist in this country. But deep down, everyone knows that it exists...you even sound bad talking about it. The people believe that if you talk about it that you are being difficult or too intense..." I clarified, "Color discrimination?" She nodded. "Nobody talks about that topic in Mexico. You sound bad and the people look at you in a bad way. But deep down, the people are thinking it even though they don't express it, right?" Jessica's interpretation of the social taboo on race mirrored my experiences in the field—if someone breaks the silence, they receive criticism, and everyone scrambles to bury the issue.

I witnessed the social hazing that follows such violations during a focus group discussion with six women. They all knew each other well, being connected by blood, marriage, or living arrangements. I had invited them over to watch *Angelitos Negros,* the 1948 classic that engages the topic of racism in Mexico. After the film ended, the group started chatting about the movie. The tone of the conversation was agreeable, even lively at times. At one point Bella, the forty-eight-year-old light-skinned high school teacher, decisively announced that racism does not exist in Mexico. This was of no surprise since the conversation had already drifted toward that con-clusion. Other participants nodded and vocalized sounds of support. But then, Rosalía, Bella's eighteen-year-old light-skinned niece spoke up: "No. There is racism. There is. But nobody is going to say it. A person is never going to say it. Never. But there is." A hush fell over the room. Rosalía and Bella locked gazes. The other women, anticipating a battle, withdrew, positioning themselves as spectators. Bella began, "Look—," but Rosalía cut her off: "There is. There is." Being challenged and then cut off was too much for Bella. Within her family, among her friends, and at work, Bella is well respected. Despite her small physical presence, she is frequently in a position of authority. She paused, composing herself, and then responded: "Look. What I *will* talk about is weight. You can be *moreno* or white but if you are overweight you can't get a job." Bella's strategy was effective. Rosalía, who is overweight and often dieting, broke eye contact and began to pick at the food on her plate, disengaging from the conversation. The silence had been restored and the national ideology maintained. Veracruzanos rarely disrupt the silence on race, with one major exception—in the context of humor.

Humor is ubiquitous in Veracruz and frequently incorporates jokes about race and color. Humor represents "a discursive space within which it becomes possible to speak about matters that are otherwise naturalized, unquestioned, or silenced."[9] Not only is the silence on race broken in humorous contexts but individuals are frequently pressured to "go along" with racial jokes since challenging humor is viewed as a breech in etiquette. I encountered this dynamic one day when I arrived at Pepe's home and asked if I could speak with his handyman, Marco. Signaling to the roof where Marco (who has dark-brown skin) was laboring, Pepe loudly exclaimed: "This guy is Memín Pinguín's uncle!,"[10] and laughed. A look of discomfort flashed across Marco's face. Marco descended the ladder. By the time he reached the bottom, he had regained his composure. Smiling, he said: "Yes, if you take a picture of me, I look like Memín." Marco is expected to "go along" with the joke not only because of social norms but also because of his position of subservience relative to Pepe.

In my observations I stumbled upon endless examples of racial humor. "They are only jokes," I was constantly told. "Don't take them seriously." "They are made in good fun." The bottom line: race humor, regardless of content, is not considered racism, a perception which also exists in other parts of Latin America.[11] Esteban, the twenty-nine-year-old light-skinned computer technician, asserted the putative harmlessness of race jokes. He has a friend who is "very dark" but Esteban told me that neither he, nor his other friends, are critical of his color. "We only call him *negrito* and make jokes like 'Hey, *negrito*, bring me whatever…I am going to put a little bone on your head like an African and you can dance.'" Esteban assured me that they never make comments to offend their friend; they only do it for fun.

Brown-skinned Veracruzanos are the most common recipients of race humor—a humor that is typically laced with derogatory sentiment. Nevertheless, brown-skinned Veracruzanos also frame race jokes as harmless. For example, Franco, the sixty-four-year-old fisherman with dark-brown skin, nonchalantly told me that whites will occasionally shout "filthy *negro*" at him, but "just as a joke." Even Bernardo, the forty-three-year-old dark-brown-skinned psychologist who demonstrated a strong pride in his blackness, adopted the "they are only kidding" frame. He shared that, in his classroom, when a black student enters, the jokes begin.[12] They call the student "Memín" or "use a phrase that has an association with being black." "The Veracruzano is very creative," he chuckled. Bernardo reassured me that the students are not "cruel" and do not hit black students or key their cars or anything like that. Sometimes the black students get upset by the jokes, he explained, but only if they come to class in a bad mood. I clarified: "When you say a black student, are you referring to someone like yourself or darker?" "Like myself," Bernardo replied. Bernardo's narrative illustrates the expansiveness of the boundary of "acceptable" joking; even in his presence and in a private educational setting, racial jokes are treated as unproblematic.

In my year in the field, I was unsuccessful in locating a case of race humor that was unequivocally deemed to be unacceptable by Veracruzanos. Alicia, a 25 twenty-five-year-old navy employee with dark-brown skin, even classified violent acts as harmless. She made this clear while relaying an incident she had witnessed. Alicia told me that a while back a "very dark" man was in the street and some people started throwing tomatoes at him. She heard them yell *negro* and slave and things like that. She shrugged it off concluding, "I took it as a joke... Here the people are really intense with their games." Alicia framed the incident as a joke—maybe a joke that had gone too far—but a joke nonetheless. Veracruzanos' energies to restore the invisibility of critical discussions of racism are not wasted on race humor. Since Veracruzanos strip race humor of any conceptual association with racism, they do not view this humor as something that needs to be managed, nor a form of discourse that needs to be silenced. Other forms of race talk and race-related incidents are potentially more threatening and when they cannot be silenced, need to be managed in other ways. In the next section I discuss how Veracruzanos use symbolic boundaries to deflect attention away from Mexican racism.

Symbolic Boundaries: The United States as the Racist "Other"

As outlined in chapter 1, post-revolutionary elites deployed symbolic boundaries in relation to the United States—an external "other"—to foster nationalist sentiment.[13] Due to the historically-contentious nature of U.S.-Mexico relations, the United States provided an easy target against which all Mexicans could assert their difference. Furthermore, defining the United States as the epitome of racism was not difficult in light of U.S. racial segregation of the time. In contemporary times, both elite and non-elite Mexicans continue to deploy symbolic boundaries between Mexico and the United States to shield Mexico from charges of racism.[14]

The Memín Pinguín Controversy

The dialogue surrounding the Memín Pinguín controversy, which I introduced in chapter 1, is a rich example of how Mexicans, both elite and non-elite, deploy symbolic boundaries vis-à-vis the United States to deflect charges of racism away from Mexico. Recall that in 2005, U.S. leaders criticized the Mexican government for its decision to issue a commemorative stamp featuring the comic book character Memín Pinguín. Whereas many in the United States view Memín, a pickaninny-type figure, as racist, Mexicans by and large do not. In Mexico, stereotypical characterizations of blacks (as well as indians) are widespread. In Veracruz, during the 2005 annual Carnival celebration, I watched as a man in black face walked in the procession, hunched over in a subservient bow. He was sporting a jacket with the image of a large watermelon and the word "Negrito" written on his back (see Figure 7.1).

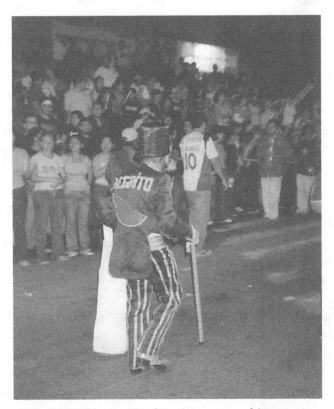

FIGURE 7.1 An individual wearing blackface who was part of the 2005 Carnival procession in Veracruz, Mexico.

In the Veracruz central market, a business advertisement reads "*Negro*, The King of Cheese" and is accompanied by an image resembling a monkey. Veracruzanos do not interpret these kinds of visual representations of blacks (or similar stereotypic depictions of indians) as racist. Therefore, they were both insulted and dismayed that "Americans" were accusing Mexicans of racism during the Memín controversy.

Amid confusion and indignation, Mexicans perceived criticism of Memín as a direct attack on Mexico's stance as a nonracist nation. In reaction, they quickly mobilized to prevent their country's image from being tarnished. Government officials, intellectuals, and the populace collectively defended Memín. The Mexican public was particularly invested in countering the charges of racism as Mexicans are avid consumers of the Memín comics. Headlines such as "There is nothing racist about Memín Pinguín!"[15] were plastered across the front pages of local and national newspapers. The fervor over the Memín scandal demonstrates how U.S. accusations of racism in Mexico struck a moral cord. Mexico is supposed to be a country free of racism, *unlike* the United States.

In response to the assault on Mexico's image of nonracism, Mexicans built a defense by erecting a symbolic boundary between Mexico and the United States. Then, they attacked the credibility of the source. They shifted the spotlight away from Mexico's alleged racism, onto U.S. racism in an attempt to discredit "American" legitimacy to weigh-in on such issues. Van Dijk (1992) describes this process as "reversal"—accusations of racism are reflected back to the accuser. The following text, illustrating this strategy, appeared in a Veracruz newspaper's editorial column during the controversy:

> It is the American Union, not Mexico that is the country that has a history of slavery and institutionalized discrimination against blacks. It is the Americans that have tried to hide their past, of which oftentimes flourishes in the present. But they will not achieve this by questioning the words and icons of popular culture.[16]

The author suspects the United States is trying to deflect attention from its own racist past by criticizing Mexico and its popular cultural icons.

Countering U.S. criticism from another angle, Mexicans proclaimed that the Memín comic, far from symbolizing racism, actually fosters anti-racist sentiment. In claiming that Memín is anti-racist, Mexicans not only restore, but further entrench, their position that Mexico is morally superior to the United States on the issue of race. Major Mexican figures rallied to support the cause. Elena Poniatowska, an acclaimed writer, applauded Memín for awakening "enormous sympathy" among Mexicans, touting him as an emblem of Mexico's "affectionate" treatment of blacks.[17] Cartoonist Ramón Valdiosera Berman, originator of the idea of the Memín stamp, explained that Memín was chosen "to show the United States and the world that in Mexico we like blacks."[18] Thus, an agenda behind the Memín selection for the stamp series was to promote Mexico as a nation free of racism.

Mexico's anti-racist identity and image of racial superiority vis-à-vis the United States was even used to contextualize the creation of the Memín comic in the 1940s. The author of a newspaper editorial resurrects this historical vision:

> The reason for creating the character was always to alert Mexicans against the evils of racism and discrimination. At one time in the southern United States blacks were prohibited access to bathrooms or public schools for whites, and at which time, when using public transport, they were made to sit in the back. Memín Pinguín, the only black character of Mexican short stories, offered lessons of racial tolerance to Mexican children.[19]

This framing was recently refreshed on the back cover of the fiftieth anniversary edition of the comic, which proclaims: "Memín Pinguín is the purest representative of a society without class, without race."

Outside of the Memín controversy, Mexican officials frequently rely on the U.S.-Mexico distinction to frame discussions of racism. For example, in the aforementioned CERD reports, not only did Mexican officials assert a lack of racism in the country, they took it upon themselves to identify issues of racism in the United States, dedicating a large section of the report to Mexicans abroad, "who face growing racism."[20] The use of symbolic boundaries extends far beyond the realm of government officials and the media—it is embedded in popular common sense.

Popular Boundary-making

Veracruzanos frequently use symbolic boundaries vis-à-vis the United States to prevent or manage contradictions that arise between their lived experiences and the national ideology. We saw how this worked in Pepe's classroom—he diverted attention away from discussion of racism in Mexico by positioning the United States as the archetype of racism. With the United States as their conceptual starting point, Veracruzanos, like other Latin Americans,[21] define racism based on the U.S. system, typically referencing Jim Crow era or other overt forms of racism. Mexicans do not generally recognize the societal changes that occurred in the United States after the Civil Rights Movement.[22] Consequently, Veracruzanos define racism as race-based segregation or blatant acts of violence, a definition that excludes experiences with nonviolent, subtle, or covert acts of discrimination. For example, Rodrigo, the thirty-seven-year-old fisherman with dark-brown skin, assured me that racism does not exist in Mexico, declaring: "Racism exists in the United States…It is where they kill Mexicans, they kill the blacks, and there continues to be groups of racists who are dedicated to killing people with dark skin." By importing a definition of racism from another country and era and superimposing it on contemporary Mexico, Veracruzanos are able to frame many forms of discrimination that they witness or experience as nonracist.

Alberto, the forty-year-old teacher with light-brown skin, also introduced the U.S. comparison to draw attention away from the examples of racism in Mexico that had surfaced across our numerous discussions. When I first met Alberto, the topic of racism came up within the first few minutes of conversation. Ana, Alberto's co-worker, introduced us, telling Alberto about my study. "There is no discrimination here," she pronounced after concluding her description of my research. She then turned to Alberto: "Right?" Alberto paused, and then gave a curt nod. I made a mental note of his less-than-enthusiastic agreement.

Alberto and I stayed in touch. We crossed paths at other informal gatherings, I observed his classes, and he was a visitor in my home. On numerous occasions Alberto spoke of the discrimination that the indigenous face in his native Oaxaca. However, he didn't discuss racism directly until we were, once again, at Ana's house. Ana's husband and Alberto were discussing a state-sponsored industrial corridor project. Alberto criticized the government for taking land from the indigenous without making good on its promise to pay them. Alberto's tone was engulfed with a rarely seen anger. Ana made a noise of both surprise and disagreement, reiterating her previous statement that there is no racism in Mexico. Again, she looked to Alberto for confirmation. He verbalized a "no," but his voice waivered. These were the only times I had heard Alberto directly respond to the question of racism in Mexico—until our interview. Based on our prior interactions, I anticipated that Alberto might be critical of the official line of nonracism.

During the interview, Alberto provided example after example of instances of racial discrimination. He reiterated his views about the government's exploitation of the indigenous but also faulted others. Alberto hears "regular people" making fun of indians, and reminded me of the student in his class who negates her African heritage. Whites are in the "privileged positions," he told me. Following them are "mestizos, mulattoes, and finally, the indians." "Is there color discrimination in Mexico?" I inquired. Alberto's critical assault and confidence faltered somewhat, as he responded: "Well, look. It is like it is not seen...it is not in the spotlight. It is not seen at the simple glance, but I think that yes, it exists." I asked him to elaborate. "People are treated poorly. Like the indians." Alberto also spoke of discrimination against people with brown skin who are not indigenous. He shared comments he had heard, describing how his mother instilled in his sister the message that she is to marry a white man. He also mentioned his white, blue-eyed neighbor who refuses to "mix" with classmates who have brown skin and who told him she would never marry an indigenous person.

With his barrage of examples regarding discrimination, Alberto appeared to be building a case for the existence of racism in the country. But this was not his agenda. He offered these examples only in response to my questions on the topic. When I asked Alberto very directly about racism in Mexico, he appeared to realize the potential depth of his contradictions if he were to negate its existence. As a preemptive management strategy, he quickly conjured up the case of the United States to shield Mexico. His first response was to tell me that, in the United States they don't accept Mexicans and that they even kill them. After Alberto had finished, I attempted to shift the conversation back to the Mexican side of the symbolic boundary he had just erected. The following exchange ensued:

CS: Do you believe that racism exists here?

ALBERTO: No.

CS: And the cases that you told me about where people were discriminated against based on their race, do you feel that is racism?

ALBERTO: Yes but—yes but no. How can I say it?...It is not seen in a scandalous form.

CS: Scandalous like...?

ALBERTO: Like the example I just told you about in the United States. That I am going to kill these people because they are not...

CS: And the example of a person that you knew who said she didn't want to marry an indigenous person?

ALBERTO: Oh, well that yes. But they are isolated cases. They are not common cases.

Here, Alberto deployed symbolic boundaries vis-à-vis the United States to reconcile his experience with racism and the national ideology. By anchoring his definition of racism in extreme examples from the United States, he was able to disqualify the instances of discrimination he had witnessed as representing racism. Additionally, he minimized the examples he provided by isolating them, a pattern I cover later in the chapter. Alberto illustrates how Veracruzanos continually create, maintain and re-construct the symbolic boundary between Mexico and the United States in a way that helps them prevent, avoid, and manage contradictions that arise between their lived experiences and Mexico's national ideology of nonracism.[23]

The restrictive definitions of racism used by Alberto and many other Veracruzanos have important institutional and legal consequences. For example, the Mexican government recently established The National Council for the Prevention of Discrimination which is tasked with investigating discrimination complaints. Out of 3,537 complaints of discrimination made between 2004 and 2010, only six were based on alleged *racial* discrimination.[24] Knowing how Veracruzanos define racism helps us to understand why institutions such as this may only be somewhat effective in combating racism.

Explaining Away the Race-Color Hierarchy with Nonracism Frames

As mentioned previously, Veracruz is stratified by race and color. In addition, many people experience or witness racial discrimination in their daily lives. Veracruzanos deal with the dilemmas that these realities pose to the national ideology by deploying nonracism frames—discourses which downplay or negate race or color as an explanation for inequality and discrimination. These discursive frames are similar to "colorblind" frames used by U.S. whites.[25] However, in Veracruz individuals of all colors adopt these frames, a finding I discuss in the chapter's conclusion.

On the topic of the race-color hierarchy, the vast majority of individuals I spoke with agreed that Veracruz is organized by race and color, although only after reflection. Tellingly, most informed me they had never thought about this before. They simply had not noticed it. Although the existence of this social arrangement was generally not a point of contention, the *cause* of the hierarchy was. If the cause is racism, the national ideology crumbles. To avoid this, Veracruzanos make sense of the race-color hierarchy in a way that does not implicate racism. They do so by adopting discourses which dismiss the importance of the race-color hierarchy or explain its existence through the use of nonracial discursive frames involving the themes of inheritance, culture, and beauty.

Veracruzanos' first line of defense is to dismiss the race-color hierarchy with a tone of complacency, framing it as unworthy of attention. This societal complacency was also documented in Twine's (1998) study of Afro-Brazilians and can be understood in the context of Bourdieu's (1977) theorization of *doxa*. He writes, "The instruments of knowledge of the social world are in this case (objectively) political instruments which contribute to the reproduction of the social world, seen as self-evident and undisputed..." (p. 164). The Mexican government's historical and contemporary refusal to recognize racial inequality has facilitated the undisputed nature of the race-color hierarchy. Unlike the United States, where social movements have created counter-ideologies around race, in Mexico, counter-discourses have been absent or ineffective in dismantling the national ideology.[26] Therefore, the hierarchy remains largely unquestioned.

Veracruzanos exercise the dismissal frame as a preemptive strategy; if they are complacent towards and accept the race-color hierarchy as part of their reality, or if they frame the hierarchy as unworthy of attention, they erase the motivation for identifying any potential mechanisms (such as racism) involved in the creation and perpetuation of the hierarchy, thereby avoiding an ideological dilemma. However, as with racial discrimination, individuals are not blind to the race-color hierarchy. They recognize it but work to ignore it or frame its existence as unremarkable. When the hierarchy becomes visible, they make active attempts to restore its status as an undisputed aspect of reality. Moreover, when attention is drawn to the race-color hierarchy, individuals explicitly refrain from addressing its *meaning*. Alfredo, the fifty-six-year-old fisherman with dark-brown skin, supplied a typical response:

ALFREDO: Generally I have observed that they [whites] have the best positions. I have noticed that it is easier for them to get a job than for the *moreno* or black person...

CS: And why do you think that is?

ALFREDO: About that, I ignore it, I ignore it... Because mainly... when they hire someone in the media they want them to have "presentation." This is the advantage of color... to be white...

CS: That is what they want?

ALFREDO: Yes, they tell you clearly in the jobs.

cs: Why?

ALFREDO: Who knows? I also ignore that. Who knows? [laughs]. That, I ignore…That is life and you have to get used to it.

Alfredo is clearly aware that Veracruz is organized around race and color. However, he chooses to accept this reality as "the way things are." Similarly, Josue, a forty-nine-year-old fisherman with medium-brown skin told me, "it is a normal thing" that whites are overrepresented in the media. For Veracruzanos, the race-color hierarchy is unworthy of question, attention, or even comment.

However, Veracruzanos did speak about the race-color hierarchy when I asked them about it directly. In this context, they frequently identified non-racial factors, such as inheritance of money or wealth, to explain its existence. Whites are on top, they argued, because Spanish immigrants brought money and resources with them, capital they subsequently passed on to their children. Bernardo, the psychology professor with dark-brown skin acknowledged that all of his students "with money" are light-skinned. I asked him why this is. He replied:

…The majority of the people who have big businesses are foreigners. The majority are Spaniards. So it isn't a secret to anyone that the Spaniards are from the white race, right? So when they come here, they know how to integrate themselves and how to help each other and that is how they form businesses and they also form families between them.

As Bernardo sees it, Spaniards offer more than just capital and resources—they also have strong social networks and reproduce their wealth by marrying within their community. The implication of this discourse is that whites are positioned at the top ranks of society because of their disproportionate access to resources derived from wealthy immigrants, and that these resources can then be passed down to later generations within the community.

Veracruzanos also deploy cultural explanations,[27] revealing a deeper set of meanings associated with white success which include ideas of white cultural superiority. Omar, the forty-four-year-old journalist with medium-brown skin, provides an example. According to Omar, whites have "heads for business," an "enterprising culture," a "strong work ethic," and are "mentally organized." Operating with a similar perspective (while directly contradicting the inheritance discourse), Gloria, the forty-eight-year-old middle-class homemaker with light-brown skin, relayed a "rags to riches" story: "The child that comes from a father in Spain comes from a different culture. That child feels above the indian and the black. So that child, even though the family is in ruins, will come out of the ruins and will return to occupy his place in the society that he claims in his own right." According to Gloria, it is not because of material resources, but an attitude of racial superiority that explains why whites, against all odds, will assume their natural, dominant place in the world.

Veracruzanos not only use cultural frames to explain success, but also to contextualize failure. They frequently fault indians' and blacks' attitudes, behaviors, and belief systems for their inability to climb the socioeconomic ladder. They describe indians as lazy, unwilling to work, and having an affinity for begging and procreation, while they characterize blacks as untrustworthy, unintelligent, and addicted to vice. However, Veracruzanos apply cultural explanations to the indigenous population with caution, at least initially. The indigenous represent an integral part of Mexico's foundational myth; indians and their culture have been placed on a symbolic pedestal and glorified for their role in Mexico's past. This national narrative commands a certain degree of respect from Mexicans, even if it is contradicted by the contemporary stigmatization of and discriminatory practices toward the indigenous population. Further complicating indigenous-related discourse is Mexico's history of indigenous social movements. The 1994 Zapatista uprising, in particular, gained international attention and forced the plight of indigenous Mexicans upon the national (and global) consciousness. Out of this, a sympathetic and politically correct discourse arose to explain the low status of the indigenous. This discourse sometimes surfaced in my initial conversations with Veracruzanos. However, after more extensive discussion, the political correctness peeled away, revealing deeply-entrenched ideas about indigenous cultural inferiority.

This transformation occurred when I asked Gabriel, a thirty-five-year-old medium-brown-skinned beer distribution center employee, about the low socioeconomic standing of the indigenous in Mexico. He first fingered a lack of educational opportunities, effectively reproducing the politically correct line. But later in our discussion, he gave another explanation: "Many indians are accustomed to asking for money. I mean, they go to the street to ask for money, help from the people…Yes, all of the indians ask for money," he told me. When I asked his opinion of this, he said, "It is not okay. The truth is they should work…People offer to have them sweep patios and do dishes, but they are already accustomed to not working." Unlike his initial response about "blocked opportunities," Gabriel delivered this secondary explanation more easily and with conviction. Like others, Gabriel was more elaborate, passionate, and convincing when forwarding cultural explanations compared to his seemingly regurgitated and emotionally stale, politically correct response. Like Gabriel, many others conveyed to me, through a host of signals, that the indigenous themselves are the source of the problem.

Roberto, the twenty-three-year-old college graduate with medium-brown skin, gave a quick nod to the politically correct response, but made little additional effort to disguise his view that the problem is indigenous culture:

> A lot of it has to do with the government, but a lot of it has to do with the indians themselves as well. Many years ago I had the opportunity to work with some people, to take them food and clothes and to chat about family planning and well, we gave them condoms, to the men, but well no...I said it was the same ignorance that does not permit them to think correctly, that they should use condoms to not impregnate the women, right? If you notice, when you go out, how many indigenous women...have four or five kids and one is tied to their backs? I mean, it is not that society makes them less...

The frustration in Roberto's voice was not aimed at the Mexican government, but at the indigenous themselves. Roberto views outside assistance as useless until indians realize the error of their ways. It is not difficult to see how these cultural explanations help shield the nonracism ideology.

The cultural perspective is even more powerful when the politically-correct gloss is removed. Bypassing the discourse of political correctness, Gael, the twenty-three-year-old university student with dark-brown skin, shared his views on why the indigenous lack higher education: "The indigenous are very stubborn and they don't like to abandon their customs or their languages or anything...They prefer to keep having many, many children instead of having two and sending them to school." Gael echoes the collective sentiment that it is not the government, nor society, nor racism, but the indians themselves who are responsible for their failings. Despite Mexico's promotion of its indigenous heritage, indigenous culture is still seen as incompatible with success. However, individuals do not reserve cultural explanations for indians alone. José, the sixty-three-year-old taco vender with dark-brown skin, told me that blacks are at the bottom rungs of society because they have not taken advantage of opportunities afforded to them. He elaborated: "If we have one hundred pesos we run to a bar or go buy drugs. We don't know how to take advantage of our money." Interestingly, José implicates himself, a dark-skinned individual with African-origin features, in this narrative.

A final nonracism frame that Veracruzanos lean on to explain the race-color hierarchy is that of beauty. They argue that it is necessary in spheres such as the media, to present a "beautiful" product. This discourse is racialized because, as discussed in chapter 2, Veracruzanos perceive light skin and European features as beautiful, while they view brown skin and indigenous or African features as less desirable. Whites are more successful in particular venues because whites are more attractive, they argue. With elegant simplicity, Omar, the journalist with medium-brown skin, illustrates this perspective. He told me that whites are overrepresented in the media because "they are the beautiful ones, right?" The viability of this discourse as a nonracism frame rests on Veracruzanos' belief that the pervasive beautification of whiteness is absent of racist underpinnings. Veracruzanos treat white beauty as a fact, not a perception.

Cristina, the twenty-year-old law student whose dyed blond hair and pale skin stand out even among her private university classmates, is known for being both fashionable and confident. Although I met Cristina on her campus, I had seen her in other venues. On one late-night occasion, I saw her lingering outside the entrance to a well-known night club. Clubbing is one of her favorite pastimes. Appearances are everything in the Veracruz discotheque world, especially when trying to get into a club. Potential clubbers crowd around those who man the entrance, waiting to be chosen. As everyone is well aware, the first to be offered admittance are the white and the wealthy; it is their faces that club owners want representing their establishments. Cristina is one of the coveted faces and she knows it. The evening I saw her, I could sense her confidence. She understands the power of being white, of being beautiful. On a different occasion Cristina explained to me how the discotheque system works: "The darkest, even those with money," she clarified, "are not allowed to enter." "They see a white person and always say 'come on in.'" These are the rules and Cristina knows she is sure to win every time. Cristina explained that power and politics are guided by "what is seen." For example, in advertising, "they prefer to have a pretty face... It is easier to look at a picture of a person with a pretty smile or a white person... instead of a *morena* with a wide nose." According to Cristina, this is why whites are on top of the social hierarchy.

The media is one of the most blatant sites of race-color inequality in Mexico. When turning on the television or flipping through a magazine, one is bombarded by white faces. Like Cristina, Bernardo, the dark-brown-skinned professor, justified the prevalence of these images, explaining: "What sells is the beautiful, the agreeable, the chic." Bernardo, like others, adopts a market ideology to contextualize the societal preference for whiteness. Under this perspective, race-color imbalances in media representations are not about racism, but about capitalism. As a high school economics teacher, Pepe, who has light-brown skin, views himself as a market expert. He explained that the market is the reason whites play central roles on television:

> It is part of the same programming, to take care of the aesthetics. It should be the most attractive product that they are promoting. In the case of soap operas, it has a lot to do with beauty and if they put a person of color on the show, well, normally he or she is not very beautiful or attractive, right? The physical characteristics of the people of color are always more coarse, more rough, more hard…In the case of a soap opera, it requires having an actor that is good-looking, right?

But image does not matter only for the media, Pepe reminded me. It matters for the job market as well:

> I have seen businesses like Liverpool [a department store]. The manager is a man who is very presentable. Physically he is thin, he is white, well-groomed…I am in agreement with them because, for an important business here in Veracruz, there should be a person who has a good image…Imagine arriving at a store and saying "Listen, can I speak to the manager because I have a question…" But I want to see a manager who has a good image, right? I mean thin like that, and what if it turns out to be a manager who is *moreno* and fat?

Pepe tailored the beauty frame to justify occupational inequality. The consolidation of the accounts of Cristina, Bernardo, and Pepe presents contrasting imagery: a brown-skinned, wide-nosed, coarse-featured, fat individual, compared to a white, chic, well-groomed, pretty-faced thin person. Whiteness and brownness are bundled together with positive and negative characteristics respectively, making the election of the white-chic-well-groomed-thin package appear reasonable and logical, not racist. Veracruzanos strip the beautification of whiteness of racist connotations, allowing for a nonconflicting coexistence between the race-color hierarchy and the national ideology.

Moving beyond abstract notions of "whiteness sells," Judy, the thirty-five-year-old light-skinned university professor, exposes the process through which a white face becomes an institution's poster child. In our conversation, Judy asked me if I had noticed that all the advertisements for her private university use pictures of white students with blond hair and blue or green eyes. I nodded. Well, she knows why:

> They go to the classrooms and they select them. The other day I was giving a class and a girl arrived...she told me, "Listen, can you loan me some students because we are going to take pictures?" "Sure, go ahead, who do you want?" She signaled exactly, to all of the whites...the girls. And for the boys, I think she did not like the ones that I had in the classroom (they are not so white) because I told her, "There are only these" and she asked me, "Only those? There is no one else?" I asked her, "Well, you want a student, right? Well, they are all students." Ahhhh, but she only wanted *white* students.

Judy's critical tone differentiated her from the vast majority of Veracruzanos who failed to question or critique such practices.

Explaining Away Racial Discrimination with Nonracism Frames

Veracruzanos are not only saddled with the responsibility of reconciling the existence of a race-color hierarchy with the national ideology but, in a much more personal way, they need to manage experiences with what *they* understand to be "racism" or "color discrimination,"[28] experiences that contradict the nonracism ideology. Individuals manage these contradictions by deploying minimization and racial projection discourses. Minimizing, or downplaying the significance of racist incidents, is an effective strategy for de-centering the importance of, and directing attention away from, inconvenient experiences and observations. Veracruzanos liberally administer minimization discourses, which are both malleable and accessible, to remedy problems of ideological contradiction. They minimize incidents of racism by relying on the power of comparison—they juxtapose such discrimination with a time (temporal minimization) or place (spatial minimization) when racism was putatively worse, a strategy also used by Brazilians.[29] Minimization discourses accomplish the double duty of leaving the national ideology intact without completely dismissing or negating lived experiences.

Martín, the sixty-year-old navy captain with dark-brown skin, used both temporal and spatial frames to minimize racism. According to Martín, he has been the target of racism, although he did not care to share the particulars of these incidents. However, when I asked him point blank about whether or not he believes racism exists in Mexico, he answered: "Right now I feel like it has been disappearing, right? It has been disappearing and now there is almost none. It is almost never seen, at least around here." Martín simultaneously places racism on a temporal trajectory towards extinction and displaces it to another region. In doing so he neither charges Mexico with, nor absolves it completely, from racism. He avoids taking a decisive stance that would contradict the national ideology, yet he injects enough ambiguity into his response to avoid negating his own experiences with racism. Minimization discourses effectively "smooth over" contradictions, robbing them of their power to challenge the dominant belief system.

Veracruzanos also isolate instances of racism, thus controlling for potential collateral symbolic damage. The underlying logic of this minimization strategy is simple: the existence of one racist individual or isolated incidents of racism does not justify a verdict of racism in Mexico. Jennifer, the forty-two-year-old working-class homemaker with light-brown skin, embraces this logic. In our conversation, she talked about a highly-educated indigenous acquaintance of hers who was unable to get a job because of racism. But later she assured me that there is no racism in Mexico. I gently requested that she reconcile these two statements. "Oh well, that yes... There are only a few people who discriminate today," she surmised, shrugging off any sense of contradiction.

My experience with Vanesa, the thirty-year-old working-class homemaker with medium-brown skin, was similar. She was adamant that, in Veracruz, whites are preferred in hiring situations. Later in our conversation, however, she told me: "There is no racism in Mexico." Unlike Jennifer, Vanesa did not wait for me to point out her contradictions. One step ahead, she clarified: "It is only... What percent would I say? Thirty. It is not a lot." In Vanesa's mind, racism on the part of thirty percent of the population does not necessitate an endorsement of the idea that there is racism in Mexico. In a final example, Carlos, the fifty-four-year-old high school teacher with dark-brown skin, shared personal experiences with racism, but later told me that racism does not exist in Mexico. As if mentally assessing the holes in his argument he waivered, softening his position: "I feel that it could be that there is racism, but in such a minimal percent that it isn't even worth considering that it exists." Carlos weakened his position only to the degree necessary to accommodate his experiences, while leaving his statement firm enough to support the national stance. When Veracruzanos minimize their experiences with racism, deflating their importance and rendering them so insignificant as to nullify their existence, they effectively reproduce the national ideology.

As another strategy, Veracruzanos project racism onto symbolically marginal sub-groups of the Mexican population; most frequently, they assign guilt to members of the upper class, whites, and foreigners. This particular frame accounts for racism in society yet absolves the Mexican nation of racism by proclaiming that working- to middle-class brown-skinned mestizos, (i.e., "typical" Mexicans) do not participate in racism. As the logic goes, if "ordinary" Mexicans do not participate in racism, the national ideology is safe. An example of the projection frame can be seen in a survey response from a sixteen-year-old female high school student, regarding a question about whether color discrimination exists in Mexico. She wrote: "People who think they are rich believe they are perfect because they are white. They don't accept people with dark skin." Responding to the same question, a seventeen-year-old student wrote: "Yes, this exists in the white people."

Alfredo, the fisherman with dark-brown skin, deployed the projection strategy at a deeper level. During our interview at the docks, Alfredo frequently paused, looking toward the sea, as he contemplated my questions. Immediately in front of us, but in the distance, was the outline of the local yacht club. However, Alfredo wasn't looking in that direction until we began discussing the club's members. "Those people," the ones who go to the yacht club, the "white and the wealthy," "they are racist," Alberto told me as he scowled in the club's direction. He knows. He has to deal with them each year during the prestigious Veracruz fishing tournaments. During these tournaments yacht owners hire local fishermen to increase their chances in the competition. This is one context where social and spatial barriers break down, where the white and wealthy interact with the brown-skinned and the poor of Veracruz. They may physically work together, but it is no better than a slave-master relationship in Alfredo's eyes. He detests the servile role he is expected to play while on the boat— serving drinks, lighting cigarettes, and cleaning up. He believes he disgusts the yacht owners by his very presence; they humiliate him and treat him "like a slave." Although Alfredo interprets this treatment as racist, when I asked him about racism in Mexico he described it as "sporadic," attributing racism to upper-class whites. In projecting racism onto wealthy whites, he plays on a preexisting script which relegates upper-class whites to the symbolic fringes of the Mexican nation.

In another case, Ana, the forty-four-year-old teacher and small business owner with dark-brown skin, shared various instances of racism she had witnessed in Veracruz. Later, in the same conversation she told me: "Here in Veracruz there is no racism." She then paused, adopting a racial projection strategy to produce a rapid, in-the-moment fix of her contradictory narratives. "But, well, the person who is really racist is the white person..." Gaining momentum with this newfound stance, she elaborated:

> ANA: The white person is really racist. One in a few *morenos*, but normally it is the white person. The white people think that since Christ is white, since they have made him white, they believe that they are the chosen ones, the rich people, right? They are the nobility, so then the high level positions are given to the white people... They are normally rich and the ones who govern the people...
>
> CS: Then would you say that there is racism in Mexico?
>
> ANA: Yes, there is, but by the upper class.

According to Ana, there is racism, but only among whites, who are also the rich; their racism is driven by a superiority complex stemming from a sense of divine right.

In a final example of projection, Omar, the journalist with medium-brown skin, mused over the possibility that there is racism against intercolor couples: "It could occur in another class, right? The upper class probably has its rules... But that is another world." Omar transports whites even further from the margins of Mexico, to another universe. Like other non-racism frames, racial projection is adept at accounting for realities which individuals perceive as instances of racism while preserving the national ideology. This strategy is situation adaptable—the category of "others" is expansive enough that individuals can pick and choose among various projection targets who vary according to color, class, and nationality.

Lastly, Veracruzanos deploy class-based frameworks to explain both the race-color hierarchy and individual experiences with racism. For anyone familiar with Mexico, or other parts of Latin America where race and class hierarchies are intertwined, this particular discourse should not be surprising. In Mexico, even the casual observer will notice that the majority of the upper class is light-skinned and that those with brown skin are generally working- to middle-class. This means that when discrimination occurs, it could hypothetically be due to race, class, both, or additional factors. Unless a specific reference is made to either race or class, it is difficult to identify the root cause. The strong interconnection between class and race creates an opening for Veracruzanos to interpret discrimination within a class-driven framework. I frequently heard the script: "It is not so much color, but class." This script effectively allows Veracruzanos to protect the national stance without invalidating their lived experiences. Note that Veracruzanos avoid saying—"It is not color but class"—a script which would comprehensively dismiss portions of their reality. Veracruzanos' careful choice of wording allows them to negotiate contradictions in a way that simultaneously permits them to stay true to themselves and maintain loyalty to their country.

Bernardo, the psychology professor with dark-brown skin, adopted this frame when discussing racial inequality in Mexico. However, he also used it to explain his own experience with discrimination when he was stopped by immigration officials in the Mexico City airport, an incident I referenced in the previous chapter. Bernardo framed his experience by explaining:

"In that time I had a little bit of an Afro hairstyle. It was longer. That was probably it…but we as Mexicans discriminate more against other Mexicans…I have realized that when I am in the airport and I have sandals on and jeans with a t-shirt, I draw the attention of the security people and [they say] "Let's see, come here to chat. Who are you and what do you do?" But when you go with a sports coat and a tie, they will even open doors for you. That signifies that, once again, it is not so much color but social condition."

Bernardo makes room for the role of race in this incident by referencing his Afro hairstyle. However, by superimposing a stronger, more carefully articulated, and definitive class-based framework, he de-centers color and privileges the explanatory power of class.

Manuel, a forty-three-year-old carwash owner with medium-brown skin, also deployed a nonracism frame rooted in class. However, he did so, not in reference to his own experiences with racism, but to preempt the responses of his employees, whom I was interviewing. I met Manuel and his workers through Laura, one of my main informants. Manuel's carwash was a half block away from her newspaper stand. About seven or eight men work for Manuel as car washers. They are poor, Laura told me. Very, very poor. When one of the men came to buy a small, tabloid-style magazine from Laura, she asked him if he would talk to me about my study. He stood there, his dirty white t-shirt draped over his thin frame and blue jeans tucked into large rubber boots, and said nothing but glanced over his shoulder toward the car wash. He left abruptly. Within minutes, Manuel, clean and nicely dressed, walked toward the stand. When he approached, Laura made the pitch to Manuel, hoping to get permission to interview his workers. He agreed, as long as I spoke with them only on their break time.

Manuel invited me to conduct the interviews in his office, a small shack equipped with a metal desk and a few metal chairs. At night, this space doubled as housing for most of his employees. I sat down in the small chair that was offered to me. Beside me was another empty chair. Across the desk sat Manuel; the information sheet about the study lay on the table between us. The interview set-up was far from ideal. Normally, I get to know respondents before interviewing them and when I solicit an interview I request that we converse in a comfortable, private space. This situation violated all of these conditions. The door opened and the first employee, Fernando, entered. Manuel motioned for him to sit. I handed Fernando the information sheet. Leaning across the table, Manuel snatched the paper out of his hands. "They don't understand," he explained, proceeding to read the information out loud.[30] Under these less than ideal conditions, we began. Manuel entered and exited the room numerous times during our conversation. At one point, while he was sitting at his desk reading a newspaper, Fernando and I began to talk about color inequality in Veracruz. Lowering the newspaper, Manuel interrupted. In Mexico we "respect different cultures." We "break bread" with anyone. There may be some racism but if there is, it is "very very little." He continued: "It is more about class than color...Here it is more about social groups and economic power. I mean if we are rich, we move in the group of the rich. If we are poor, we move in the group of the poor." Manuel's interjection preemptively framed any instances of racism that Fernando might share with me. He managed his workers' responses just like Pepe managed those of his students.[31]

Veracruzanos sometimes offered the existence of successful dark-skinned individuals as a testament to the power of class over race. However, when details surfaced about the *form* of existence of these societal outliers, it became clear that there are limits to the power of class. For example, Lili, the forty-seven-year-old light-skinned upper-class homemaker, told me that, within high society, "people differentiate" and "appearance counts a lot." There are no set guidelines or boundaries but "the blonder or whiter you are, and higher status, the better." Lili provided a concrete example, making her point: "If you enter a social club and they see you are *morenito*, they won't accept you as much as a stunning blond. Here in Veracruz, that is how it is." The testimony of Roberto, the college graduate, on the same point was even more convincing because Roberto's medium-brown skin has been a constant source of jokes and nicknames despite his family's upper-class standing. Roberto wasn't one to focus on racism but, when I asked, he told me, with no degree of uncertainty, that his family's financial status is not a colorblind pass into economically privileged circles. Finally, the most visible test case of the experience of dark brown-skinned individuals penetrating the elite is that of former Veracruz Governor Fidel Herrera Beltrán. During his campaign and while he was in office, I repeatedly witnessed a barrage of racial insults and jokes directed at the governor. Class certainly matters in Veracruz society, but so does race and color. To conclude, the nonracism frames that form part of Veracruzanos' racial common sense largely mirror the colorblind discourses used by U.S. whites. However, in Veracruz it is individuals in all color categories who embrace these perspectives.

Counter-Discourses: Rare Challenges to the National Ideology

When discussing the societal norm of silence, I introduced Jessica and Rosalía, individuals who boldly defied this norm by breaking the taboo on critical discussions of racism. Out of one hundred and twelve respondents, only fourteen diverged from the depiction of the racial attitudes I have presented thus far; these individuals consistently asserted that racism *does* exist in Mexico. As part of this minority, Julieta, the light-skinned university student in her twenties, matter-of-factly informed me that people with brown skin are not represented in the top positions of society because of racism. Julieta continually implicated all Mexicans in racist behaviors, thereby directly challenging the national ideology. Rosalía, the university student with light skin who confronted her aunt, Bella, in the focus group session, also held a counter-perspective on race. In our conversation, she did not flinch when making the blanket statement that whites occupy the top positions in society because of racism. She also shared that a good friend of hers is forced to date her boyfriend in secret because his brown skin makes him an unacceptable partner.

Individuals who employed counter-perspectives were lighter, of higher socioeconomic status, and more educated than other respondents, thereby implicating a potential color, class, or education influence. Bailey (2002, 2004) and Beck et al. (2011), in their research on racial attitudes in Brazil and Ecuador respectively, also found a correlation between perspectives on racism and education. Bailey argues education (which he uses as a proxy for class) is the best predictor of differences in attitudes regarding racism. However, in Veracruz, this perspective does not explain why the majority of light-skinned, upper-class, and highly educated respondents negated the presence of racism in society. Upon closer analysis, I discovered a striking similarity among those who held counter-perspectives—they all had *extensive* foreign connections. The content of these ties varied widely and included having a foreign partner who held a counter-perspective on race, having close personal ties to individuals living in the United States (where close contact was maintained *and* respondents discussed the topic of racism with these individuals), having extensive travel experience outside of Mexico (usually living in another country or engaging in repeated international travel).[32] Therefore, in Veracruz, class and education may be proxies for another underlying phenomenon that drives differences in racial attitudes—extensive ties with non-Mexicans and/or non-Mexican contexts. Color, class, and education may correlate with perspectives on racism because light-skinned, well-off, highly educated individuals are more likely to have the opportunity to develop and maintain foreign ties.[33]

Despite the tendency for those holding counter-perspectives to be lighter, better off, and better educated, some cases diverged from these patterns. For example, Aracely, the forty-eight-year-old working-class homemaker with a middle-school education and medium-brown skin, was adamant that racism exists in Mexico. She has never discussed the topic with anyone in Mexico, but she has talked about racism during telephone conversations with her sister in Texas. Silvia, the fifty-four-year-old daycare worker with dark-brown skin, did not finish elementary school but also challenged the national ideology. Silvia told me she had conversed extensively about racism while dating (and almost marrying) a U.S. citizen. Finally, three male respondents, ranging from medium- to dark-brown in skin tone, held counter-perspectives. Although not from economically-privileged backgrounds, they all traveled extensively while in the navy.

My conversation with Lupe, the thirty-five-year-old medium-brown skinned middle-class homemaker with a high-school education, provided a window into how these ties can be influential. When talking to Lupe, I was struck by how drastically her views on racism diverged from those of other Veracruzanos. Trying to locate the source of this divergence, I asked her how and when she had begun to think about racism. It all started when she met Mike, her African American partner. She explained: "Little by little you get to know things and you reflect... what has helped me a lot is Mike. He has taught me a lot."

Given the close ties between the United States and Mexico and the strength and duration of their human migratory flows, it makes sense that most of Veracruzanos' foreign contact is with the United States However, other types of foreign contact also appeared to influence individuals' thoughts on racism. For example, two respondents who expressed a counter-perspective, a light-skinned female and a medium-brown-skinned male, members of the upper-middle and upper class respectively, both studied abroad in Canada. In other cases, the culmination of a variety of experiences appeared to facilitate the development of a counter-ideology; two individuals with foreign travel experience had also participated in activities that engaged the issue of race. One, a journalism student, reported on the conditions of indigenous street vendors. The other designed a school project on the topic of racism in Mexico. These experiences possibly enhanced the development of a counter-perspective.

The existence of foreign ties alone was not sufficient to create counter-discourses. Not every Veracruzano I spoke with who had travel experience or family outside of Mexico challenged the national ideology. Instead, these ties appear to create the *potential* for the development of a counter-perspective. In nearly all of the fourteen cases, not only did extensive ties exist but respondents reported discussing the issue of racism with non-Mexicans or reflecting on the issue in non-Mexican contexts. In the case of intimate relationships with foreigners, it was not only that these individuals were in these relationships but that their partners held a critical perspective on race. My findings resonate with those of Roth (2008) based on her research with Puerto Ricans and Dominicans—that the strength of ties to the United States, not one's color, is most influential in determining perspectives on racism. They also build on her argument, by suggesting that this dynamic may apply to other, non-U.S. foreign environments such as Canada.

Conclusion

In this chapter I demonstrated how Veracruzanos navigate a sea of contradictions that arise between their racialized experiences and the state-sponsored belief of nonracism. In their navigation efforts they deploy silencing strategies which render racism invisible when its putative invisibility is challenged; they use symbolic boundaries to divert attention away from racism in Mexico and re-direct it towards the United States and they adopt nonracism discourses to manage contradictions between the national ideology, the race-color hierarchy, and their personal experiences with racism. These strategies all serve the common goal of protecting, maintaining, and reproducing the national belief that there is no racism in Mexico.

The findings presented in this chapter have two implications with respect to theoretical frameworks related to boundaries and ideology, as well as racial attitudes. First, the fact that Veracruzanos use symbolic boundaries as a mechanism for ideological reproduction should encourage scholars of race in Latin America to attend to the use of symbolic boundaries vis-à-vis the United States not only in the original development of national ideology, but also in the contemporary, common-sense version of these ideologies. Currently, many Latin American scholars acknowledge the historic role of symbolic boundary-making with the United States, but they then proceed to treat contemporary Latin America and the United States as ideologically insular entities, each with their own distinct systems of race.[34] By focusing exclusively on how racial ideologies in Latin America and the United States differ, we overlook how ideologies in one region continue to define and shape ideologies in the other. As the case of Veracruz illustrates, U.S. racial ideology has historically influenced and continues to influence elite and non-elite racial ideology in Mexico. Therefore, it is not sufficient to simply state that the Mexican and the U.S. ideological systems of race are different; they are different precisely because their difference is actively reproduced on an everyday basis.

Second, my findings contribute to the literature on racial attitudes, in particular, those involving perceptions of racism. The fact that Veracruzanos, independent of color, generally negate the existence of racism, even when it is not in their best interest to do so, calls into question some of the fundamental assumptions embedded in interest-based theories of racial attitudes—that it is primarily those in positions of race-color privilege who adopt discourses that uphold the status quo and that colorblind discourses are primarily tools used by those at the top of race-color hierarchies. Although mestizos in Mexico represent the dominant group vis-à-vis indians, throughout the book I have argued that 1) the mestizo-indigenous distinction oversimplifies racial dynamics in Mexico and 2) the color hierarchy within the *mestizo* population is very important with respect to distribution of resources. In Veracruz, the socioeconomic hierarchy is almost entirely comprised of mestizos. Therefore, to examine interest-based theories, it makes sense to look at color.

Contrary to the predictions of interest-based theories of racial attitudes, the vast majority of respondents, independent of color and placement in the socioeconomic hierarchy, displayed attitudes which protect the status quo. The finding that brown-skinned individuals downplay racism in society, silence discussions of racism, and render racial discrimination invisible, runs counter to U.S. academic and popular understandings of racial attitudes. In the United States, it is assumed that whites, not racial minorities, minimize or negate racism. Illustrating this view, Charles Mills (1997) writes: "In a racially structured polity, the only people who can find it psychologically possible to deny the centrality of race are those who are racially privileged..." (p. 75). I suspect that the weakness of U.S.-based perspectives in the Veracruz context is due, in part, to the fact that these theories do not account for the strength of ideological forces and the power of nationalist sentiment.

As mentioned previously, Bailey assessed the applicability of U.S racial attitude theories to Brazil using survey data. His finding that Brazilians' race did not significantly influence their perceptions of racism suggests that U.S.-derived theories, which contend that racial attitudes should vary based on individuals' or groups' best interest, are ineffective in the Brazilian context. Interestingly, Bailey found that most Brazilians, regardless of race, claimed racism *does* exist in society, whereas I found that most Veracruzanos, regardless of color, claimed racism *does not* exist. We do not have adequate data to explain this divergence, although it could be due to methodological and/or national-context differences. The fact that my findings are consistent with some ethnographic work in Brazil—for example, Twine (1998) found that Brazilians overwhelmingly perceived their country to be racism-free—suggests that varying methodological approaches may be driving these differences. Alternatively, the divergence may be due to differences and shifts in the national ideologies themselves. Although Brazil has long held a nonracism-type national ideology, within the past decade or so this ideology has moved towards recognizing racism in the country.[35] Thus, under contemporary Brazilian ideology, recognizing racism would not threaten the national identity of Brazilians. Therefore, the differences between my findings and those of Bailey may reflect recent divergences between Mexican and Brazilian national ideology.

Although the similarity of racial discourses across race-color categories found among Mexicans and Brazilians may seem contrary to understandings of race more broadly, the fact that these similarities exist is significant. Whereas the interesting story of racial discourse in the United States has been defined as the *difference* in attitudes between racial groups, my findings have revealed a story about *similarities* in racial discourse. Sidanius and Pratto (1999) argue that data that show agreement, not disagreement, between racial groups' attitudes are the most telling. Similarities, or the consensual component of opinion, demonstrate that members share the same ideological framework. It is precisely this shared ideology that promotes the stability of a social system and helps to maintain the status quo. To highlight this point, we can draw on a question posed by Bonilla-Silva (2003), which he presents as an interesting conundrum in the U.S. context: *How is it possible to have a tremendous degree of racial inequality in a country where most whites claim that race is no longer relevant?* (p. 2). However, the more interesting question may be one adapted to the Mexican situation: *How is it possible to have a high degree of race-color inequality in a country where Mexicans, regardless of color, claim that race and color are not relevant?* Perhaps our academic common sense, which supposes that the interesting story about racial attitudes is one of differences, rather than similarities, is misguided. That being said, although the finding that non-elite Veracruzanos of all colors participate in reproducing a social structure that benefits elites seems to resonate with a false consciousness perspective, I do not adopt this interpretation. As I elaborate in the next chapter, I believe that Veracruzanos engage in the reproduction of Mexico's racial ideology, in part, to protect their national identities as Mexicans. In other words, in deploying nonracism frames, they may be asserting and defending their national identities as Mexican.

8 | What's at Stake? Racial Common Sense and Securing a Mexican National Identity

O N JUNE 25, 2004, while engaged in my habitual reading of *El Dictamen*, a local Veracruz newspaper, an editorial caught my eye. It was titled "The Next Benito Juárez Will Not be President of Mexico... but of the United States."[1] The article seemed destined to strike the chords of deep-seated nationalist sentiment. In it, Mexican journalist César Fernando Zapata not only asserted that racism is rampant in Mexico but also suggested that the Mexican strain of racism is worse than that which exists in the United States. In making this claim, Zapata challenged the national ideology of nonracism, delegitimized Mexico's claim of racial superiority vis-à-vis the United States, and broke the silence on race.

Following his proclamation that the future Benito Juárez is more likely to be from the United States than from Mexico, Zapata asked rhetorically: "Why gringo and not Mexican?" "Isn't Mexico the country that exalts the indigenous figure?" Zapata responded to these questions by suggesting that if one looks at the "facts," one will conclude that a Mexican American of indigenous descent has more opportunities to climb the social ladder than an indigenous Mexican. He argued that Mexican Americans are less marginalized than indigenous Mexicans and that they have the opportunity to compete in a country where "minority politicians continue gaining ground." In Mexico, in contrast, Zapata observes that politicians are getting "whiter and whiter." Elaborating on the theme of Mexico's privileging of whiteness, Zapata explained that in Mexico:

The whiter one is the better. You obtain the best jobs, are the most photogenic. It doesn't matter if you do not know how to do anything, just by smiling and showing your Aryan face, is enough of a credential. Surely, if you are white, you are already assured a promissory future as a model, actor, or singer. If not, at least on the street, people respect you more if you are white and have blue eyes than if you have dark skin....

Zapata also expressed concern that, in a country where 90 percent of the inhabitants are mestizos or indians, the governing class is white. In this context, he sees the country as running the "risk of falling into suspicions of racism." Adding insult to injury, Zapata locates these racist tendencies in the Mexican citizenry-at-large.

In his article, Zapata bluntly draws attention to the ironies, contradictions, and hypocrisies that surround Mexican national ideology and the everyday realities of Mexican society. In doing so, he trespasses on a host of social norms and he does so at a cost. His critical stance represents a major offense for a Mexican national. By challenging Mexico's official ideology, he places his own patriotism in question. More damning still is the fact that, although Zapata was born in Mexico, as an adult he moved to Texas to work as an editor of a Spanish-language newspaper.

Zapata's stance regarding racism in Mexico garnered an impassioned response from the Mexican community. Through personal email communication, Zapata shared with me the reactions he received from some of his readers. He characterized the feedback as representing the "extremes"—he was either congratulated for his sincerity and for being "right on the mark" or he was insulted for being pro-Yankee, anti-Mexican, and a sell-out. In our correspondence, Zapata expressed sadness regarding the negative responses but tried to remain empathetic, explaining: "They have been filling us with revolutionary dogmas and patriotisms for so long that we have believed the story." The varied reactions to Zapata's article are telling and largely encapsulate the complications and ironies surrounding Veracruz racial common sense that I have addressed throughout the book. The "right on the mark" flavor of response suggests there is a latent, unspoken truth about the existence of racism in Mexico—a truth known to Mexicans but seldom discussed. Supporting this interpretation is the fact that, although Zapata's critics attacked the symbolism of his words—words privileging the United States and challenging Mexican national ideology—they did not dispute his substantive claims of racism within Mexico. In other words, it was his patriotism, not his assessment of the situation, which came under attack.

Like some of my more outspoken Veracruz respondents, Zapata disrupted the silence surrounding critical discussions of race in Mexico.

Reactions to such disruptions expose the strength of the taboo against discussing racism in Mexico, a taboo that not only operates in the popular sphere but also extends into the academic realm. As Zerubavel (2007) reminds us, "What we ignore socially is also ignored academically, and conspiracies of silence are therefore still an under-theorized as well as understudied phenomenon" (p. 182). It is not surprising then that the topic of Mexican racial common sense has not been sufficiently explored. In examining race and color in Veracruz, I have ventured to speak of the unspoken, expose that which has been buried, and theorize the undertheorized. Ultimately, I have attempted to demystify the process surrounding the everyday reproduction of racial ideology.

Navigating Contradictions through Ideological Work

Interrogating the relationship between common sense and national ideology is not an easy task. Although ethnography is well suited to detecting and understanding the pulse of a community, establishing a direct link between popular thought and elite ideology is a tricky endeavor. It is particularly difficult when dealing with topics such as racial inequality, which "may rarely be overtly expressed, and, indeed, may be deliberately disguised or disingenuously denied" (Knight 1990, p. 71). While I certainly appreciate the challenges associated with this task, I also recognize the importance of understanding how elite ideas interact with and manifest in popular consciousness.

To understand the relationship between elite ideology and common sense, or the *process* of ideological reproduction, we need to identify the *mechanisms* through which individuals socially reproduce ideology. As I have consistently demonstrated, ideology does not simply "legitimize itself" through some mystical process; there are clear and identifiable actors and mechanisms driving the process of ideological reproduction. "Regular" people continuously create and remake a common sense, which, when strategically deployed, serves to legitimize and reproduce dominant ideology. Through an investigation of the inner workings of Veracruzanos' racial common sense, I was able to identify popular-level discourses related to the *mestizaje*, nonracism, and nonblackness pillars of Mexican national ideology. I presented countless examples of how "ordinary" Veracruzanos make elite ideas their own in a way that is meaningful to them and how they use national ideology to make sense of the world around them. This sense making is complicated, however, especially given that Mexican ideology is wrought with disorganization and contradiction. Therefore, Veracruzanos must develop and continually recreate a common sense that accounts for contradictions embedded in the elite ideology as well as the incongruities that surface between their lived realities and this national ideology. In this book I demonstrated how these ideological struggles play out in Veracruzanos' everyday discourses, attitudes, and behaviors.

Among other things, my examination of Veracruzanos' racial common sense reveals the problems inherent in treating the relationship between elite ideology and common sense in a dichotomous fashion; rarely do they neatly align or wholly conflict. Instead, individuals' responses to hegemonic ideologies are oftentimes varied and nuanced. Swidler (2001) has encouraged scholars to identify and understand the multiple manifestations of culture, including its partial, ambivalent, or incomplete uses and forms. We saw how mixed-race Veracruzanos, in the process of constructing their identities, use the *mestizaje* pillar in a partial sense, relying on it as a tool to inform their identities under certain conditions. Additionally, the discussion of Veracruzanos' attitudes on race mixture revealed an incomplete adoption of the *mestizaje* ideal—individuals did not embrace race mixture in and of itself but instead embraced it insofar as it helped them achieve their goal of whitening the next generation. On the topic of blackness, Veracruzanos of African descent displayed unstable black identities, thus not fully accepting or completely challenging the nonblackness ideological pillar. Finally, Veracruzanos overwhelmingly embraced the ideology of nonracism despite the existence of the race-color hierarchy and widespread practices of racism. Taken as a whole, these different slices of Veracruz racial common sense reveal the vast and variegated manifestations of the interconnection between common sense and elite ideology.

Beyond False Consciousness

Despite the complex and non-dichotomous nature of the relationship between common sense and national ideology, much of Veracruzanos' racial common sense fuels the social reproduction of inequality, an unfavorable outcome for the vast majority of the population. One then wonders why non-elites actively work to construct and maintain a racial common sense that protects and reinstates the national ideology, when it is seemingly not in their best interest to do so. A superficial perusal of the data presented in this book could lead one to conclude that Veracruzanos are blind to the realities surrounding inequality and that they simply regurgitate messages promulgated by their leaders; in other words, one could perceive them as being "falsely conscious" and participating in their own exploitation.

The concept of false consciousness has received heavy criticism as of late and has fallen out of favor for epistemological and political reasons.[2] Hanchard's (1994) sardonic summary of a false consciousness perspective lends insight into its overly simplistic, and thus problematic, nature: "The dominant class simply hurls an ideological pellet upon the stage of civil society. An impenetrable mist arises, enshrouds the dominant class, and obscures its movements before a captive audience (the masses), who reel back in their collective seats, transfixed, spellbound" (p. 22). Criticizing the theory of false consciousness by addressing its politically distasteful nature, Eagleton (1991) explains: "The belief that a minority of theorists monopolize a scientifically grounded knowledge of how society is, while the rest of us blunder around in some fog of false consciousness, does not particularly endear itself to the democratic sensibility" (p. 11). Aside from being politically and epistemologically objectionable, false consciousness perspectives are also unequipped to explain many social realities.

The theory of false consciousness cannot account for the complex dynamics I witnessed in Veracruz; it is particularly inefficient on two fronts. First, a false consciousness perspective assumes non-elites are *blind* to particular social realities. As such, we would expect falsely conscious individuals to be oblivious to mechanisms such as racial discrimination that sustain the racial hierarchy. However, Veracruzanos are far from blind to such realities. They recognize contradictions with the national ideology, including societal objections to marrying someone darker, the existence of racial discrimination, and a black presence in Mexico, but they choose to manage these inconsistencies in a way that protects the ideology. Thus, it would be far more accurate to say that Veracruzanos *turn a blind eye* to realities that threaten the status quo. Because of their awareness, they engage in active attempts to minimize or render such realities invisible or unimportant, which brings me to my second point regarding the inability of a false consciousness perspective to explain Veracruz race dynamics.

Classic treatments of false consciousness imply a *passive* acceptance of elite ideology by the populace. It is assumed that the "masses" "reel back in their collective seats" because it is easier for them to do so then to challenge the established order. However, the empirical realities of the Veracruz case paint a different picture. Veracruzanos go to great lengths to *actively* engage in sophisticated conceptual work, to silence, minimize, reframe, and naturalize realities that conflict with the national ideology. This is not, I would argue, an empirical demonstration of false consciousness.

Veracruzanos are not duped or deceived by elite ideology. They do not passively accept the dominant ideology, completely dismissing all that they see and know. Instead, they demonstrate high levels of situational creativity in developing, recreating, and articulating a racial common sense that allows them to manage the host of ideological contradictions that they confront on a daily basis. Through this process of ideological management, they craft a series of discourses that carefully finesse contradictions in a way that maintains a truth both to the ideology and to their identities and lived experiences. Therefore, the reach of elite ideology is ultimately determined by the way that non-elites actively incorporate this ideology into their worldviews and allow it to influence their thoughts, discourses, and behaviors.

If we reject a false consciousness framing, we are still left with the puzzle of why non-elites work to reproduce elite ideology even when it is seemingly not in their best interest to do so. Addressing a similar conundrum presented by the Brazilian case, Sheriff (2001) posits that the racial democracy myth supplies a powerful vision of hopes and dreams of what Brazil could be. She argues that Brazilians accept the myth of racial democracy not because they believe it represents reality but because of the potential reality that it portrays. Whereas this dynamic may also be at work in Mexico, I believe that two additional factors help explain the paradox of Veracruz racial common sense: (1) the "shreds of truth" embedded in Mexican ideology; and (2) the importance of nationalism.

Shreds of Truth in Ideological Myths

> In order to be truly effective, ideologies must make at least some minimal sense of people's experience, must conform to some degree with what they know of social reality from their practical interaction with it....In short, successful ideologies must be more than imposed illusions, and for all their inconsistencies they must communicate to their subjects a version of social reality which is real and recognizable enough to not be simply rejected out of hand.
> —TERRY EAGLETON (1991, pp. 14–15)

Dominant ideologies that are successfully incorporated into popular thought need to resonate, at some level, with individuals' sense of reality.[3] In the case of Mexico, the country does possess certain elements of racial inclusiveness that dovetail with the ideologies of nonracism and *mestizaje*, especially when juxtaposed against the U.S. racial situation. Although Mexico has experimented with racial segregation,[4] these practices are not comparable to Jim Crow segregation laws that existed in the United States. Furthermore, Mexico has a history of openness to race mixture, which starkly contrasts with the U.S. situation, where anti-miscegenation laws were in effect in some states until 1967.

At the political level, Mexico has a powerful racially progressive claim to fame—the mid-nineteenth-century ascendancy of Benito Juárez, an impoverished indigenous Mexican, to the presidency. When in Veracruz, I had the privilege of listening to the ten-year-old nephew of my informant Laura, narrate Juárez's personal history in rehearsal for a school event. Adrián, the jewel of the family, is loquacious, articulate, and wise beyond his years. His short stature belies his powerful voice. As I sat on a couch alongside Laura and her sister, Ana, I took note of Adrián's dark-brown skin and indigenous features, especially in the context of his pending speech about Mexico's brown-skinned indigenous president. Adrián stood, facing us, poised and ready. He paused, in dramatic fashion, and then began: "I am going to talk to you about a great man...Mr. Benito Juárez García, who was born in a little town in the state of Oaxaca, on March 21, 1806." In biographical form, Adrián proceeded to introduce Juárez's parents, emphasizing their impoverished status as indians. He spoke of their death and Juárez's new life with his uncle. Adrián then led us through Juárez's educational trajectory, beginning when a local man took Juárez under his wing, teaching him to read and write and ending with his formal training as a lawyer. In 1858 he became the president of Mexico. Adrián concluded by reciting Juárez's famous motto: "The respect of others' rights is peace." The story of Benito Juárez was retold to me by many Veracruzanos and was repeatedly evoked as a testament to the inclusive and nonracist character of the Mexican nation. This narrative, coupled with other symbols of racial openness, facilitates the palatability of the national ideology, which contends that the country is free of racism.

The Relationship Between Mexican Nationalism and Racial Ideology

Recognizing the powerful sway of Mexican nationalism can further elucidate the conceptual conundrums that surround Veracruzanos' racial common sense. More specifically, understanding the role of nationalist sentiment in Mexico can help demystify the enigmatic nature of non-elites' participation in the reproduction of the country's racial ideology. Mexico has long been preoccupied with defining what it means to be Mexican and developing its own national narrative about race, especially when faced with negative European racial stereotypes regarding Latin America.[5] As explained previously, racialization in twentieth-century Mexico was deeply intertwined with the process of building and defining the nation. As a result, being Mexican implies being mestizo (descending from Spanish and indigenous populations) and living in a nation where racism does not exist. Illustrating this is Rodrigo, the thirty-seven-year-old fisherman with dark-brown skin. When I asked him what it means to be Mexican, he simply stated: "Here, racism does not exist." Illustrating how nationalist sentiment is tied to understandings of race and nation is José, the sixty-three-year-old taco vendor with dark-brown skin who shared, "It is a great pride to be Mexican because here there is no distinguishing between race and color. We are all the same." Many other Veracruzanos echoed these sentiments during our conversations.

Racial ideology, ideas of nation, and nationalist sentiment are so intertwined in Mexico that, in reproducing the substantive basis of official racial ideology, Mexicans secure their national identities as Mexican. On the flip side, engaging in critical discussions of racism and thus challenging the national ideology, could be easily construed as antinationalistic, as we saw in the reactions to Zapata's article. Therefore, in defending and reproducing national ideology, Mexicans potentially fulfill something much more immediate than a dream or a hope—they achieve a sense of belonging to the national community. National community membership is far from insignificant in Veracruz. Although Veracruzanos' identity as Mexican was not a focal point of my research, I discovered that it was among the most salient of all identities.

Viewed through the lens of nationalism, there is ample motivation for Mexicans to reproduce the *mestizaje*, nonracism, and nonblackness pillars of Mexican national ideology, despite the numerous complications that arise in the process. When Mexicans exalt the practice of race mixture, negate racism in the country, and displace blackness, they fortify their national identities. Or, viewed differently, in the process of asserting their Mexicanness, individuals articulate a racial common sense that reproduces elite ideology on race. Because of the interconnection between racial ideology and state formation in Mexico, the social reproduction of national ideology reinforces the meaning of Mexicanness and vice versa. Consequently, Mexicans' engagement with state-sponsored ideologies is not merely a negotiation with elite beliefs about race but also what it means to be Mexican. Finally, it is also possible that Veracruzanos, especially those with a brown phenotype, use national ideology as a tool to protect and manage their psychological and emotional integrity in the face of the "everyday wounds of color" (Burdick 1998).[6] In other words, by embracing the vision of a mixed race nation free of racism they are able to avoid directly confronting and acknowledging their experiences with discrimination. Certainly, the "shreds of truth," nationalism, and psychological protection explanations are not mutually exclusive elements; it is likely that they all play a role in explaining the paradox of Veracruz racial common sense presented in this book.

Implications for Race Studies

Throughout the book, I addressed themes that are of central concern for race scholars, including boundary dynamics, identities, attitudes, discrimination, and inequality. Interrogating these themes in the Mexican context allows us to broaden our understanding of race. For example, I have argued that we cannot fully understand Mexican racial dynamics without looking at color and that any theorizing that addresses the topic of race in Mexico should address the color dynamics that exist within the mestizo boundary. More broadly, I have encouraged all race scholars to interrogate the potential role that color plays within the boundaries of racial categories or groups. Although research on color is increasing, scholars have only begun to scratch the surface of this issue. The limited research that does exist in the U.S. context, for example, has revealed the relevancy of color to racial dynamics.[7] Some race theorists argue that color is becoming increasingly salient in the United States,[8] which would make a focus on color even more pressing.

My findings forward the standing literature on race in additional ways. In the book I engaged methodological and substantive debates related to race-color terminology and the race versus color distinction. My empirical approach to these issues allowed me to build upon existing understandings of race-color schema and systems of classification in Latin America. Furthermore, I demonstrated how folk understandings of race and color diverge; Veracruzanos prefer color over racial identities as they associate color with descriptive characteristics and race with hierarchy and inequality. Additionally, I illustrated that, although Veracruzanos' race-color identities are not determined by ancestry to the degree seen in the United States, ancestry still matters; individuals evoke and ignore particular ancestral lineages to achieve various identity goals such as wedding oneself to a Mexican identity or establishing a connection to whiteness.

My discussion of individuals' attitudes and behaviors regarding inter-racial relationships and multiracial families also contributes to scholarly knowledge on race. I challenged the thesis embedded in both the Latin American and U.S. literatures that the intimate crossing of race-color boundaries signals that race and color are of minimal importance. I fur-ther suggested that scholars of interracial marriage pay attention to the race-color of family units when studying dating and marriage market dynamics; in Veracruz, the race-color background of family members appears to influence partner choice. I also examined the processes of race-color identity formation and group construction in a context where blackness is minimized. Based on my findings, I argued that we need to go beyond the boundaries of the nation-state to fully understand racial-ization processes. I further demonstrated how race-color categories are both fixed and fluid in Veracruz and proposed that we reevaluate the standing generalization that Latin American systems of race are always fluid and ambiguous. Finally, I used my findings regarding Veracruzanos' discourses on racism to critique U.S.-based theories on racial attitudes, arguing that an individual's position within the race-color hierarchy does not necessarily determine racial attitudes in the way that current theories suggest.

The findings presented in this book also speak to current debates regarding the future of U.S. race relations.[9] In particular, they inform the recent theory proposed by Eduardo Bonilla-Silva (2004), and espoused by others,[10] that the U.S. racial terrain is reconfiguring to resemble that of Latin America. Bonilla-Silva sees the United States as moving away from a binary black–white model toward a tri-racial model comprised of three tiers: whites; honorary whites; and a collective black. Furthermore, he predicts that color will play an increasing role in U.S. racial dynamics. However, it seems premature to propose a Latin Americanization thesis if we do not yet have a clear understanding of race-color dynamics through-out Latin America, especially given the heavy emphasis on Afro-Latin America.[11] This bias is particularly problematic since most countries in Latin America are *not* part of Afro-Latin America but instead are part of mestizo America. Recent research suggests that race functions somewhat differently across Latin American nations. For example, while the rate of black-brown/white interracial marriage is high in Brazil,[12] in Guatemala Ladino/indigenous interracial marriages are exceedingly rare.[13] To pro-vide another contrast, similar to my findings involving Veracruzanos,

Ecuadorians do not perceive racism in their country[14]; however, the same cannot be said for Afro-Cubans[15] or for Afro-Brazilians.[16]

Even traditional claims about how race operates in Latin America are being revisited. For example, the generalizability of the idea that "money whitens" has recently been scrutinized.[17] In Veracruz, the "money whitens" effect is weak at best, suggesting this dynamic may not be present (or only mildly so) in Mexico or at least not in some regions of the country. Furthermore, the long-standing notion that race is fluid and continuous (as opposed to fixed and bi-polar) across Latin America has recently been challenged.[18] Although race is generally fluid in Veracruz, it can also be fixed.

At any rate, the verdict is still out regarding the degree to which particular race-color dynamics are similar or different across Latin America. Increasingly, however, scholars are highlighting important national distinctions.[19] In this book I addressed the case of Mexico, the largest country in mestizo America. My findings certainly do not resolve the issue in any definitive way, but they do supply additional pieces to the puzzle. As I noted throughout the book, there is much overlap between my findings and those from Afro-Latin American countries. However, it is premature to assess whether this signifies a similarity between mestizo and Afro-Latin American countries or whether the similarities are a result of the fact that race-color dynamics in Veracruz contain an African element. Either way, additional research within and across a variety of Latin American countries is necessary to assess whether the "Latin American racial system" is a productive unit of analysis.

Finally, my research informs recent debate over how immigrants and their descendants are altering the U.S. racial terrain.[20] Mexico sends more immigrants to the United States than any other country. In 2010, Mexicans accounted for 30 percent of all U.S. immigrants.[21] In order to assess how Mexican immigrants are fitting into and shaping U.S. racial dynamics, it is imperative to understand the racial identities and conceptualizations of race that Mexicans hold in their own country,[22] especially since racial frameworks are not immediately shed after migration and may even be transmitted across generations.[23] That being said, the racial common sense of Mexicans is not a static variable, impermeable to change. As Mexican migrants leave their home country, they take with them the understandings of race that they developed during their time in Mexico. These notions of race then interact with those they encounter in the United States; this process results in the creation of a new, hybrid racial common sense.

However, while this transformation among the U.S. Mexican immigrant population is occurring, the racial ideologies of Mexico and the racial common sense of those who stayed behind are also subject to change. Although Mexican national ideology related to race has remained fairly stable since the Mexican Revolution, the smell of ideological change is in the air.[24] Because elite racial discourse may in fact be shifting, it is not clear what the future holds in terms of the meanings and manifestations of race in Mexico. What is clear, however, is that, although the racial ideology promulgated by Mexico's post-revolutionary leaders has, in many respects, been successfully incorporated into mainstream popular thought, the vision and hope of Mexican revolutionaries—that they could obliterate race—has failed; over a century later, race still matters in Mexico, and significantly so. Therefore, the pressing question is not *if* but *how* race matters and, more importantly, how it will matter in the future. In looking forward it is imperative to acknowledge the power that the Mexican citizenry wields in determining the future of race in Mexican society. If the ideological current indeed shifts course, non-elite Mexicans will undoubtedly develop new management skills and strategies to construct a racial common sense that adapts to and incorporates these changes. The resulting racial common sense will then hold the potential to fuel or undermine any new national ideological stance. Although current and future leaders of Mexico will undoubtedly shape racial ideology, the nation's racial future will ultimately be determined by the Mexican populace in *their* land of the cosmic race.

9 | Epilogue

THE TURN OF THE TWENTY-FIRST CENTURY: A NATIONAL IDEOLOGICAL SHIFT?

IDEOLOGIES ARE CONSTANTLY IN FLUX, reacting to internal and external influences as well as changing circumstances. That being said, the ideological pillars of *mestizaje*, nonracism, and nonblackness have shown immense resilience over time. I have provided various examples of elites reproducing these pillars throughout the twentieth century. Even at the beginning of the twenty-first century, these ideologies appear to be alive and well. However, there are signs that Mexican leaders may be shifting their stance, particularly with respect to the nonracism pillar. For example, the government recently established legislation and organizations to combat racial discrimination.[1] These changes were likely facilitated by Mexico's move toward democratization, a shift reflected in the end of the seventy-one-year rule of the Institutional Revolutionary Party (PRI) in 2000. This momentous change in the Mexican political scene provided additional openings for demands for equality and inclusion.

There has also been a noticeable shift in Mexico's stance on racism in international contexts, including the UN International Convention on the Elimination of All Forms of Racial Discrimination (CERD). My prior reference to CERD reports submitted by Mexico in the early 1990s showcased the government's unequivocal denial of racism in Mexico. However, in the 1996, 2004, and 2008 reports, the Mexican government no longer pursued this position and instead publicly acknowledged the existence of racism in the country.[2] An excerpt from the 2004 report illustrates this new stance: "Mexico acknowledges that racism, racial discrimination, xenophobia and related intolerance continue to exist at all levels of Mexican society." Although these recent departures from the nonracism pillar are far from insignificant, it is important to keep in mind that these reports were produced for an international body dedicated to combating racism. Moreover, these changes occurred only after Mexico was strongly reprimanded by the United Nations for failing to acknowledge racism in the country. Therefore, it is important to also look at other recent race-related events and discourses, which are removed from this context, when attempting to assess any potential ideological changes at the national level.

The stance of the administration of Mexican President Felipe Calderón (2006-2012) with respect to race was somewhat difficult to evaluate. In part, this was because Calderón, since he took office, was consumed with issues related to the drug war. Furthermore, he tended to be cautious and deliberate when making public statements, helping him to evade political quagmires on the race topic, unlike his predecessor, Vicente Fox. That being said, a few events that occurred during Calderón's presidency provided clues regarding the state of official discourse on race. These include the 2010 bicentennial celebration of Mexico's independence from Spain and a controversial broadcast by Televisa during the 2010 Soccer World Cup held in South Africa.

Throughout the bicentennial celebrations which were carried out across the country, there was evidence of continued reproduction of twentieth-century ideology. In these celebrations, Mexico was consistently portrayed as an egalitarian, multicultural, and mixed-race (indigenous–Spanish) country. For example, a monument erected for bicentennial purposes was designed to symbolize "the two cultures that are the essence of our *mestizaje*." This characterization not only portrays the Mexican population as mixed race but once again excludes any African influence in the mixture. To commemorate the bicentennial, the Mexican government also instituted a plan to send every Mexican household a state-approved book on Mexican history (González and González 2010). This book contains a number of statements reiterating twentieth-century racial ideology and reaffirming the connection between understandings of race and nation. For example, one passage describes the offspring of indigenous–Spanish mixture as "a new racial group generically known as mestizos, that was not Spanish nor indigenous, but Mexican" (p. 25).

Thus, in recognizing and celebrating Mexico's bicentennial, Mexican government officials recycled many of the same ideological themes popularized by their elite counterparts a century earlier; they portrayed Mexico as a mixed-race country unified by shared indigenous–Spanish blood and culture. Given that the bicentennial celebrations were held over the course of a year and targeted Mexican nationals in all regions of the country, these events had considerable potential to affect popular thought. Furthermore, since they were aimed at reinvigorating nationalist sentiment, it is probable that they were successful in intensifying Mexicans' expressions and feelings of patriotism. If Mexican leaders' efforts to heighten national sentiment were indeed successful, we might expect that, given the strong connection between understandings of race and national identity, the nationalist focus may have also strengthened Mexicans' efforts to defend and reproduce the country's official racial ideology.

Also in 2010, a race-related event occurred within the context of the World Cup soccer finals held in South Africa. Mexico found itself at the center of controversy following a broadcast by Televisa, a major Mexican media conglomerate. During the morning coverage of the soccer matches, Televisa aired a programming segment in which actors wore blackface to portray a South African theme. These images drew international attention and criticism related to the stereotypic portrayal of blacks that once again threatened Mexico's image as a nonracist nation. Reminiscent of the Memín controversy, much of the criticism came from the United States. For example, Tracey Wilkinson published an article in the *Los Angeles Times* titled "Racism in Mexico Rears Its Ugly Head."[3] As part of the article, she made the powerful and unapologetic assertion that racism is "alive and well in Mexico." Although the Mexican government was fairly silent on the issue, Ricardo Bucio, the head of Mexico's National Council for the Prevention of Discrimination (CONAPRED), issued a public statement protesting the use of actors in blackface and further asserted: "Racism in Mexico is covered up...There is a lot of denial about it."

The response by both Televisa and Mexicans who were following the story, however, largely mirrored the racial common sense of Veracruzanos. In an attempt to fend off critics, a spokesperson from Televisa argued that the characters in blackface "do not signify anything bad" and that "they should not be taken seriously,"[4] signaling an "it's only a joke" framing. Similar discourses surfaced after an article detailing the controversy was printed in a major Mexican newspaper. Many readers reacted with indignation regarding the charges that the Televisa skits were racist. One reader criticized the United States, citing a "disgusting double standard for an imperialist and invading country,"[5] erecting a U.S.–Mexico symbolic boundary in a manner similar to that used by Veracruzanos and those involved in the Memín debate six years prior. Popular discourse surrounding this event largely reproduced twentieth-century national ideology. That being said, there is evidence that some Mexican government institutions are trying to change these popular perspectives on racism.

CONAPRED has made recent efforts to identify racial discrimination in Mexico and increase popular awareness of racism.[6] For example, the First National Survey of Discrimination in Mexico was carried out in 2005 and repeated in 2010 and included questions about individual experiences with racial discrimination. Additionally, in 2011, CONAPRED launched a campaign about racism in Mexico under the slogan "For a Society Free of Racism," with the goal of disseminating information to the Mexican public about how to recognize and combat racism. The campaign plan included circulating information about racism through short video clips aired on television and in movie theaters; radio, Internet, and billboard announcements; and workshops targeting children. CONAPRED's strategy has been to create messages that resonate with Mexicans' everyday experiences. For example, one of the video campaigns opens with the rhetorical question "Sound familiar?" and proceeds to introduce a series of "real-life" scenarios:

A parent telling her daughter, "Honey, get out of the sun. You are going to get darker."

A young female being scolded about her choice of partner, "How did you end up with him? Don't you see that we have to 'better the race'?"

A businessman shouting out of his car window to a dark-skinned pedestrian: "You don't even know how to cross the street! You are acting like an indian!"

A young man telling his date: "They didn't let me into the club because I'm brown."

The video then cuts to the statement: "In Mexico, the majority of us say we are not racist." It then displays the results from a CONAPRED survey that challenge this perception by providing evidence of racism. This particular government campaign directly confronts the ideology of nonracism.

It is too soon to tell whether recent changes, including Mexico's recognition of racism in the CERD reports and the activities of CONAPRED, foreshadow a broader, more permanent shift. If the ideological terrain is indeed reconfiguring, it is not doing so in a linear fashion. Although recent changes may be harbingers of a new national ideology, the dominant ideological strands of the post-revolutionary era are still present. Such inconsistencies make it difficult to assess the future direction of the ideological current. Further complicating predictions is the fact that the political current has once again shifted with the 2012 election of Enrique Peña Nieto to the presidency. Despite these uncertainties, what we do know is that the final outcome of this particular ideological struggle will likely be determined by the actions and discourses of non-elite Mexicans.

APPENDIX

TABLE A.1 Number of interviewees according to
selected characteristics

Sex	
Female	59
Male	53
Age groups	
18–27	21
28–37	21
38–47	27
48–57	26
58–67	8
68–77	1
78–87	8
Social class*	
Lower/working	46
Middle	48
Upper	18
Educational attainment	
None	3
Some elementary	19
Some middle school	13
Some high school	13
Technical education	7
Some college	17
College graduate	27
Post-graduate education	7
No data	6

continued

Nativity	
Mexican-born	107
Born abroad**	5
Color***	
Light	22
Light brown	29
Brown	31
Dark brown	30
N	112

*Class categories based on living standards, reported income, and occupation.

**Immigrants from Cuba and Panama with long-term residence in Mexico.

***Based on author's classification.

NOTES

Chapter 1

1. This was part of a broader series of postage stamps issued to commemorate Mexican comic books. The still popular comic book was first published in 1947 and has been exported to many Latin American countries.

2. Memín is reminiscent of derogatory figures used in reference to African American children in the U.S. South in the 1900s. Memín was modeled after a Cuban child and therefore "speaks" with a coastal or Caribbean accent.

3. *El Dictamen*, 7/1/05.

4. *El Dictamen*, 7/1/05.

5. I define *elites* as government officials and state-sponsored intellectuals and *non-elites* as members of the populace who are not in charge of creating national ideology. I define *national ideology* as the ideology promulgated by elites (as defined above). I use the terms national ideology, *official ideology, elite ideology, dominant ideology*, and *state-sponsored ideology* interchangeably.

6. The use of quotation marks signals that race (like related terms) is a social construction. However, I drop this practice in the remainder of the text for ease of reading.

7. Although mestizo typically refers to individuals of European and indigenous heritage, I include individuals of partial African descent in this category because my respondents of African descent identified as mixed race.

8. All names are pseudonyms.

9. In Spanish, words characterizing specific individuals end in an "a" to reference a female and an "o" to reference a male.

10. Because of the ambiguity surrounding the term *moreno*, I sometimes leave the term in Spanish. I further discuss the meaning of the term in chapter 2.

11. *Negrito/a* is the diminutive form of *negro/a*. The literal translation of the noun-form of these terms is "blackie." However, *negrito/a* and *negro/a* have various connotations, including ones related to endearment, paternalism, or derogatory sentiment. The diminutive form is typically used to emphasize endearment or paternalism. Because the English translation does not capture these varied connotations and because the term "blackie" is rarely used in English, I leave these terms in Spanish.

12. She is referring to *Angelitos Negros,* a movie where a black girl puts white powder on her face because she is unhappy with her color.

13. Throughout the text, I use the term *race mixture* as a translation for *mestizaje,* and use these terms interchangeably. I consider race mixture to be an umbrella term that includes both interracial and intercolor mixture.

14. In the text I use the term *racism* as an umbrella term to refer to both racism and colorism.

15. I use the term *racial attitudes* as an umbrella term to refer to attitudes regarding both race and color.

16. I use the term *interracial* to refer to both race- and color-related dynamics.

17. In the text I use the term *racial discrimination* to refer to discrimination related to race or color.

18. For a discussion regarding causal mechanisms in interpretive social research, see Reed (2011).

19. For an overview of this literature, see de la Peña and Vázquez (2002).

20. For examples, see Friedlander (1975), Frye (1996), and Saldívar (2008).

21. There is very limited data on the mestizo population in Mexico. Mestizo is generally treated as a default category for non-indians (Eshelman 2005). In 2010, roughly 7 percent of the population spoke an indigenous language (http://www.inegi.org.mx), a common measure of indigenous status (Corona 2001; Fernández et al. 2002). This could put the mestizo population somewhere around 90% according to Mexican census numbers. However, in a recent nationally representative survey of race in Mexico, Martínez Casas et al. (2011) found that 64.3% of respondents identified as mestizo when asked: "Do you consider yourself…mulatto, black, indigenous, mestizo, white or other?" Although this number is well below 90%, since respondents were only able to mark one category, it is likely that some of those identifying in other categories would also identify as mestizo, which would increase the self-identified mestizo population.

22. Furthermore, the dominant frame for analyzing inequality in Mexico is class, not race.

23. Katzew (2004), Martínez Casas et al. (2011), Flores and Telles (2012); Villarreal (2010, 2012).

24. CONAPRED (2010, http://www.conapred.org.mx/redes/userfiles/files/Enadis-2010-RG-Accss-002.pdf); Castellanos Guerrero (2003); Cruz Carretero (1989); Friedlander (1975); Harvey (1998); Hernández-Cuevas (2001); Lewis (2000); Martínez Maranato (1994); Martínez Novo (2006); Moreno Figueroa (2008a); Vaughn (2001).

25. Barth [1969]1998, p. 15

26. See, for example, Lamont and Molnár (2002); Nagel (1994); Wimmer (2008).

27. This emphasis reflects my broader plea for race scholars to pay attention to color (Sue 2009b).

28. Bonilla-Silva (1999); Cornell and Hartmann (1988); Loveman (1999); Omi and Winant (1994); Wimmer (2008).

29. Golash-Boza (2010); Harris (2009); Nakano Glenn (2009); Sue (2009a, 2009b); Telles (2004).

30. Wade (1997).

31. Alba (2009).

32. Gramsci (1971); Hanchard (1994); Jackman (1994); Omi and Winant (1994).

33. Jackman (1994).

34. For a critique, see Bailey (2009); Hasenbalg and Silva (1999); Sidanius and Pratto (1999); Twine (1998); Winant (1992).

35. Burdick (1998); Sawyer (2006); Twine (1998).

36. Gramsci (1971).

37. Foucault (1990); Roseberry (1996).

38. Eagleton (1991); Hanchard (1994).

39. Gramsci (1971).

40. Eagleton (1991); Hall (1986); Hanchard (1994).

41. Although Gramsci did not write about race, consistent with others (Hall 1986; Hanchard 1994; Omi and Winant 1994), I see Gramsci's work as relevant to studies of racial ideology.

42. Bourdieu (2001); Sidanius and Pratto (1999).

43. In illuminating this process, I highlight the "gray" areas on the continuum of ideological acceptance; the relationship between common sense and ideology is oftentimes not dichotomous, with common sense perfectly aligning or comprehensively conflicting with elite ideology (Swidler 2001).

44. Telles and Paschel (n.d.).

45. Telles (2004).

46. Tilley (2005).

47. For exceptions and critique, see Castellanos Guerrero (2000); Moreno Figueroa (2008a, 2010); Lomnitz (2005); Urías Horacasitas (2007).

48. Aguirre Beltrán (1944).

49. Aguirre Beltrán [1946]1989; Martínez Montiel (1994).

50. Vaughn (2001). For overviews of the Afro-Mexican experience, see Martínez Montiel (1994); Muhammad (1995); Vinson and Restall (2009); Vinson and Vaughn (2004).

51. Aguirre Beltrán (1946). The 1810 Spanish census marked the last official treatment of blacks as a separate category. Recently, in a nationally representative survey, 3.1% of the Mexican population identified as either black or mulatto (Martínez Casas et al. 2011).

52. Cope (1994); Katzew (2004); Knight (1990).

53. Cope (1994); Martínez (2009); Mörner (1967).

54. Mörner (1967).

55. Katzew (2004).

56. Cope (1994); Katzew (2004); Mörner (1967); Swarthout (2004).

57. Swarthout (2004).

58. Lomnitz (1992).

59. Lomnitz (2001).

60. Archer (2000); Martínez Casas et al. (2011).

61. Vázquez (2000).

62. Vanderwood (2000).

63. Buffington and French (2000).

64. Tilley (2005).

65. Knight (1990); Stern (2003).

66. Stepan (1991).

67. Knight (1990).

68. Buchenau (2001); Knight (1990); Stern (2003). This practice occurred in other parts of Latin America (Golash-Boza 2011; Loveman 2001; Telles 2004; Wright 1990).

69. Buchenau (2001); Cook-Martín and Fitzgerald (2010).

70. Basave Benítez (1992); Buffington (2000); Knight (1990); Stern (2003); Tilley (2005).

71. Buffington and French (2000); Hart (2000).

72. Hart (2000).

73. Hart (2000).

74. Knight (1990).

75. Knight (1990).

76. Swarthout (2004).

77. Buffington (2000); Knight (1990).

78. Swarthout (2004); Tilley (2005).

79. Across Latin America, *mestizaje* projects have held different meanings. In countries with significant indigenous populations, *mestizaje* ideologies have emphasized acculturation, whereas in countries with large black populations *mestizaje* has generally referred to the establishment of interracial unions (Golash-Boza 2011). In the case of Mexico, conceptions of *mestizaje* have involved notions of both cultural and biological mixture (Moreno Figueroa 2011; Knight 1990; Swarthout 2004). My focus in this book is on the element of *mestizaje* that refers to interracial unions and mixed-race offspring.

80. Implicitly, the nonracism ideology suggests an absence of colorism in Mexico. Therefore, my discussion of the nonracism pillar includes dynamics associated with both racism and colorism.

81. These pillars do not represent all strands of twentieth-century national ideology. Most notably, *indigenismo*, an elite ideology that promoted the "respectful" integration of indians into the national community, was also present (Knight 1990; Wade 1997).

82. Gonzalez Navarro (1970); Stepan (1991); Stern (2009); Vasconcelos ([1925]1997).

83. Knight (1990); Stern (2003); Swarthout (2004).

84. Basave Benítez (1992).

85. Appelbaum et al. (2003); Loveman (2001); Martínez-Echazábal (1998).

86. Delpar (2000); Paz (1985).

87. Gutiérrez (1999); vom Hau (2009).

88. Benjamin (2000); Gutiérrez (1999).

89. Delpar (2000).

90. Tilley (2005).

91. Only the 1921 Mexican national census asked about race, with the following results: indian race (29.16%); mixed race (*raza mezclada*) (59.33%); white race (9.8%); other race or no reply (1%); and foreigner, without racial distinction (0.71%). However, the Mexican government has fairly consistently made attempts to estimate the size of the indigenous population based on cultural and, only recently, self-identification measures.

92. Lamont and Molnár (2002) define symbolic boundaries as "conceptual distinctions made by social actors to categorize objects, people, practices, and even time and space" (p. 168).

93. Brading (1985). The use of territorial borders to construct difference is a common nation-building strategy (Lamont and Molnár 2002). Other Latin American leaders have used the United States as a symbolic backdrop for the construction of their nation's ideology (Bailey 2009; Beck, Mijeski, and Stark 2011; Candelario 2007; Telles 2004; Wright 1990).

94. Vazquez (2000).

95. Béjar Navarro (1969); Knight (1990).

96. Golash-Boza (2011).

97. Deans-Smith and Katzew (2009).

98. The supposed disappearance of the black population was questioned in the writings of Gonzalo Aguirre Beltrán (1946, 1958). As part of his research, Aguirre Beltrán studied a black population residing in the Costa Chica, a southern coastal region lying within the states of Guerrero and Oaxaca.

99. Gonzalez-El Hilali (1997); Hernández Cuevas (2004, 2005).

100. Hoffman (2007).

101. Some shifts have taken place, which I address in the conclusion.

102. CERD/C/260/Add.1. I discuss this report in further detail in chapter 7.

103. Appelbaum et al. (2003); Graham (1990); Telles and Flores (2013); Wade (1997).

104. Hernández Cuevas (2004, 2005); Knight (1990); Stepan (1991); Tilley (2005); Wade (1997).

105. When referencing these relationships I use the term *intercolor couples* and *mixed-color families* because Veracruzanos think of these units as crossing color, not racial, boundaries.

106. According to the 2010 Census, the Veracruz metropolitan area has 742,169 inhabitants (www.inegi.org.mx). Compared with other metro areas of similar size (i.e., 500,000–1 million inhabitants; www.inegi.org.mx/est/contenidos/espanol/metodologias/otras/zonas_met.pdf, Table 4), the number of people ages three and over who speak an indigenous language, per 1,000 inhabitants, in the Veracruz metro area (7.4) lies close to the middle of the range, according to 2010 census data. The metro areas of Aguascalientes (2.3), Saltillo (2.5), San Luis Potosí-Soledad de G.S. (5.0), Xalapa (5.1), Morelia (5.5), and Querétaro (5.7) had lower numbers of people ages three and over who spoke an indigenous language per 1,000 inhabitants, while Chihuahua (8.8), Reynosa-Río Bravo (10.9), Tampico (11.8), Acapulco (14.5), Cuernavaca (17.4), and, most notably, Villahermosa (51.3) and Mérida (110.6) had higher rates than Veracruz. As such, the number of indigenous language speakers per capita in the Veracruz metro area seems fairly comparable to that of similarly sized urban areas across Mexico. Although these counts are surely underestimates given the stigmatized nature of status, they give a rough comparative sense of estimates across metropolitan areas.

107. For details on the experience of Africans and their descendants in colonial Veracruz, see Carroll (2001); García Bustamante (1987); Motta Sánchez (2001); Naveda Chávez-Hita (1987); Winfield Capitaine (1988).

108. In the early 1800s, many Cuban expatriates associated with the independence movement resided in Veracruz. Furthermore, during the Cuban wars of independence, a number of Cuban refugees fled to Veracruz (García Díaz 2002; García Díaz and Guerra Vilaboy 2002). During the largest wave of Cuban migration (1870–1900), approximately

2,716 Cuban individuals immigrated to Mexico; Veracruz received the largest number of these migrants (García Díaz 2002). Despite their relatively small numbers, Cubans were highly visible in particular arenas such as baseball and popular music (Flores Martos 2004; García Díaz 2002; Martínez Montiel 1993; Vaughn 2001).

109. African slavery, however, was not unique to Veracruz. African slaves migrated throughout Mexico, including the states now known as Yucatán, Michoacán, Tlaxcala, México, Campeche, Chiapas, Puebla, Querétaro, Guerrero, and Oaxaca (Aguirre Beltrán [1946]1989). Today, there is a visible African-origin presence in other regions of Mexico, most notably in the Costa Chica, but also in Coahuila and Quintana Roo (Martínez Montiel 1994; Rout 1976).

110. The Port of Veracruz has been and continues to be an integral part of transnational networks, connecting a mercantile flow between Mexico, the Caribbean Islands, Colombia, Venezuela, and Panama (García de León 1992). It has a particularly strong connection with La Havana, Cuba. These sister ports have been intricately linked by commerce, culture, and human migratory flows (García Díaz and Guerra Vilaboy 2002).

111. Vaughn (2001).

112. The 2006 Mexican census showed that 78.3% percent of Mexicans currently reside in urban areas (see Table 2 in Riosmena and Massey 2012). Despite the potential that Veracruz holds for illuminating studies of race-color, the Port of Veracruz has rarely been an object of anthropological study (Flores Martos 2004). The scant literature on the contemporary experience of Mexicans of African descent focuses primarily on the Costa Chica (e.g., Aguirre Beltrán 1958; Althoff 1994; Campos 2005; Díaz Pérez et al. 1993; Flanet 1977; Gutiérrez Ávila 1988; Lewis 2000, 2001, 2004; Moedano Navarro 1988; Tibón 1961; Vaughn 2001). The even more limited work on Veracruz has primarily focused on rural areas within the state (e.g., Cruz Carretero 1989; Hall 2008; Martínez Maranto 1997), with only a few recent studies addressing urban Veracruz (e.g., Malcomson 2010; Sue 2010; Sue and Golash-Boza 2009).

113. Weiss (1994).

114. See Table A.1 for a breakdown of respondents by various characteristics.

115. The focus group method relies on group interaction while minimizing the direct influence of the researcher, which can lead to greater emphasis on participants' point of view (Krueger 1988; Langford and McDonagh 2003; Morgan 1988).

116. This justification has been used by others (Roth 2010; Telles 2004).

117. Color, like race, is socially constructed. I relied on my ethnographic experience to understand the Veracruz color schema when making these classifications. See Table A.1 for a breakdown of respondents' color.

118. *Indígena* is a socially acceptable term to refer to the indigenous population in Mexico. *Indio/a*, on the other hand, while also referring to the indigenous population, is sometimes used with paternalistic or derogatory sentiment. When using the English translations, I use the term that best captures the original meaning. Outside of translation issues, I use indian or indigenous depending on which term is best suited to the particular context (e.g., historical time period).

119. Baca Zinn (1979); Riessman (1987); Waters (1999).

120. Beoku-Betts (1994); Blee (2000); Zavella (1996).

121. Rhodes (1994); Martínez-Novo (2006). For a more detailed discussion, see Chavez (2008); Twine (2000).

Chapter 2

1. In this chapter I leave many race-color terms in Spanish since I am analyzing the manner in which such terms are used in Veracruz.

2. Bourdieu and Wacquant (1999); Loveman (1999).

3. Golash-Boza (2010, 2011); Roth (2012).

4. The term race does not translate smoothly from Mexican Spanish into English. In Mexico, *raza* or *la raza* (race or the race) has a variety of meanings that are more expansive than the English term, including common folk, the people, or breed. When Mexicans use *raza* in a manner similar to English speakers' use of race, it connotes notions of ancestry, hierarchy, and groupness. Because of the subject matter of our conversations, when I asked Veracruzanos about *raza*, they generally treated it in this more narrow racialized sense.

5. Bailey (2009); Telles (2004).

6. For examples see Bailey (2009); Golash-Boza (2011); Roland (2006); Roth (2012).

7. The literal translation of *güero/a* (as well as *güerito/a*) is "whitie" or "blondie" These terms can connote endearment or respect and are sometimes used for the purpose of flattery. Unlike *negro/a,* they typically do not carry derogatory sentiment. Because *güero/a* is used as a noun and does not easily translate into English, I leave it in Spanish throughout the book.

8. Vaughn (2001) also found that residents of the Costa Chica, Mexico, were more comfortable using *moreno* than *negro*. He attributed this preference to their interaction with him as an African American. However, the fact that I also encountered a strong hesitancy by Veracruzanos to use the term *negro* suggests that Mexicans' gravitation toward the term *moreno* is not simply due to a race-of-the-interviewer effect.

9. This association has been noted both directly and indirectly in previous work on Mexico (Flores Martos 2004; Friedlander 1975; Moreno Figueroa 2012; Vaughn 2001; Velázquez Gutiérrez 2008; Villarreal 2010) as well as in work on other parts of Latin America (Burdick 1998; Golash-Boza 2011; Goldstein 2003; Hoetink 1967; Roland 2006; Sheriff 2001; Twine 1998; Warren 2001). However, less attention has been paid to how this association manifests discursively in everyday talk, which is what I focus on in this section.

10. There is a parallel discourse in Veracruz about dark-skinned women that is highly sexualized, but I consider this distinct from more traditional understandings of beauty.

11. In this section, I italicize words that mark linguistic slips.

12. Andrews (1991); Roth (2012); Twine (1998); Warren (2001).

Chapter 3

1. Moreno Figueroa (2012).

2. For research on identity and authenticity, see Cornell and Hartmann (1998); Erickson (1995); Fine (2003); Grazian (2003); King-O'Riain (2006); Peterson and Anand (2004).

3. In this chapter, when I reference "light-skinned individuals," I am referring to those individuals I classified as "light." When I discuss "brown-skinned individuals," I am referring to those individuals I classified as "light-brown," "medium-brown," or "dark-brown."

4. I exclude individuals of African descent from this discussion as they face a different set of identity-related dilemmas, which I cover in chapter 6.

5. Golash-Boza (2011); Telles (2004); Warren (2001).

6. Daniel (2002).

7. For more on this distinction, see Bakalian (1993).

8. This is a reference to a region in the Mexican state of Chiapas that is predominately indigenous.

9. Degler (1971); Friedlander (1975), Twine (1998); Villarreal (2010); Wade (1993).

10. To reiterate, I exclude individuals of African ancestry from this discussion and thus do not engage identities that reference the racialized version of *moreno*.

11. Twine (1998).

12. Telles and Paschel (n.d.).

13. Swidler (2001).

14. For an analysis of representations of indians in Mexican school textbooks, see Gutiérrez (1999).

15. Warren (2001).

16. This is similar to how labels related to blackness operate in Veracruz, a point covered in chapter 6.

Chapter 4

1. To reiterate, Mexican national ideology has highlighted both biological and cultural aspects of *mestizaje*. In this book I narrow the discussion and focus on interracial relationships.

2. The desire for lighter-skinned partners has been documented in other Latin American contexts (Burdick 1998; Golash-Boza 2011; Twine 1998).

3. A similar stereotype exists for *serrano* men (hillbillies) in Peru (Golash-Boza 2011).

4. Frankenberg (1993); Sullivan (2005); Thornton (1996).

5. Gordon (1964a); Hall (1992); Reuter (1931). For further discussion, see Johnson and Nagoshi (1986); Telles and Sue (2009).

6. Burdick (1998); Golash-Boza (2011); Sheriff (2001); Twine (1998); Wade (1993).

7. Osuji (2011); Twine (1998).

8. Given the importance of eye color in Veracruz discourse, it is interesting that eye color has not been highlighted in the broader literature on race in Latin America, which has primarily emphasized the importance of skin color (e.g., Golash-Boza 2011; Nogueira 1985; Roth 2008; Villarreal 2010) and hair (e.g., Burdick 1998; Candelario 2007; Osuji 2011; Roland 2006).

9. Golash-Boza (2011); Osuji (2011); Roth (2008, 2012); Sheriff (2001); Wade (1993).

10. The participants were women of varying shades of brown and from working- to middle-class backgrounds.

Chapter 5

1. http://www.ameasite.org/factsheet.pdf

2. As mentioned previously, when referencing the case of Veracruz, I generally use the terms *intercolor couples* and *mixed-color families* because Veracruzanos think

of these units as crossing color, not racial, boundaries. However, when discussing the literature and more general dynamics, I use the terms *interracial relationships* and *multiracial families*.

3. Tannenbaum ([1946]1992); Vasconcelos ([1925]1997); for discussions see Telles and Sue (2009); Wade (2004).

4. Degler (1971); Hoetink (1985); Mörner (1967).

5. Gordon (1964b); Kalmijn (1998); Lieberson and Waters (1988); Park (1950).

6. Daniel (2002); D'Souza (1995); Fernández (1996); Gay (1987); Kalmijn (1998); Nakashima (1992); Patterson (2000); Zack (1993).

7. This is similar to what Osuji (2011) documented in her qualitative study of black–white couples in Rio de Janeiro, Brazil. However, she found that interracial couples perceived onlookers as understanding their relationships through the lens of status exchange, although they did not think about their relationships in that way.

8. Davis (1941); Merton (1941). Scholars have consistently found status exchange dynamics at work in interracial marriages. For the U.S. case, see Fu (2001); Kalmijn (1993); Lichter and Qian (2004); Qian (1997); for Brazil see Telles (2004).

9. Burdick (1998); Osuji (2011); Telles (2004); Wade (1993).

10. Osuji (2011); Sheriff (2001); Twine (1998).

11. Howard (2001).

12. Burdick (1998); Rangel (2007); Sheriff (2001).

13. Moreno Figueroa (2008a, 2008b, 2012) had a similar finding regarding expectations of sameness in her study of Mexican families.

14. This song is performed by *La Sonora Dinamita*, an internationally-recognized Colombian group.

15. For elaboration of this argument see Warren and Sue (2011).

Chapter 6

1. *La Jornada*, 5/30/05.

2. Vaughn (2001).

3. In this chapter I refer to individuals of African descent or African origin as those socially marked as such in Veracruz society. To avoid cumbersome language, I generally reference an individual's ancestry only if he or she has clear phenotypic markers of African descent.

4. This minimization is significant as slavery discourses can impact understandings of blackness and facilitate the development of racial consciousness. In other words, collective memories about slavery oftentimes (but not always) foster the development of a black identity.

5. Aguirre Beltrán (1946); Carroll (2001); Palmer (1976).

6. Carroll (2001).

7. Vaughn (2001).

8. Cruz Carretero (n.d.).

9. Ibid.

10. Ibid.

11. Bailey (2009); Golash-Boza (2011).

12. Wagley and Harris (1958).

13. Vila (2000).

14. Pérez Montfort (2007).

15. Lewis (2004).

16. *"Más Mexicano que el nopal."* This phrase references the cactus plant, oftentimes evoked as a symbol of being authentically Mexican.

17. Among everyone I interviewed, Bernardo was the only native Veracruzano who adopted a strong and consistent black identity. As he is just one individual, it is difficult to know why his identification significantly deviates from those of his fellow Veracruzanos, but I suspect that his training in psychology and his personal focus on the concepts of self-esteem and pride are contributing factors.

18. http://mexico.cnn.com/nacional/2011/04/01/afrodescendientes-en-mexico-la-poblacion-invisible

19. Interestingly, Sawyer (2006) found that Cubanness is racialized even within Cuba—Cubans are perceived to be black and foreigners white.

20. Martínez Montiel (1993); Vaughn (2001).

21. Hoffman (2009); Lewis (2004).

22. Vaughn (2001).

23. *El Dictamen* 8/6/05.

24. Similar to Mexicans in other regions, Veracruzanos stereotype blacks as being lazy, unintelligent, poor, violent, untrustworthy, and unattractive (Flanet 1977; Lewis 2004; Vaughn 2001). Less overtly negative stereotypes portray blacks as hard workers, physically strong, happy-go-lucky, and outgoing.

25. Degler (1971); Hanchard (1994); Harris (1952); Twine (1998); Winant (2001).

26. Bailey (2002); Duany (2002); Harris (1952); Hoetink (1985); Mörner (1967); Telles (2004).

27. CERD/C/SR.1731.

28. CERD/C/MEX/CO/15.

29. This question was not included in the final questionnaire.

30. Many of these points were reiterated in Mexico's 2008 report (CERD/C/MEX/16–17). In this report, the Mexican government also highlighted additional cultural events dedicated to recognizing Mexicans of African descent.

31. For elaboration on this argument, see Golash-Boza (2011); Sue and Golash-Boza (2009).

Chapter 7

1. Duany (2002); Guimarães (2001); Hanchard (1994); Twine (1998); Winant (2001).

2. Bailey (2002, 2009); Frye (1996); Sheriff (2001).

3. Bakanic (1995); Bobo and Kluegel (1993); Hunt (2007); Kinder and Sanders (1996); Kluegel (1990); Safron and Broman (1997).

4. Scholars have developed various models to explain racial group attitudes including classical prejudice, stratification belief, group position, and self-interest (Bobo and Hutchings 1996). In this chapter I focus on the self-interest model because, unlike some of the others, it is not dependent on a strong sense of race-color groupness, something which is absent in Veracruz.

5. For recent work on colorblindness, see Bonilla-Silva (2003); Feagin (2001); Frankenberg (1993); Gallagher (2003); Moras (2010).

6. That being said, Bonilla-Silva (2003) describes blacks as "slightly" colorblind, and O'Brien (2008) found that Asians and Latinos also use colorblind frames, but to a lesser degree than whites.

7. Zerubavel (2007: 181).

8. Beck et al. (2011); Goldstein (2003); Moraes da Silva and Reis (2011); Sheriff (2001); Twine (1998); Wade (1993).

9. Goldstein (2003: 10).

10. Memín is a black comic book character (see Figure 1, chapter 1).

11. Golash-Boza (2011); Sheriff (2001); Telles (2004); Twine (1998).

12. Such jokes were not confined to Bernardo's class. In one high-school classroom where I distributed surveys, of twenty-seven students, nine mentioned their black classmate being made fun of because of his color.

13. Other scholars such as Bail (2008), Lamont and Molnár (2002), and Wimmer (2008) have also used the concept of symbolic boundaries to understand racial dynamics.

14. A similar dynamic exists in other Latin American countries (Beck, Mijeski, and Stark 2011; Roth 2008, 2009, 2012; Sawyer 2006; Twine 1998; Wright 1990).

15. *El Planeta*, 7/1/05.

16. *El Dictamen*, 7/1/05.

17. *La Jornada*, 7/1/05.

18. *La Jornada*, 7/3/05.

19. *El Dictamen*, 7/1/05.

20. CERD/C/260/Add.1.

21. Golash-Boza (2011); Roth (2008); Sawyer (2006); Twine (1998).

22. Lomnitz (2005). A student's survey response provides insight as to how the media may reinforce this perception: "I saw something on the television. Police in the U.S.A. were beating a man with black skin."

23. Given my findings regarding how the United States is "othered" in Mexico, it is important to revisit the issue of my positionality. Logical questions are: How common is it for Veracruzanos to evoke symbolic boundaries vis-à-vis the United States? Are they using this discourse merely in reaction to my presence as a U.S. citizen? Or is this a more entrenched part of their racial common sense? Although my positionality is clearly relevant and likely triggers cognitive reactions related to the United States, it is important to note that the "othering" of the United States in Mexico has been well-documented by non-U.S. researchers as well (Brading 1985; González-Casanova 1970; Gonzalez Navarro 1993; Lomnitz 2005; van den Berghe 1967; Vázquez 2000; Velázquez Gutiérrez 2008). Moreover, I presented examples of U.S. boundary construction outside of my presence (e.g., during the Memín controversy) although these were in direct response to U.S. criticism. Given the long-standing relationship between Mexico and the United States, it should not be surprising that the United States serves as a common conceptual backdrop for Mexicans, and that symbolic boundary-making with the United States plays an important role in their racial common sense.

24. CERD/C/MEX/16-17.

25. Bonilla-Silva (2003); Frankenberg (1993).

26. The 1994 indigenous-based Zapatista uprising in Chiapas had the potential to disrupt Mexico's national ideological pillar of nonracism as it drew attention to the indigenous plight in Mexico. However, inequality related to the indigenous population is typically framed as being the result of class- or culture-based, not race-based discrimination (see, e.g., Caso 1971: 108–109; CERD/C/260/Add.1; CERD/C/296/Add.1). Consequently, the uprising did not significantly destabilize the nonracism pillar.

27. This is similar to discourses identified by Twine (1998) and Bonilla-Silva (2003) under the terms *cultural inferiority* and *cultural racism*.

28. In my conversations with Veracruzanos, both terms were used. Furthermore, Veracruzanos treated both practices as presenting challenges to the national ideology of nonracism.

29. Osuji (2011); Twine (1998).

30. Fernando is not only literate but also an avid reader.

31. The rest of my interviews with Manuel's employees were conducted in his absence.

32. The idea that geographic moves or changes in environment stimulate shifts in race frames is supported by other research (Golash-Boza 2011; O'Brien 2008; Roth 2009, 2012; Twine 1997).

33. An exception would be individuals having migrant relatives in the United States. However, I did not find these relationships to be a common source of counter-discourses.

34. Degler (1971); Marx (1998); Telles (2004); van den Berghe (1967).

35. Bailey (2009); Telles (2004).

Chapter 8

1. http://www.cesarfernando.blogspot.com/2004/06/el-prximo-benito-jurez-no-ser.html. Juárez was the twenty-sixth president of Mexico and is revered among Mexicans. Among other things, he is known for being the first (and only) indigenous president of Mexico. This article was published in various Mexican newspapers.

2. For details see Eagleton (1991); Thompson (1984).

3. Burdick (1998); Jackman (1994).

4. Cope (1994).

5. Swarthout (2004).

6. This interpretation is supported by evidence from other Latin American countries (Roth 2008; Sheriff 2001; Twine 1998).

7. Edwards (1973); Gullickson (2005); Herring (2002); Hill (2000); Hughes and Hurtel (1990); Keith and Herring (1991); Murguía and Telles (1996); Telles and Murguía (1990).

8. Alba and Nee (2003); Bonilla-Silva (2004); Bonilla-Silva and Glover (2004).

9. Alba (2009); Bonilla-Silva (2004); Bonilla-Silva and Glover (2004); Gans (1999); Lee and Bean (2004); Warren and Twine (1997); Yancey (2003).

10. Alba (2009); Daniel (2006); Roth (2012).

11. Sue (2009a).

12. Telles (2004).

13. Ishida (2003).

14. Beck, Mijeski, and Stark (2011).

15. Sawyer (2006).

16. Bailey (2009); Osuji (2011).

17. Golash-Boza (2010); Schwartzman (2007); Telles (2004); Telles and Paschel (n.d.).

18. Bailey (2008, 2009); Daniel (2006); Golash-Boza (2011); Roth (2012); Sheriff (2001); Skidmore (1993); Telles and Paschel (n.d.).

19. Telles and Paschel (n.d.).

20. Alba and Nee (2003); Bonilla-Silva (2004); O'Brien (2008); Warren and Twine (1997); Yancey (2003); Zhou (2001).

21. Passel, Cohn, and Gonzalez-Barrera (2012).

22. For elaboration of this point, see Sue (2011).

23. Portes and Bach (1985); Roth (2012); Telles and Ortiz (2008).

24. I discuss this further in the Epilogue.

Chapter 9

1. In 2001, Mexico made constitutional reforms related to indigenous rights. Additionally, prohibitions against discrimination gained constitutional status. Also in 2001, the Mexican government established the Citizens' Commission on Discrimination Studies, which influenced the drafting of the Federal Act to Prevent and Eliminate Discrimination, promulgated in 2003 (CERD/C/473/Add.1). In 2004, CONAPRED, the National Council for the Prevention of Discrimination, was created. These changes have paralleled those in other Latin American countries that have developed and implemented new public institutions, governmental policies, and legislation aimed at combating ethnic and racial discrimination (Escobar 2008; Hooker 2008; Sieder 2002; Telles 2004).

2. CERD/C/296Add.1, CERD/C/473/Add.1, CERD/C/MEX/16-17.

3. http://articles.latimes.com/2010/jul/05/world/la-fg-mexico-racism-20100705

4. http://www.eluniversal.com.mx/notas/693533.html

5. Daniel Hernandez documented and published a commentary on these responses: http://latimesblogs.latimes.com/laplaza/2010/07/mexico-race-racism-black-face-televisa.html

6. http://www.conapred.org.mx/

REFERENCES

Aguirre Beltrán, Gonzalo. 1944. "The Slave Trade in Mexico." *Hispanic American Historical Review* 24(3):412–30.

———. 1946. *La Población Negra de México: Estudio Ethnohistórico*. Veracruz: Fondo de Cultura Económica.

———. 1958. *Cuijla: Esbozo Etnográfico de un Pueblo Negro*. México, D.F.: Fondo de Cultura Económica.

Alba, Richard. 2009. *Blurring the Color Line: The New Chance for a More Integrated America*. Cambridge, MA: Harvard University Press.

Alba, Richard, and Victor Nee. 2003. *Remaking the American Mainstream: Assimilation and Contemporary Immigration*. Cambridge, MA: Harvard University Press.

Althoff, Daniel. 1994. "Afromestizo Speech from Costa Chica, Guerrero: From Cuaji to Cuijla." *Language Problems and Language Planning* 18(3):242–56.

Andrews, George Reid. 1991. *Blacks and Whites in São Paulo Brazil, 1888-1988*. Madison: The University of Wisconsin Press.

Appelbaum, Nancy, Anne Macpherson, and Karin Alejandra Rosemblatt (Eds.). 2003. *Race and Nation in Modern Latin America*. Chapel Hill: The University of North Carolina Press.

Archer, Christon I. 2000. "Fashioning a New Nation." Pp. 301–39 in *The Oxford History of Mexico*, edited by Michael C. Meyer and William H. Beezley. Oxford: Oxford University Press.

Baca Zinn, Maxine. 1979. "Insider Field Research in Minority Communities." *Social Problems* 27(2):209–19.

Bail, Christopher A. 2008. "The Configuration of Symbolic Boundaries against Immigrants in Europe." *American Sociological Review* 73(1):37–59.

Bailey, Stanley R. 2002. "The Race Construct and Public Opinion: Understanding Brazilian Beliefs about Racial Inequality and Their Determinants." *American Journal of Sociology* 108(2):406–39.

———. 2004. "Group Dominance and the Myth of Racial Democracy: Antiracism Attitudes in Brazil." *American Sociological Review* 69:728–47.

————. 2008. "Unmixing for Race Making in Brazil." *American Journal of Sociology* 114(3):577–614.

————. 2009. *Legacies of Race: Identities, Attitudes, and Politics in Brazil.* Stanford: Stanford University Press.

Bakalian, Anny. 1993. *Armenian-Americans: From Being to Feeling Armenian.* New Brunswick, NJ: Transaction.

Bakanic, Von. 1995. "I'm not Prejudiced, But...: A Deeper Look at Racial Attitudes." *Sociological Inquiry* 65(1):67–86.

Barth, Fredrik. 1969. "Introduction." Pp. 9–38 in *Ethnic Groups and Boundaries: The Social Organization of Culture Difference*, edited by Fredrik Barth. Prospect Heights, NY: Waveland Press.

Basave Benítez, Agustin. 1992. *México Mestizo: Análisis del Nacionalismo Mexicano en Torno a la Mestizofilia de Andrés Molina Enríquez.* México, D.F.: Fondo de Cultura Económica.

Beck, Scott H., Kenneth Mijeski, and Meagan M. Stark. 2011. "¿Qué Es Racismo?: Awareness of Racism and Discrimination in Ecuador." *Latin American Research Review* 46(1):102–25.

Béjar Navarro, Raúl. 1969. "Prejuicio y discriminación racial en México." *Revista Mexicana de Sociología* 31(2):417–33.

Benjamin, Thomas. 2000. "Rebuilding the Nation." Pp. 467–503 in *The Oxford History of Mexico*, edited by Michael C. Meyer and William H. Beezley. Oxford: Oxford University Press.

Beoku-Betts, Josephine. 1994. "When Black Is Not Enough: Doing Field Research among Gullah Women." *NWSA Journal* 6(3):413–33.

Berger, Bennett. 1981. *The Survival of a Counterculture: Ideological Work and Everyday Life Among Rural Communards.* Berkeley: University of California Press.

Blee, Kathleen M. 2000. "White on White: Interviewing Women in U.S. White Supremacist Groups." Pp. 93–110 in *Racing Research, Researching Race: Methodological Dilemmas in Critical Race Studies*, edited by France Winddance and Jonathan Warren Twine. New York: New York University Press.

Bobo, Lawrence D., and Vincent L. Hutchings. 1996. "Perceptions of Racial Group Competition: Extending Blumer's Theory of Group Position to a Multiracial Social Context." *American Sociological Review* 61(6):951-72.

Bobo, Lawrence D., and James R. Kluegel. 1993. "Opposition to Race-Targeting: Self-Interest, Stratification Ideology, or Racial Attitudes?" *American Sociological Review* 58(4):443–64.

Bonilla-Silva, Eduardo. 1999. "The Essential Social Fact of Race." *American Sociological Review* 64(6):899–906.

————. 2003. *Racism Without Racists: Color-Blind Racism and the Persistence of Racial Inequality in the United States.* Lanham, MD: Rowman & Littlefield Publishers, Inc.

————. 2004. "From Bi-racial to Tri-racial: Towards a New System of Racial Stratification in the USA." *Ethnic and Racial Studies* 27(6):931–50.

Bonilla-Silva, Eduardo, and Karen S. Glover. 2004. "'We Are All Americans': The Latin Americanization of Race Relations in the United States." Pp. 149–83 in *The Changing Terrain of Race and Ethnicity*, edited by Maria Krysan and Amanda E. Lewis. New York: Russell Sage Foundation.

Bourdieu, Pierre. 1977. *Outline of a Theory of Practice*. London: Cambridge Studies in Social Anthropology.

———. 2001. *Masculine Domination*. Stanford: Stanford University Press.

Bourdieu, Pierre, and Loïc Wacquant. 1999. "On the Cunning of Imperialist Reason." *Theory, Culture & Society* 16(1):41–57.

Brading, David A. 1985. *The Origins of Mexican Nationalism*. Cambridge: University of Cambridge.

Buchenau, Jürgen. 2001. "Small Numbers, Great Impact: Mexico and Its Immigrants." *Journal of American Ethnic History* 20(3):23–49.

Buffington, Robert M. 2000. *Criminal and Citizen in Modern Mexico*. Lincoln: University of Nebraska Press.

Buffington, Robert M., and William E. French. 2000. "The Culture of Modernity." Pp. 397–433 in *The Oxford History of Mexico*, edited by Michael C. Meyer and William H. Beezley. Oxford: Oxford University Press.

Burdick, John. 1998. *Blessed Anastacia: Women, Race, and Popular Christianity in Brazil*. New York: Routledge.

Cabrera, Luis. 1977. *La Revolución es la Revolución*. Guanajuato: Gobierno del Estado de Guanajuato.

Campos, Luis Eugenio. 2005. "Caracterización étnica de los pueblos de negros de la Costa Chica de Oaxaca: Una Visión etnográfica." Pp. 411–27 in *Poblaciones y culturas de origen africano en México*, edited by María Elisa Velázquez Gutiérrez. Roma, México. D.F.: Instituto Nacional de Antropología e Historia.

Candelario, Ginetta E.B. 2007. *Black behind the Ears: Dominican Racial Identity from Museums to Beauty Shops*. Durham, NC: Duke University Press.

Carroll, Patrick J. 2001. *Blacks in Colonial Veracruz: Race, Ethnicity, and Regional Development*. Austin: University of Texas Press.

Caso, Alfonso. 1971. *La Comunidad Indígena*. México, D.F.: SEP/SETENTAS.

Castellanos Guerrero, Alicia. 2000. "Antropología y Racismo en México." *Desacatos* 4.

———.(Ed.). 2003. *Imágenes del Racismo en México*. México, D.F.: Universidad Autónoma Metropolitana.

Chavez, Christina. 2008. "Conceptualizing from the Inside: Advantages, Complications, and Demands on Insider Positionality." *Qualitative Report* 13(3):474–94.

Cook-Martín, David, and David Fitzgerald. 2010. "Liberalism and the Limits of Inclusion: Race and Immigration Law in the Americas, 1850-2000." *Journal of Interdisciplinary History* 41(1):7–25.

Cope, R. Douglas. 1994. *The Limits of Racial Domination: Plebeian Society in Colonial Mexico City, 1660-1720*. Madison: University of Wisconsin Press.

Cornell, Stephen, and Douglas Hartmann. 1998. *Ethnicity and Race: Making Identities in a Changing World*. Thousand Oaks, CA: Pine Forge Press.

Corona, Rodolfo (Ed.). 2001. *Tamaño de la Población Indígena Mexicana*. México, D.F.: CONAPO.

Cruz Carretero, Sagrario del Carmen. 1989. "Identad en una Comunidad Afromestiza del Centro de Veracruz; La Población de Mata Clara." PhD diss., Universidad de las Américas-Puebla.

———. n.d. "Past and Presence of Blacks in Mexico." Unpublished manuscript.

da Silva, Graziella Moraes, and Elisa P. Reis. 2011. "Perceptions of Racial Discrimination among Black Professionals in Rio de Janeiro." *Latin American Research Review* 46(2):57–78.

Daniel, Reginald G. 2002. *More than Black? Multiracial Identity and the New Racial Order*. Philadelphia: Temple University Press.

———. 2006. *Race and Multiraciality in Brazil and the United States: Converging Paths?* University Park: Pennsylvania State University Press.

Davis, Kingsley. 1941. "Intermarriage in Caste Societies." *American Anthropologist* 43(3):376–95.

De la Peña, Guillermo, and Luis Vázquez (Eds.). 2002. *La antropología sociocultural en el México del milenio. Búsquedas, encuentros y transiciones*. México, D.F.: Fondo de Cultura Económica.

Deans-Smith, Susan, and Ilona Katzew. 2009. "Introduction: The Alchemy of Race in Mexican America." Pp. 1–24 in *Race and Classification: The Case of Mexican America*, edited by Ilona Katzew and Susan Deans-Smith. Stanford: Stanford University Press.

Degler, Carl N. 1971. *Neither Black nor White: Slavery and Race Relations in Brazil and the United States*. New York: MacMillan Publishing Co. Inc.

Delpar, Helen. 2000. "Mexican Culture: 1920–1945." Pp. 543–73 in *The Oxford History of Mexico*, edited by Michael C. Meyer and William H. Beezley. Oxford: Oxford University Press.

Díaz Pérez, María Cristina, Francisca Aparicio Prudente, and Adela García Casarrubias (Eds.). 1993. *Jamás Fandango al Cielo: Narrativa Afromestiza*. México, D.F.: Dirección General de Culturas Populares.

D'Souza, Dinesh. 1995. *The End of Racism: Principles for a Multiracial Society*. New York: Free Press.

Duany, Jorge. 2002. *The Puerto Rican Nation on the Move: Identities on the Island and in the United States*. Chapel Hill: University of North Carolina Press.

Eagleton, Terry. 1991. *Ideology: An Introduction*. London: Verso.

Edwards, Ozzie L. 1973. "Skin Color as a Variable in Racial Attitudes of Black Urbanities." *Journal of Black Studies* 3(4):473–83.

Erickson, Rebecca J. 1995. "The Importance of Authenticity for Self and Society." *Symbolic Interaction* 18:121–44.

Escobar, Arturo. 2008. *Territories of Difference: Place, Movements, Life, Redes*. Durham, NC: Duke University Press.

Eshelman, Catharine Good. 2005. "El Estudio Antropológico-histórico de la Población de Origen Africano en México: Problemas Teóricos y Metodológicos." Pp. 141–60 in *Poblaciones y Culturas de Origen Africano en México*, edited by María Elisa Velázquez Gutiérrez and Ethel Correa Duró. México, D.F.: Instituto Nacional de Antropología e Historia.

Feagin, Joe R. 2001. *Racist America: Roots, Current Realities, and Future Reparations*. New York: Routledge.

Fernández, Carlos A. 1996. "Government Classification of Multiracial/Multiethnic People." Pp. 15–36 in *The Multiracial Experience: Racial Borders as the New Frontier*, edited by Maria P.P. Root. Thousand Oaks, CA: SAGE.

Fernández, Patricia, Juan Enrique García, and Diana Esther Ávila. 2002. "Estimaciones de la Población Indígena en México." Pp. 169–82 in *La Situación Demográfica de México*, edited by CONAPO. México, D.F.: CONAPO.

Fine, Gary Alan. 2003. "Crafting Authenticity: The Validation of Identity in Self-Taught Art." *Theory and Society* 32:153–80.

Flanet, Véronique. 1977. *Viviré si Dios Quiere. Un Estudio de la Violencia en la Mixteca de la Costa*. México, D.F.: Instituto Nacional Indigenista.

Flores Martos, Juan Antonio. 2004. *Portales de Múcara: Una Etnografía del Puerto de Veracruz*. Xalapa: Universidad Veracruzana.

Flores, René and Edward E. Telles. 2012. "Social Stratification in Mexico: Disentangling Color, Ethnicity, and Race." *American Sociological Review* 77:486–94.

Foucault, Michel. 1990. *The History of Sexuality*. New York: Vintage Books.

Frankenberg, Ruth. 1993. *The Social Construction of Whiteness: White Women, Race Matters*. Minneapolis: University of Minnesota Press.

Friedlander, Judith. 1975. *Being Indian in Hueyapan: A Study of Forced Identity in Contemporary Mexico*. New York: St. Martin's Press.

Frye, David. 1996. *Indians into Mexicans: History and Identity in a Mexican Town*. Austin: University of Texas Press.

Fu, Vincent Kang. 2001. "Racial Intermarriage Pairings." *Demography* 38(2):147–59.

Gallagher, Charles A. 2003. "Miscounting Race: Explaining Whites' Misperceptions of Racial Group Size." *Sociological Perspectives* 46(3):381–96.

Gans, Herbert J. 1979. "Symbolic Ethnicity: The Future of Ethnic Groups and Cultures in America." *Ethnic and Racial Studies* 2:1–20.

———. 1999. "The Possibility of a New Racial Hierarchy in the Twenty-First-Century United States." Pp. 371–90 in *The Cultural Territories of Race: Black and White Boundaries*, edited by Michèle Lamont. Chicago: University of Chicago Press.

García Bustamante, Miguel. 1987. "El Esclavo Negro y el Desarrollo Económico en Veracruz durante el Siglo XVII." MA Thesis., Universidad Nacional Autónoma de México.

García de León, Antonio. 1992. "El Caribe Afroandaluz: Permanencias de una Civilización Popular." *La Jornada Semanal* 12:27–33.

García Díaz, Bernardo. 2002. "La Migración Cubana a Veracruz 1870-1910." Pp. 297–320 in *La Habana/Veracruz, Veracruz/La Habana: Las Dos Orillas*, edited by Bernardo García Díaz and Sergio Guerra Vilaboy. Xalapa: Universidad Veracuzana.

García Díaz, Bernardo, and Sergio Guerra Vilaboy. 2002. "Introducción." Pp. 13–20 in *La Habana/Veracruz, Veracruz/La Habana: Las Dos Orillas*, edited by Bernardo García Díaz and Sergio Guerra Vilaboy. México: Universidad Veracruzana.

Gay, Kathlyn. 1987. *The Rainbow Effect: Interracial Families*. London: Franklin Watts.

Godreau, Isar P. 2006. "Folkloric "Others": Blanqueamiento and the Celebration of Blackness as an Exception in Puerto Rico." Pp. 171–87 in *Globalization and Race*, edited by Kamari Maxine Clarke and Deborah A. Thomas. Durham, NC: Duke University Press.

Golash-Boza, Tanya. 2010. "Does Whitening Happen? Distinguishing between Race and Color Labels in an African-Descended Community in Peru." *Social Problems* 57(1):138–56.

———. 2011. *Yo Soy Negro: Blackness in Peru*. Gainesville: University Press of Florida.

Goldstein, Donna. 2003. *Laughter Out of Place: Race, Class, Violence, and Sexuality in a Rio Shantytown*. Berkeley: University of California Press.

González y González, Luis. 2010. *Viaje por la Historia de México*. México, D.F.: Secretaría de Educación Pública.

González Navarro, Moisés. 1970. "Mestizaje in Mexico during the National Period." Pp. 145–69 in *Race and Class in Latin America*, edited by Magnus Morner. New York: Columbia University Press.

———. 1993. *Los Extranjeros en México y Los Mexicanos en el Extranjero, 1821–1970*. México, D.F.: El Colegio de México.

González-Casanova, Pablo. 1970. *Democracy in Mexico*. New York: Oxford University Press.

González-El Hilali, Anita. 1997. "Performing Mestizaje: Official Culture and Identity in Veracruz, Mexico." PhD diss., University of Wisconsin.

Gordon, Albert. 1964a. *Intermarriage: Interfaith, Interracial, Interethnic*. Boston: Beacon Press.

Gordon, Milton. 1964b. *Assimilation in American Life: The Role of Race, Religion, and National Origins*. New York: Oxford University Press.

Graham, Richard. 1990. "Introduction." Pp. 1–5 in *The Idea of Race in Latin America, 1870–1940*, edited by Richard Graham. Austin: University of Texas Press.

Gramsci, Antonio. 1971. *Selections from the Prison Notebooks*. New York: International Publishers.

Grazian, David. 2003. *Blue Chicago: The Search for Authenticity in Urban Blues Clubs*. Chicago: University of Chicago.

Guimarães, Antonio. 2002. "Democracia Racial: El Ideal, El Pacto, y El Mito." *Estudios Sociológicos* 20(59):305–33.

Gullickson, Aaron. 2005. "The Significance of Skin Color Declines: A Re-analysis of Skin Tone Differentials in Post Civil Rights America." *Social Forces* 84(1):157–80.

Gutiérrez Ávila, Miguel Angel. 1988. *Corrido y Violencia entre los Afromestizos de la Costa Chica de Guerrero y Oaxaca*. Chilpancingo: Universidad Autónoma de Guerrero.

Gutiérrez, Natividad. 1999. *Nationalist Myths and Ethnic Identities: Indigenous Intellectuals and the Mexican State*. Lincoln: University of Nebraska Press.

Hall, Christine Iijima. 1992. "Please Choose One: Ethnic Identity Choices for Biracial Individuals." Pp. 250–64 in *Mixing it Up: Multiracial Subjects*, edited by Maria P.P. Root. Newbury Park, CA: SAGE.

Hall, Ronald E. (Ed.). 2008. *Racism in the 21st Century: An Empirical Analysis of Skin Color*. New York: Springer.

Hall, Stuart. 1986. "Gramsci's Relevance for the Study of Race and Ethnicity." *Journal of Communication Inquiry* 10(2):5–27.

Hanchard, Michael George. 1994. *Orpheus and Power: The Movimento Negro of Rio de Janeiro and São Paulo, Brazil, 1945–1988*. Princeton, NJ: Princeton University Press.

Harris, Angela P. 2009. "Introduction: Economies of Color." Pp. 1–6 in *Shades of Difference: Why Skin Color Matters*, edited by Evelyn Nakano Glenn. Stanford, CA: Stanford University Press.

Harris, Marvin. 1952. "Race Relations in Minas Velhas, a Community in the Mountain Region of Central Brazil." Pp. 47–81 in *Race and Class in Rural Brazil*, edited by Charles Wagley. Paris: UNESCO.

———. 1964. *Patterns of Race in the Americas*. New York: The Norton Library.

Hart, John Mason. 2000. "The Mexican Revolution 1910–1920." Pp. 435–67 in *The Oxford History of Mexico*, edited by Michael C. Meyer and William H. Beezley. Oxford: Oxford University Press.

Harvey, Neil. 1998. *The Chiapas Rebellion: The Struggle for Land and Democracy*. Durham, NC: Duke University Press.

Hasenbalg, Carlos, and Nelson do Valle Silva. 1999. "Notes on Racial and Political Inequality in Brazil." Pp. 154–79 in *Racial Politics in Contemporary Brazil*, edited by Michael George Hanchard. Durham, NC: Duke University Press.

Heine, S. 2006. "'Black America'—The Ultimate Anachronism." Pp. 1–5 in *Interracial Voice*. http://interracia/voice.com/sheine10.html.

Hernández Cuevas, Marco Polo. 2001. "The Erasure of the Afro Element of Mestizaje in Modern Mexico: The Coding of Visibly Black Mestizos According to a White Aesthetic in and through the Discourse on Nation during the Cultural Phase of the Mexican Revolution, 1920–1968." PhD diss., University of British Colombia.

———. 2004. *African Mexicans and the Discourse on Modern Nation*. Dallas: University Press of America.

———. 2005. *África en el Carnaval Mexicano*. México, D.F.: Plaza y Valdes Editores.

Herring, Cedric. 2002. "Bleaching out the Color Line? The Skin Color Continuum and the Tripartite Model of Race." *Race & Society* 5:17–31.

Hill, Mark E. 2000. "Color Differences in the Socioeconomic Status of African Men: Results of a Longitudinal Study." *Social Forces* 78(4):1437–60.

Hoetink, Harry. 1967. *The Two Variants in Caribbean Race Relations: A Contribution to the Sociology of Segmented Societies*. New York: Oxford University Press.

———. 1985. "'Race' and Color in the Caribbean." Pp. 55–84 in *Caribbean Contours*, edited by Sidney W. Mintz and Sally Price. Baltimore: John Hopkins University Press.

Hoffman, Odile. 2006. "Negros y Afromestizos en México: Viejas y Nuevas Lecturas de un Mundo Olvidado." *Revista Mexicana de Sociología* 68(1):103–35.

———. 2007. "De las "Tres razas" al Mestizaje: Diversidad de las Representaciones Colectivas acerca de lo "Negro" en México." Pp. 98–109 in *Africanos y Afrodescendientes en Acapulco y la Costa Chica de Guerrero y Oaxaca*, edited by María Elisa Valázquez and Ethel Correa. México: INAH.

———. 2009. "De 'Negros' y 'Afros' en Veracruz." in *Atlas del Patrimonio Histórico y Cultural de Veracruz*, edited by Rosío Cordoba and Juan Ortiz. Xalapa: Universidad Veracruzana.

Hooker, Juliet. 2008. "The Institutional Design of Multiculturalism in Nicaragua: Effects on Indigenous and Afro-descendant Collective Identities and Political Attitudes." Pp. 337–74 in *New Voices in Studies in the Study of Democracy in Latin America*, edited by Guillermo O'Donnell, Joseph S. Tulchin, and Augusto Varas. Washington DC: Woodrow Wilson International Center for Scholars.

Howard, David. 2001. *Coloring the Nation: Race and Ethnicity in the Dominican Republic*. Oxford: Signal Books.

Hughes, Michael, and Bradley Hertel. 1990. "The Significance of Color Remains: A Study of Life Chances, Mate Selection, and Ethnic Consciousness among Black Americans." *Social Forces* 68(4):1105–20.

Hunt, Matthew O. 2007. "African American, Hispanic, and White Beliefs about Black/White Inequality, 1977–2004." *American Sociological Review* 72(3):390–415.

Ishida, Kanako. 2003. "Racial Intermarriage between Indígenas and Ladinos in Guatemala" MA Thesis, University of California, Los Angeles.

Jackman, Mary R. 1994. *The Velvet Glove: Paternalism and Conflict in Gender, Class, and Race Relations.* Berkeley: University of California Press.

Johnson, R., and C. Nagoshi. 1986. "The Adjustment of Offspring of Within-Group and Interracial/Intercultural Marriages: A Comparison of Personality Factor Scores." *Journal of Marriage and the Family* 48: 279–84.

Kalmijn, Matthijs. 1993. "Trends in Black/White Intermarriage." *Social Forces* 72(1):119–46.

———. 1998. "Intermarriage and Homogamy: Causes, Patterns and Trends." *Annual Review of Sociology* 24:395–421.

Katzew, Ilona. 2004. *Casta Painting: Images of Race in Eighteenth-Century Mexico.* New Haven, CT: Yale University Press.

Keith, Verna, and Cedric Herring. 1991. "Skin Tone and Stratification in the Black Community." *American Journal of Sociology* 97(3):760–78.

Kinder, Donald, and Lynn Sanders. 1996. *Divided by Color: Racial Politics and Democratic Ideals.* Chicago: University of Chicago Press.

King-O'Riain, Rebecca Chiyoko. 2006. *Pure Beauty: Judging Race in Japanese American Beauty Pageants.* Minneapolis: University of Minnesota Press.

Kluegel, James R. 1990. "Trends in Whites' Explanations of the Black-White Gap in Socioeconomic Status, 1977–1989." *American Sociological Review* 55(4):512–25.

Knight, Alan. 1990. "Racism, Revolution, and Indigenismo: Mexico, 1910-1940." Pp. 71–113 in *The Idea of Race in Latin America, 1870–1940*, edited by Richard Graham. Austin: University of Texas Press.

Krauze, Enrique. 2009. "The Mexican Evolution." in *The New York Times.* http://www.nytimes.com/2009/03/24/opinion/24krauze.html?pagewanted=all

———. Enrique. 2011. "Mexico's Strengths Still Shine Through the Gloom" in Bloomberg.com
http://www.bloomberg.com/news/2011-12-30/mexico-s-strengths-still-peak-through-gloom-commentary-by-enrique-krauze.html

Krueger, Richard A. 1988. *Focus Groups: A Practical Guide for Applied Research.* Newbury Park, CA: SAGE.

Lamont, Michèle, and Virág Molnár. 2002. "The Study of Boundaries in the Social Sciences." *Annual Review of Sociology* 28:167–95.

Langford, Joe, and Deana McDonagh (Eds.). 2003. *Focus Groups: Supporting Effective Product Development.* London: Taylor and Francis Group.

Lee, Jennifer, and Frank D. Bean. 2004. "America's Changing Color Lines: Immigration, Race/Ethnicity, and Multiracial Identification." *Annual Review of Sociology* 30:221–42.

Lewis, Laura A. 2000. "Blacks, Black Indians, Afromexicans: The Dynamics of Race, Nation, and Identity in a Mexican Moreno Community (Guerrero)." *American Ethnologist* 27(4):898–926.

————. 2001. "Of Ships and Saints: History, Memory, and Place in the Making of Moreno Mexican Identity." *Cultural Anthropology* 16(1):62–82.

————. 2004. "Modesty and Modernity: Photography, Race, and Representation on Mexico's Costa Chica (Guerrero)." *Identities: Global Studies in Culture and Power* 11:471–99.

Lichter, D. T., and Z. C. Qian. 2004. "Marriage and Family in a Multiracial Society." New York: Russell Sage Foundation.

Lieberson, Stanley, and Mary C. Waters. 1988. *From Many Strands: Ethnic and Racial Groups in Contemporary America.* New York: Russell Sage Foundation.

Lomnitz, Claudio. 1992. *Exits from the Labyrinth: Culture and Ideology in the Mexican National Space.* Berkeley: University of California Press.

————. 2001. *Deep Mexico, Silent Mexico: An Anthology on Nationalism.* Minneapolis: University of Minnesota Press.

————. 2005. "Mexico's Race Problem: The Real Story Behind Fox's Faux Pas." *Boston Review,* November–December. http://bostonreview.net/BR30.6/lomnitz.php

Loveman, Mara. 1999. "Is 'Race' Essential?" *American Sociological Review* 64(6):891–98.

————. 2001. Nation-State Building, "Race," and the Production of Official Statistics: Brazil in a Comparative Perspective. PhD Diss., University of California, Los Angeles.

Malcomson, Hettie. 2010. "La configuración racial del danzón: Los imaginarios raciales del puerto de Veracruz." Pp. 267–298 in *Mestizaje, Diferencia y Nación*, edited by Elizabeth Cunin. México, D.F.: INAH, UNAM, CEMCA, IRD.

Martínez Casas, Regina, Emiko Tanaka Saldívar, René Flores, and Christina A. Sue. 2011. "Informe PERLA México 2010: Etnicidad y Raza en México: La Construcción Social de la Diferencia." New York: Ford Foundation.

Martínez Maranato, Alfredo. 1994. "Dios Pinta como Quiere: Identidad y Cultura en un Pueblo Afromestizo de Veracruz." Pp. 525–73 in *Presencia Africana en México*, edited by Luz María Martínez Montiel. México, D.F.: Consejo Nacional para la Cultura y las Artes.

Martínez, María Elena. 2009. "The Language, Genealogy, and Classification of 'Race' in Colonial Mexico." Pp. 25–42 in *Race and Classification: The Case of Mexican America*, edited by Ilona Katzew and Susan Deans-Smith. Stanford, CA: Stanford University Press.

Martínez Montiel, Luz María. 1993. "La Cultura Africana: Tercera Raíz." Pp. 111–80 in *Simbiosis de Culturas: Los Inmigrantes y su Cultura en México*, edited by Guillermo Bonfil Batalla. México, D.F.: Fondo de Cultura Económica.

————. (Ed.). 1994. *Presencia Africana en México.* México, D.F.: Consejo Nacional Para la Cultura y las Artes.

Martínez Novo, Carmen. 2006. *Who Defines Indigenous?: Identities, Development, Intellectuals, and the State in Northern Mexico.* New Brunswick, NJ: Rutgers University Press.

Martínez-Echazabal. 1998. "Mestizaje and the Discourse of National/Cultural Identity in Latin America, 1845-1959." *Latin American Perspectives* 25(3):21–42.

Marx, Anthony. 1998. *Making Race and Nation: A Comparison of the United States, South Africa, and Brazil.* Cambridge: Cambridge University Press.

Merton, Robert. 1941. "Intermarriage and the Social Structure." *Psychiatry* 4:361–74.

Mills, Charles W. 1997. *The Racial Contract.* Ithaca, NY: Cornell University Press.

Moedano Navarro, Gabriel. 1988. "El Arte Verbal Afromestizo de la Costa Chica de Guerrero. Situación Actual y Necesidades de su Investigación." *Anales de Antropología* 25:283–96.

Moras, Amanda. 2010. "Colour-Blind Discourses in Paid Domestic Work: Foreignness and the Delineation of Alternative Racial Markers." *Ethnic and Racial Studies* 33(2):233–52.

Moreno Figueroa, Mónica G. 2008a. "Historically Rooted Transnationalism: Slightedness and the Experience of Racism in Mexican Families." *Journal of Intercultural Studies* 29(3):283–97.

———. 2008b. "Negociando la pertenencia: Familia y mestizaje en México." Pp. 403–430 in *Raza, Etnicidad y Sexualidades: Ciudadanía y Multiculturalismo en América Latina*, edited by Peter Wade, Fernando Urrea Giraldo, and Mara Viveros Vigoya. Bototá: Centro de Estudios Sociales, Universidad Nacional de Colombia.

———. 2010. "Distributed Intensities: Whiteness, Mestizaje and the Logics of Mexican Racism." *Ethnicities* 10(3):387–401.

———. 2011. "Naming Ourselves: Recognising Racism and Mestizaje in Mexico." Pp. 122–43 in *Contesting Recognition*, edited by J. McLaughlin, P. Phillimore, and D. Richardson. Basingstoke, UK: Palgrave.

———. 2012. "'Linda Morenita': Skin Colour, Beauty and the Politics of Mestizaje in Mexico." Pp. 167–189 in *Cultures of Colour: Visual, Material, Textual*, edited by C. Horrocks. Oxford and New York: Berghahn Books.

Morgan, David L. 1988. *Focus Groups and Qualitative Research*. Newbury Park, CA: SAGE.

Mörner, Magnus. 1967. *Race Mixture in the History of Latin America*. Boston: Little, Brown and Company.

Motta Sánchez, José Arturo. 2001. "Familias Esclavas en Ingenio de San Nicolás." Pp. 117–37 in *Pardos, Mulatos, y Libertos: Sexto Encuentro de Afromexicanistas*, edited by Adriana Naveda Chávez-Hita. Xalapa: Universidad Veracruzana.

Muhammad, Jameelah S. 1995. "Mexico." Pp. 163–80 in *No Longer Invisible: Afro-Latin Americans Today*, edited by Pedro Peréz Sarduy and Jean Stubbs. London: Minority Rights Group.

Murguía, Edward, and Edward E. Telles. 1996. "Phenotype and Schooling Among Mexican Americans." *Sociology of Education* 69:279–89.

Nagel, Joane. 1994. "Constructing Ethnicity: Creating and Recreating Ethnic Identity and Culture." *Social Problems* 41(1):152–76.

Nakano Glenn, Evelyn (Ed.). 2009. *Shades of Difference: Why Skin Color Matters*. Stanford, CA: Stanford University Press.

Nakashima, Cynthia L. 1992. "An Invisible Monster: The Creation and Denial of Mixed-Race People in America." Pp. 162–80 in *Racially Mixed People in America*, edited by Maria P.P. Root. Newbury Park, CA: SAGE.

Naveda Chávez-Hita, Adriana. 1987. *Esclavos Negros en las Haciendas Azucareras de Córdoba, Veracruz, 1690–1830*. Xalapa: Universidad Veracruzana.

Nogueira, Oracy. 1985. *Tanto preto, Quanto Branco: Estudo de Relações Raciais*. São Paulo: EDUSP.

O'Brien, Eileen. 2008. *The Racial Middle: Latinos and Asian Americans Living beyond the Racial Divide*. New York: New York University Press.

Omi, Michael, and Howard Winant. 1994. *Racial Formation in the United States from the 1960s to the 1990s*. New York: Routledge.

Osuji, Chinyere. 2011. *Marriage and Mistura: Black–White Interracial Couples in Los Angeles and Rio de Janeiro*. Los Angeles: University of California Press.

Palmer, Colin. 1976. *Slaves of a White God: Blacks in Mexico, 1570–1650*. Cambridge, MA: Harvard University Press.

Park, Robert E. 1950. *Race and Culture*. Glencoe, IL: Free Press.

Passel, Jeffrey S., D'Vera Cohn, and Ana Gonzalez-Barrera. 2012. "Net Migration from Mexico Falls to Zero—and Perhaps Less." Pew Hispanic Center: http://www. pewhispanic.org.

Patterson, Orlando. 2000. "Race Over." *New Republic* 222:6.

Paz, Octavio. 1985. *The Labyrinth of Solitude and Other Writings*. New York: Grove Press.

Pérez Montfort, Ricardo. 2007. "El 'Negro' y la Negritud en la Formación del Estereotipo del Jarocho Durante los Siglos XIX y XX." Pp. 175–210 in *Expresiones Populares y Estereotipos Culturales en México. Siglos XIX y XX. Diez Ensayos*, edited by Ricardo Pérez Montfort. México, D.F.: CIESAS.

Peterson, Richard A., and N. Anand. 2004. "The Production of Culture Perspective." *Annual Review of Sociology* 30:311–34.

Portes, Alejandro, and Robert Bach. 1985. *Latin Journey: Cuban and Mexican Immigrants in the United States*. Berkeley: University of California Press.

Qian, Zhenchao. 1997. "Breaking the Racial Barriers: Variations in Interracial Marriage between 1980 and 1990." *Demography* 34(2):263–76.

Rangel, M. A. 2007. "Ownership Rights, Family Formation and Family Decision-Making: Evidence from US Historical Data." Harris School of Public Policy: University of Chicago.

Reed, Isaac. 2011. *Interpretation and Social Knowledge: On the Use of Theory in the Human Sciences*. Chicago: University of Chicago Press.

Reuter, Edward Byron. 1931. *Race Mixture: Studies in Intermarriage and Miscegenation*. New York: Whittlesey House, McGraw-Hill Book Company, Inc.

Rhodes, Penny. 1994. "Race-of-Interviewer Effects: A Brief Comment." *Journal of the British Sociological Association* 28(2):547–58.

Riessman, Catherine Kohloer. 1987. "When Gender is not Enough: Women Interviewing Women." *Gender and Society* 1(2):172–207.

Riosmena, Fernando, and Douglas Massey. 2012. "Pathways to El Norte: Origins, Destinations, and Characteristics of Mexican Migrants to the United States." *International Migration Review* 46(1):3–36.

Roland, L. Kaifa. 2006. "Tourism and the Negrificación of Cuban Identity." *Transforming Anthropology* 14(2):151–62.

Roseberry, William. 1996. "Hegemony, Power, and Languages of Contention." Pp. 71–84 in *The Politics of Difference: Ethnic Premises in a World of Power*, edited by Edwin N. Wilmsen and Patrick McAllister. Chicago: The University of Chicago Press.

Roth, Wendy D. 2008. "'There Is No Discrimination Here': Understanding Latinos' Perceptions of Color Discrimination through Sending-Receiving Society Comparison." Pp. 205-234 in *Racism in the 21st Century: A Question of Color*, edited by Ronald E. Hall. New York: Springer Press.

————. 2009. "Transnational Racializations: The Extension of Racial Boundaries from Receiving to Sending Societies." Pp. 228–44 in *How the United States Racializes Latinos: At Home and Abroad*, edited by Jose A. Cobas, Jorge Duany, and Joe R. Feagin. Boulder, CO: Paradigm Publishers.

————. 2012. *Race Migrations: Latinos and the Cultural Transformation of Race.* Palo Alto, CA: Stanford University Press.

Rout, Leslie B. 1976. *The African Experience in Spanish America.* New York: Cambridge University Press.

Safron, Deborah J. and Clifford L. Broman. 1997. "Racial Differences in Perceptions of Discrimination." *National Journal of Sociology* 11:61–79.

Saldívar, Emiko. 2008. *Prácticas cotidianas del estado: Una etnografía del indigenismo.* México: UIA/Plaza y Valdés.

Sawyer, Mark. 2006. *Racial Politics in Post-Revolutionary Cuba.* Cambridge: Cambridge University Press.

Schwartzman, Luisa. 2007. "Does Money Whiten? Intergenerational Changes in Racial Classifications in Brazil." *American Sociological Review* 72(6):940-63.

Sheriff, Robin E. 2001. *Dreaming Equality: Color, Race and Racism in Urban Brazil.* New Brunswick, NJ: Rutgers University Press.

Sidanius, Jim, and Felicia Pratto. 1999. *Social Dominance: An Intergroup Theory of Social Hierarchy and Oppression.* Cambridge: Cambridge University Press.

Sieder, Rachel (Ed.). 2002. *Multiculturalism in Latin America: Indigenous Rights, Diversity and Democracy.* New York: Palgrave MacMillan.

Skidmore, Thomas. 1993. "Bi-racial U.S.A. vs. Multi-racial Brazil: Is the Contrast Still Valid?" *Journal of Latin American Studies* 25(2):373–86.

Stepan, Nancy Leys. 1991. *The Hour of Eugenics: Race, Gender and Nation in Latin America.* Ithaca, NY: Cornell University Press.

Stern, Alexandra Minna. 2003. "From Mestizophilia to Biotypology: Racialization and Science in Mexico, 1920–1960." Pp. 187–210 in *Race and Nation in Modern Latin America*, edited by Nancy Appelbaum, Anne Macpherson, and Karin Alejandra Rosemblatt. Chapel Hill: University of North Carolina Press.

————. 2009. "Eugenics and Racial Classification in Modern Mexican America." Pp. 151–73 in *Race and Classification: The Case of Mexican America*, edited by Ilona Katzew and Susan Deans-Smith. Stanford, CA: Stanford University Press.

Sue, Christina. 2009a. "An Assessment of the Latin Americanization Thesis." *Ethnic and Racial Studies* 32(6):1058–70.

————. 2009b. "The Dynamics of Color: Mestizaje, Racism, and Blackness in Veracruz, Mexico." Pp. 114–28 in *Shades of Difference: Transnational Perspectives on How and Why Skin Color Matters*, edited by Evelyn Nakano Glenn. Palo Alto, CA: Stanford University Press.

————. 2010. "Racial Ideologies, Racial-Group Boundaries, and Racial Identity in Veracruz, Mexico." *Latin American and Caribbean Ethnic Studies* 5(3):273–99.

————. 2011. "Raceblindness in Mexico: Implications for Teacher Education in the United States." *Race, Ethnicity, and Education* 14(4):537–59.

Sue, Christina A. and Tanya Golash-Boza. 2009. "Blackness in Mestizo America: The Cases of Mexico and Peru." *Latino(a) Research Review* 7:30–58.

Sullivan, Rachel E. 2005. "Contemporary Racism and Family Approval of Black/White Interracial Relationships." PhD Diss., University of Connecticut.

Swarthout, Kelley. 2004. *"Assimilating the Primitive": Parallel Dialogues on Racial Miscegenation in Revolutionary Mexico*. New York: Peter Lang.

Swidler, Ann. 2001. *Talk of Love: How Culture Matters*. Chicago: The University of Chicago Press.

Tannenbaum, Frank. [1946]1992. *Slave and Citizen*. Boston: Beacon Press.

Telles, Edward E. 2004. *Race in Another America: The Significance of Skin Color in Brazil*. Princeton, New Jersey: Princeton University Press.

Telles, Edward E., and René Flores. 2013. "Not Just Color: Whiteness, Nation, and Status in Latin America." *Hispanic American Historical Review*, in press.

Telles, Edward E., and Edward Murguía. 1990. "Phenotypic Discrimination and Income Differences among Mexican Americans." *Social Science Quarterly* 71(4):682–96.

Telles, Edward E., and Vilma Ortiz. 2008. *Generations of Exclusion: Mexican Americans, Assimilation, and Race*. New York: Russell Sage Foundation.

Telles, Edward E., and Tianna Paschel. n.d. "Beyond Fixed or Fluid: Viscosity in Racial Identification across Latin America." Unpublished manuscript.

Telles, Edward E., and Christina A. Sue. 2009. "Race Mixture: Boundary Crossing in Comparative Perspective." *Annual Review of Sociology* 35:129–46.

Thompson, John B. 1984. *Studies in the Theory of Ideology*. Berkeley: University of California Press.

Thornton, Michael C. 1996. "Hidden Agendas, Identity Theories, and Multiracial People." Pp. 101–20 in *The Multiracial Experience: Racial Borders as the New Frontier*, edited by Maria P.P. Root. Thousand Oaks, CA: SAGE.

Tibón, Gutierrez. 1961. *Pinotepa Nacional: Mixtecos Negros y Triques*. México, D.F.: UNAM.

Tilley, Virginia Q. 2005. "Mestizaje and the "Ethnicization" of Race in Latin America." Pp. 53–68 in *Race and Nation: Ethnic Systems in the Modern World*, edited by Paul Spickard. New York: Routledge.

Twine, France Winddance. 1997. "Brown-Skinned White Girls: Class, Culture, and the Construction of White Identity in Suburban Communities." Pp. 214-43 in *Displacing Whiteness: Essays in Social and Cultural Criticism*, edited by Ruth Frankenberg. Durham: Duke University Press.

———. 1998. *Racism in a Racial Democracy: The Maintenance of White Supremacy in Brazil*. New Brunswick, NJ: Rutgers University Press.

———. 2000. "Racial Ideologies and Racial Methodologies." Pp. 1–34 in *Racing Research, Researching Race: Methodological Dilemmas in Critical Race Studies*, edited by France Winddance and Jonathan Warren Twine. New York: New York University Press.

Urías Horcasitas, Beatriz. 2007. *Historias Secretas del Racismo en México, 1920–1950*. México, D.F.: Tusquets Editores México.

Van den Berghe, Pierre L. 1967. *Race and Racism: A Comparative Perspective*. New York: John Wiley & Sons, Inc.

Van Dijk, Teun A. 1992. "Discourse and the Denial of Racism." *Discourse and Society* 3:87–118.

Vanderwood, Paul. 2000. "Betterment for Whom? The Reform Period: 1855-1875." Pp. 371–97 in *The Oxford History of Mexico*, edited by Michael C. Meyer and William H. Beezley. Oxford: Oxford University Press.

Vasconcelos, José. [1925]1997. *The Cosmic Race, La Raza Cósmica*. Baltimore: The John Hopkins University Press.

Vásquez, Josefina Zoraida. 2000. "War and Peace with the United States." Pp. 339–69 in *The Oxford History of Mexico*, edited by Michael C. Meyer and William H. Beezley. New York: Oxford University Press.

Vaughn, Bobby. 2001. "Race and Nation: A Study of Blackness in Mexico." PhD Diss., Stanford University.

———. 2005. "Afro-Mexico: Blacks, Indígenas, Politics, and the Greater Diaspora." Pp. 117–36 in *Neither Enemies nor Friends*, edited by Anani Dzidzienyo and Suzanne Oboler. New York: Palgrave Macmillan.

Velázquez Gutiérrez, María Elisa. 2008. "Memín Pinguín: Tres Años Después." *E-misférica* 5(2): http://hemisphericinstitute.org/hemi/en/e-misferica-52/velazquezgutierrez

Vila, Pablo. 2000. *Crossing Borders, Reinforcing Borders*. Austin: University of Texas Press.

Villarreal, Andrés. 2010. "Stratification by Skin Color in Contemporary Mexico." *American Sociological Review* 75(5):652–78.

Vinson III, Ben, and Matthew Restall (Eds.). 2009. *Black Mexico: Race and Society from Colonial to Modern Times*. Albuquerque: University of New Mexico Press.

Vinson III, Ben, and Bobby Vaughn. 2004. *Afroméxico: Herramientas para la Historia*. México, D.F.: Fondo de Cultura Económica.

Vom Hau, Matthias. 2009. "Unpacking the School: Textbooks, Teachers, and the Construction of Nationhood in Mexico, Argentina, and Peru." *Latin American Research Review* 44(3):127–54.

Wade, Peter. 1993. *Blackness and Race Mixture*. Baltimore: The John Hopkins University Press.

———. 1997. *Race and Ethnicity in Latin America*. London: Pluto Press.

———. 2004. "Images of Latin American Mestizaje and the Politics of Comparison." *Bulletin of Latin American Research* 23(3):355–66.

Wagley, Charles, and Marvin Harris. 1958. *Minorities in the New World: Six Case Studies*. New York: Columbia University Press.

Warren, Jonathan W. 2001. *Racial Revolutions: Antiracism and Indian Resurgence in Brazil*. Durham, NC: Duke University Press.

Warren, Jonathan W., and Christina A. Sue. 2011. "Comparative Racisms: What Antiracists Can Learn from Latin America." *Ethnicities* 11(1):32–58.

Warren, Jonathan W., and France Winddance Twine. 1997. "White Americans, the New Minority?: Non-Blacks and the Ever-Expanding Boundaries of Whiteness." *Journal of Black Studies* 28(2):200–18.

Waters, Mary. 1990. *Ethnic Options: Choosing Identities in America*. Berkeley: University of California Press.

———. 1999. *Black Identities: West Indian Immigrant Dreams and American Realities*. Cambridge, MA: Harvard University Press.

Weiss, Robert S. 1994. *Learning from Strangers: The Art and Method of Qualitative Interview Series*. New York: Free Press.

Wimmer, Andreas. 2008. "The Making and Unmaking of Ethnic Boundaries: A Multilevel Process Theory." *American Journal of Sociology* 113(4):970–1022.

Winant, Howard. 1992. "Rethinking Race in Brazil." *Journal of Latin American Studies* 24:173–92.

———. 2001. *The World Is a Ghetto: Race and Democracy since World War II*. New York: Basic Books.

Winfield Capitaine, Fernando. 1988. "La Vida de los Cimarrones de Veracruz." Pp. 85–88 in *Jornadas de Homenaje a Gonzalo Aguirre Beltrán*, edited by Instituto Veracruzano de Cultura. Veracruz: Instituto Veracruzano de Cultura.

Wright, Winthrop. 1990. *Café con Leche: Race, Class and National Image in Venezuela*. Austin: University of Texas Press.

Yancey, George. 2003. *Who Is White?: Latinos, Asians, and the New Black/Nonblack Divide*. Boulder: Lynne Rienner.

Zack, Naomi. 1993. *Race and Mixed Race*. Philadelphia: Temple University Press.

Zavella, Patricia. 1996. "Feminist Insider Dilemmas: Constructing Ethnic Identity with Chicana Informants." Pp. 138–59 in *Feminist Dilemmas in Fieldwork*, edited by Diane L. Wolf. Boulder, CO: Westview Press.

Zerubavel, Eviatar. 2007. "The Social Structure of Denial: A Formal Sociological Analysis of Conspiracies of Silence." Pp. 181–89 in *Culture, Society and Democracy: The Interpretive Approach*, edited by Isaac Reed and Jeffrey Alexander. Boulder, CO: Paradigm Publishers.

Zhou, Min. 2001. "Contemporary Immigration and the Dynamics of Race and Ethnicity." Pp. 200–42 in *America Becoming: Racial Trends and Their Consequences*, edited by Neil Smelser, William Julius Wilson Wilson, and Faith Mitchell. Washington, DC: National Academy Press.

INDEX

Beltrán, Fidel Herrera, 138, 171
Beltrán, Gonzalo Aguirre, 201n98
"Bettering the race," 76–77
  and mixed-color families, 87
  mixed-color families, privileging
    whiteness, 95–96
Blackface, Veracruz Carnival, 153
"Black is foreign" concept, 133–36
Blackness, 26, 114–44. *See also* African
    descent, Veracruzanos of
  distancing Mexico from, 133–36
  distancing Veracruz from, 128–33
  metaphor of, 122
  stereotypes, 1–2, 140, 153–54, 206n24
Blackness-as-a-moving target
    phenomenon, 124–25, 143
Blanco, use of term, 36–38
Bonilla-Silva, Eduardo, 186, 206n6
Boundaries
  of blackness, Veracruzanos of African
    descent, 128–41
  ethnic boundaries, Latin America, 7
  national boundaries, crossing of by
    mixed-color families, 91–92
Boundary-making, popular, 155–58
  racial discrimination, explaining away,
    155–58, 174
  racist "other," United States as, 155–58,
    207n23
Bourdieu, Pierre, 159
Brazil
  Afro-Brazilians, 159
  applicability of U.S.-based racial
    attitudes, 147
  interracial marriage, 186
Brown identities (mixed-race identity
    construction), 55–57
  European descent, 55–57
  interfamily transmission, 57
Brown-skinned Mexicans
  downplaying of racism, 175
  mixed-color families, differentiation
    within, 105–6
  mixed-color families, privileging
    whiteness, 95–97
  mixed-race identity construction, 47–48
Bucio, Ricardo, 191

Cabrera, Luis, 16
Calderón, Felipe, 190
Cárdenas, Lázaro, 114–15
Carretero, Cruz, 136
Caso, Alfonso, 16
CERD. *See* UN International Convention
    on the Elimination of All Forms of
    Racial Discrimination (CERD)
Children. *See* "Consider the children"
    discourse, attitudes on *mestizaje*
Civil Rights Movement, United States,
    156
Class-based frameworks explaining racial
    discrimination, 168–70
  power over race, examples of, 170
Classifications
  discourse of relativity, race-color
    continuum and, 33–34
  outside classifications, whiteness and,
    53
  white identities (mixed-race identity
    construction), 53
Colonial period (1519–1821), 10–11
Color. *See also* Race-color
  outliers, mixed-color families, 109–11
  role of in Mexico, 6–8
Colorblind discourse, 147, 158, 206n6
Common sense
  elite ideology and, 179–80
  nonracism and, 26
  overview, 8–10
  and status exchange, 88–93
CONAPRED. *See* National Council for
    the Prevention of Discrimination
    (CONAPRED)
Conceptual association, race-color
    terminology, 40
"Consider the children" discourse,
    attitudes on *mestizaje,* 73–79
  "bettering the race," 76–77
  eye color preferences, 74
  and partner choice, 75–79
  race-color of next generation,
    73–79
  "staying white," 76–81
  ugly, classification as, 74–75
The Cosmic Race (Vasconcelos), 15

Counter-discourses, 143
    racial discrimination, explaining away, 171–73
Criollos, 54
Cuba, expatriates, 201–2n108
Cuban-black relationship, 38–39
Cuban, use of term, 38–39

Descriptive discourse, 33
Díaz, Porfirio, 12–14
Differentiation, mixed-color families, 101–12
Discourse of relativity, race-color continuum and, 32–35
    classifications, 33–34
    descriptive discourse, 33
    discourses on race, 32–33
    labels arising from, 34–35
    pragmatic discourse, 33
Discursive slippage, race-color terminology, 40, 42–43
Discursive swap, race-color terminology, 41–42
Displacing blackness, 131–33
Distancing, racial, 128–41. *See also* Racial distancing, Veracruzanos of African descent
Dominican Republic, race relations, 143
Dominicans
    color discrimination, perceptions of, 147
    ties to United States, 173
Doxa, 159
D'Souza, Dinesh, 88

Eagleton, Terry, 181, 182
Educational settings, 148–49
El Dictamen, 177
Elites
    colonial period, 12
    ideologies, 8, 179–80, 182
    nonracism, belief of, 15–16
    post-revolutionary, 15
The End of Racism (D'Souza), 88
Enríquez, Andrés Molina, 13
Ethnicity, role of in Mexico, 6–8

European descent
    brown identities, 55–57
    white identities, 51, 54
"Everyday wounds of color," 185
Expatriates, Cuba, 201–2n108
Eye color preferences, 74, 204n8

False consciousness, 180–82
Families, mixed-color. *See* Mixed-color families, intercolor relationships of members of
Fieldwork issues, 21–22
First National Survey of Discrimination in Mexico, 192
Foreign, blackness as, 133–36
Foreign ties, counter-discourses and, 173
Fox, Vicente, 114, 190

Gamio, Manuel, 13
Gatekeeping dynamics, mixed-color families, 93–95, 112
Gender, status exchange and, 90–91
Gente blanca, use of term, 37
Güero, use of term, 36
Guerrero, Vicente, 114–15

Hidalgo, Miguel, 117

Identity
    African descent, Veracruzanos of, 121–28
    Mexican national identity. *See* Mexican national identity, securing
    mixed-race identity construction, 25, 47–63. *See also* Mixed-race identity construction for detailed treatment
    non-elites, 9
    self-identity by color, 30
Ideological pillars
    nonracism, 15–16
    mestizaje, 15
    nonblackness, 16–17
Ideology. *See also* Racial ideology
    contradictions, navigating through, 179–80
    elites, 8, 182
    mestizaje, 57–59

CPSIA information can be obtained
at www.ICGtesting.com
Printed in the USA
BVHW031715141221
623939BV00020B/137

9 780199 925506